Keaton Mills Family Cemetery Egeria-An Era Family Stories and Cookbook

Gloria Mills Mallamas

McClain Printing Company
212 Main Street
Parsons, West Virginia 26287

International Standard Book Number 0-87012-585-0
Library of Congress Catalog Card Number 97-092635
Printed in the United States of America
Copyright © 1998 by Gloria Mallamas
Beckley, West Virginia
All Rights Reserved

Some History of the Keaton Mills Family

Egeria

Family Stories and Cookbook

Mills Coat of Arms	vi
Walker Coat of Arms	vii
Preface	ix
Acknowledgments	xiii
The Keaton Mills Cemetery	1
Family Reunion	13
List of people buried in the Keaton Mills Family Cemetery	17
Egeria School	25
The Genealogy and History of the Mills family	31
Family Pictures	37
Marriage certificate	41
Keaton Mills	42
Rev. John B. Mills	45
Will of Robert Mills	49
Will of William Mills	51
Census List	66
Deed of Rev. J.B. Mills	73
Benjamin (Ben) Mills-Glennis Walker	75
Pioneer Mills Family-William Sanders	78
Grandma Mills-Five Generations of Indian Ancestry	81
Indian Claims	82
Indian Trails	101
The Trail of Tears-Glennis Walker	103
Children of Martha and Keaton	107

1. Stella Mae 107
2. Alvirdie Elizabeth 121
3. Lydia Anner 134
4. Ivory Mae 140
5. Dora Hessie 141
6. George Winfrey 152
7. Oley Johnson 159
8. Della Dessie 173
9. John Corbit 180
10. Autie Ester 210
11. Nathan Crandall 215
12. Kelly Alderman 227
13. Laurence Evestus 231
A Tribute To My Late Husband 236
Modern Mountain Man-Olive Fielding Marrical 240
James Peyton Mills-Virginia Graham 249
Foley Family in Egeria-Rachel Foley Vogtsberger 251
Old Timey Sayings 263
Some Sensible Observations 266
Stories 268
Grandma's Arthritic Medicine 271
The "Association" 273
Trip to Burton's Store 276
Hair Rollers 278
Molasses Making Time 279
Stackpole Temple to Heaven 282
Respected Teacher 283
The Green Beads 285
Pork and Bean Sandwiches 288
Family Recipes 289

What's in your name?

MILLS

Mills Coat Of Arms

The whole milling business produced a high score of surnames during the Middle Ages. These names have survived in their original forms, all with the same original meaning, not the least of which is Mills.

Although Mills is generally thought of as a "place" name given to one who lived near a mill, there was often an overlapping of categories where surnames were concerned. For instance, Mill overlaps into Miller, an "occupational" name given to one who worked at the mill.

During Medieval times, this name was more commonly Myles or Miles and Mills became a modern representative of the two. Miles was also known as a common personal name, as was Mild. The Old English word for Mills was "Mylen," from which this great variety of trade names sprang. Milles, Millis, Milne, Mell and Milner are only a few variations of this surname. One of the earliest recordings found is for John Myls on London records of 1336.

As the Mills name became popular, illustrious families of the name once held residence and title in Essex, Suffolk, Kent, Gloucester, Hertford, and Knightington.

Several Mills ancestors can be found on early colonial records in America. Peter Mills, a tailor, came from Amsterdam to Windsor, Connecticut. John Mills was a freeman in Boston in 1630. Samuel Mills arrived in Weymouth, Massachussetts, from Lancashire before 1640. Simon Mills resided in Windsor, Connecticut, in 1639.

Family coats of arms often bore symbols which referred to the trade from which the name originated. On the center of the Mills shield there appears a black millrind, which was a device used to hold the wheel stone on the stand. The shield background is divided in six parts in colors of silver and blue.

Walker Coat of Arms

"Per chevron argent and azure, three annulets within orle of cinquefoils all counter changed."

A name of occupation from one who cleaned and thickened cloth. The surname Walker is occupational in origin being derived from the old English Wealcere, a "filler" or "walker". In this modern world, "a Coat-Of-Arms is a personalized link with the past"- - a decorative badge for individual recognition of a family name that had it's origin centuries ago.

However, with the vast immigration move into the American Colonies following the discovery of the new world different blazons came into being, not necessarily traceable to medieval origins.

Once everyone was known by a single name, but this led to confusion and so an extra name was adopted. Thus a man named John who was a Walker of cloth might be known as "John (the) Walker" the additional name eventually becoming hereditary as a surname.

Early records mention Richard Le Walker in the Warwickshire Abbey records of 1248 and Robert Le Walker in the Yorkshire Assize rolls of 1260.

John Walker who died in 1588 was Archdeacon of Essex and author of many theological tracts.

Among early emigrants from England to America was Roger Walker who is recorded in Virginia in 1623.

Joseph Reddford Walker (1798-1276) was a famous American trapper and guide.

The arms may be described heroldically as: Or three pallets gules, surmounted of a sattire argent on a chief azure three mullets, of the gules, surmounted of a sattire argent on a chief azure, three mullets of the first; Crest: A cirnicioia proper; and for Motto: "Cura of Industria".

Writers in the past have attributed symbolism to the tintcures and charger of heraldry - thus, or (gold), is said to denote generosity, gules (red) maganonimity and argent (silver) sincerity. The pallet is said to denote military strength and fortitude. The motto may be translated as - "By care and industry".

Preface

My philosophy of life is: If you have a lot of things to do, get the most important one out of the way first – your nap! Consequently, it has taken me ten years to put this book together when I could have, and should have, done it in much less time.

I have written letters, made phone calls and gathered information in person. I have asked family members to write stories of their family and provide information as to dates of births, deaths, marriages, where they lived, their work, etc. The information I have been able to obtain is included in this book.

There are stories I heard over the years and incidents that happened as I was growing up. Although I have included much about my immediate family, I feel that most of my cousins can relate to the times and places.

I owe a big chunk of gratitude to Glennis Walker for allowing me to use information from his book, *The History of the Walker Family 1734-1990*. Since our grandmother, Martha Ann Charity Walker Mills, came from his family, much of our family history on the Walker side was in his book. Dates and information that he labored twenty-five years to collect have been very beneficial.

Family charts can be attributed to Jesse Walker. He has done extensive research, worked with me several summers and cheerfully made necessary changes. I am grateful for his help.

In writing about the children of Martha Ann and Johnson Keaton Mills, I used the human touch, telling of their and their children's lives as I knew them. Perhaps my cousins will see a different side or learn something about an uncle or aunt that they had not known. History of nothing but dates is dull. I have tried to locate accurate dates relating to our ancestors, but also to include something about their lives, along with that of later generations. If someone is not mentioned, it is because I received no response and had no information about them.

Records of our family date back to 1637, when John Mills

came to America from England. We have black sheep, white sheep, moonshiners (who wondered why they couldn't turn their corn crop into a paying proposition without the "givormint" taking a tax and even making it illegal), farmers, coal miners, teachers, preachers, merchants and chiefs. They were all real people from hardy stock, and survived rough times.

Although we had little in material things, we had so much: Family, first always; good neighbors always ready to help when needed; our own land, twenty acres, thirty acres or more depending on where we moved and how we traded; a house with no mortgage, usually not so fancy, but a roof to keep the rain out, a fireplace for heat and a kitchen stove to cook on. Sometimes we leased more land from the coal company holding to the farm. It seems we were always clearing "new ground," which was not easy as trees had to be cut and stumps "grubbed out" before crops could be planted. We would have felt hemmed-in by present-day seventy-five-by-fifty-foot lots.

We had woods to roam in, and clean, clear streams to wade in. The big treat in the spring was when we were allowed to take our shoes off and go wading. We had to wait until it was warm enough. We could sit on logs and listen to the trees talk. Nature was clean and perfect, and we had everything!

We may have been poor in material things, but we were rich in culture, wealthy in nature's beauty. We had the woods, wild flowers, butterflies, clear clean water, ripe blackberries and blue-purple huckleberries to pick. What a day we would make of going into the "flats" to pick huckleberries (a kind of blueberry, but much tastier). We packed something to eat, took our buckets and went in a group. We made a contest of seeing who could fill their bucket first. If you haven't eaten a huckleberry cobbler, you haven't eaten a cobbler!

Music was always with us. A boy in the group always had a French harp and would play when we rested. On Saturday nights we had violin, banjo and guitar players. A Mr. Foley was an excellent violinist. He would come to our house and play into the night, and was much in demand for dances. To us he was a "fiddler" and he sure could fiddle. I am certain he never had a formal music lesson, just natural talent.

Did you ever catch fireflies and put them in a jar? Magic! Did you ever pick sarvis (servis) berries right off the tree, stuff them in your mouth until your "tummy" was comfortably filled?

Nothing like it.

It has been my intent to keep this narrative about people and incidents positive. Maybe I should have spent more time and research when I was younger. Today my mind sometimes goes blank as I search for words. Years ago they flowed like water. But that period in time is gone forever, and I have endeavored to do the best that I can. I just hope that my book will be interesting and beneficial to the family now and families to come.

Although the Mills family names appear countless times in historical records, surprisingly little information concerning their background can be found.

Simon Mills is considered to be the progenitor of the family in America. He came from Yorkshire, England early in the 17th century and settled in Windsor, Connecticut.

Persons bearing this name can be found in all parts of our land and are represented in the arts and professions as well as in the world of business.

Gloria Mills Mallamas – 1995

Acknowledgments

Olive Fielding Marrical, San Marcos, California, formerly of Charleston and Beckley, West Virginia; with gratitude for writing, editing and publishing assistance.

Jesse Walker, Shady Spring, West Virginia. He went the extra mile in checking lists and materials and sharing his extensive research. He prepared all the charts.

Glennis Walker, Cool Ridge, West Virginia; with gratitude for permission to use any material from his book, *The History of the Walker Family 1734-1990*.

Shirley Hoskins, Chattanooga, Tennessee; with gratitude for providing information regarding Indian claims by Sizemore family members.

Chief Robert Youngdeer, Cherokee, North Carolina, retired former Chief of the Eastern Nation, Cherokee, North Carolina, who assisted in obtaining information about Indian claims.

Patricia Chambers Schaffer, Virginia Beach, Virginia; with gratitude for providing Mills family genealogy information.

William Sanders, Princeton, West Virginia; with gratitude for giving permission to use material from his book, *A New River Heritage Volume IV*.

Rachel Foley Vogtsberger, Bloomington, Minnesota; with gratitude for her narrative on the Foley family growing up in Egeria.

Virginia Midkiff Graham, Huntington, West Virginia; with gratitude for her narrative on the family of James Peyton Mills.

The many cousins, whose continuing interest inspired me to compile information and to produce this book.

Beulah L. Mills Shuemake, Beckley, West Virginia, my sister, who gave me access to her large file of genealogical information.

James Vincent Mallamas, Jr., my late husband; with love and gratitude for his patient understanding and most of all, his encouragement in this endeavor. He kept telling me that I COULD do it!

The Keaton Mills Cemetery

This cemetery is located on the main county line at the base of Bluff Mountain in Egeria.

This cemetery is the largest of all the family cemeteries in a general area of the old Indian trail county line road which is along the proposed route of the Shawnee Parkway.

The cemetery is enclosed with a chain link fence and has an adjacent parking area laid out, with tables for annual homecoming in a very pretty setting. It tells the story of the Egeria community of old.

Johnny, Thelma and Lorena's resting place – Picture by Aunt Dessie Mills Cole – July 1970.

September 17, 1981
Martha Ann Charity Walker (b) February 25, 1865,
(d) April 11, 1936
Johnson Keaton Mills (b) May 16, 1865, (d) July 15, 1924
Married September 9, 1886

1. Stella Mae (b) June 3, 1881, (d) May 5, 1913
2. Alvirdie Elizabeth (b) February 12, 1885,
   (d) February 19, 1965
3. Lydia Anner (b) March 1, 1887, (d) March 9, 1972
4. Ivory Mae (b) November 22, 1888, (d) June 15, 1890
5. Dora Hessie (b) April 8, 1890, (d) March 8, 1936
6. George Winfrey (b) June 5, 1892, (d) November 27, 1948
7. Oley Johnson (b) August 26, 1894, (d) November 1, 1952
8. Della Dessie (b) March 16, 1896, (d) March 4, 1980
9. John Corbit Keaton (b) March 17, 1898,
   (d) November 6, 1937
10. Autie Easter Anthrim (b) April 25, 1900,
    (d) December 23, 1921
11. Nathan Crandall (b) June 25, 1902, (d) July 4, 1967

12. Kelly Alderman (b) February 16, 1904,
    (d) November 26, 1931
13. Laurence Evestus (b) October 18, 1905, (d) October 25, 1929

The Keaton Mills Cemetery is located in Egeria, West Virginia, at the foot of Bluff Mountain. It is in a level area, beautiful, quiet and peaceful. It is a serene place to meditate and truly "God's acre". One cannot help but feel good after a visit there.

Our family cemetery is a bond that ties our family together. Since each of us must finally claim our six feet of ground, we are thankful that Grandfather Keaton reserved a plot of ground for this purpose when he sold the homeplace in 1923. We hold family reunions there on Memorial Day, which are happy occasions. The young and the old meet. The young ask questions and learn about their "kin" buried there and thereby build bonds to their ancestors.

The cemetery is on the Foley farm, formerly the homeplace of Johnson Keaton and Martha Ann Charity Mills until the year 1923, almost thirty-three years. They lived, worked, and raised their thirteen children there.

The family cemetery was started when their fourth daughter, Ivory Mae, died June 15, 1890. She was the first to be buried there. Since that time, mother, father, brothers, sisters, aunts, uncles, and cousins by the dozens have joined her.

Grandpa Mills sold the farm to B.R. Foley by deed dated May 1, 1923, and recorded July 26, 1923, (the year that I was born). At that time surface and mineral rights were conveyed. Grandpa Mills reserved the cemetery.

I have been working on family history for some time; however, due to my husband's illness and other pressing matters, I have not been able to concentrate or take the time to complete the work. I have included birth and death dates of Grandpa and Grandma Mills and their children, so hopefully this will be of some help or interest to family members.

The history of the cemetery is 108 (1998) years old, and I do not presume to know all about it. I am sure there are family members older than I am who could add a lot; however, no one has felt inclined to put it in writing, so I am trying my humble hand. Since I served as co-chairman with Buford Foley in 1964 in the fund-raising and erecting of the first chain link fence and subsequent maintenance and record keeping, I do have records for the last few years.

You all suffered with me during the heartbreaking experience of getting new gates (twice) after they were stolen and getting the new fence after it was torn down and part of the wire stolen.

Much of our family history is in the cemetery. Tombstones of various sizes, shapes, and colors, and graves just marked with fieldstones (some unknowns), make the family cemetery a little more dear than the acres and acres of perfectly-laid out, lined-up graves in the commercial cemeteries.

The only tombstone in the cemetery at present with a picture of the grave's occupant imbedded in it is Uncle Fred Sneed. He was the husband of Hessie Mills. Their only child to live to adulthood, Eulalia Caudill, is buried near them. Their four babies who died at birth are buried near.

I remember when Uncle Fred died at our house in Spanishburg. The hushed voices as Aunt Hessie and Mom valiantly tried to nurse him back to health. The doctor came and went, but there was no medicine for pneumonia then, so he left us as a young man. We children were sent over the bridge to Grandma's house and did not quite understand how Uncle Fred could come up to the house driving the buggy, seemingly strong and able, and be dead within a few days.

There was a heart-shaped double stone with the pictures of Aunt Dessie's two children, who died one day apart from the terrible membranes croup which swept the area in 1923 and wiped out most of the young children. Vandals pried the pictures out and Aunt Dessie had a new stone installed and put the heart-shaped little stone at the foot of the twin graves.

I would like to pay homage to Aunt Dessie, the eighth child of Johnson Keaton and Martha Ann Mills, who left us a trust of two thousand dollars, the interest to be used for the maintenance of the cemetery. We are thankful and hope that no further vandalism occurs and that we will not find it necessary to ask for donations as often.

I think that a little history of Aunt Dessie's life is in order. She was the eighth child, born March 16, 1896. She married Elmer Cole, December 10, 1916. To them were born two children, Lemma Lavada (b) January 4, 1918, (d) Feb. 27, 1923. Beulah Lorado (b) June 30, 1919, (d) February 26, 1923. Uncle Elmer worked in timbering and mining. They moved about, finally settling in Besoco, West Virginia, where they raised Arbrie

Mills, son of Ella and Oley Mills. Aunt Ella died soon after the birth of their third child, Lila Allastia. Grandma Mills raised Delmer and Allastia.

She used to tell me about the time Beulah and Lemma died. The company doctor told her that she was just being an over-anxious mother and that the children would be all right in a day or so. Within a day and night they were both dead.

After her two natural children were buried in the family cemetery, her loss was not to be over. Arbrie was killed in a mining accident in the Besoco mines in 1942, and joined his mother, father, grandparents, aunts, and uncles in the family cemetery. His grandson, Michael Edward Mills, son of Elmer Kelly and Margaret Mills is also there with him.

In later years, Aunt Dessie and Uncle Elmer moved to MacArthur, where they were very active in church work. Uncle Elmer died in 1969, and was buried near their children. When Aunt Dessie died, March 5, 1980, only the date had to be added to the big, pink stone when we laid her to rest beside Uncle Elmer, the man she was married to for fifty-three years before his death.

She had a special place in her heart for children. She was always interested in all nieces and nephews and great-nieces and nephews. She left her estate to the Freewill Baptist Church Orphan's home in Greenville, Tennessee, and the trust to the cemetery. These two interests must have been closest to her heart.

Aunt Dessie's grandmother, my great-grandmother, Martha Adeline Sizemore Walker, who was Indian, is buried in the far corner of the cemetery. The writing on the stone is so worn that it is just barely visible. The tall, thin stone has not weathered so well. The top broke off and has been repaired. There is no date on the stone. The best records that I have been able to obtain show that she was born in 1835 and died in the early 1900s. The inscription "With Christ in Heaven" can just barely be read. Aunt Dessie told me that she could remember when great-grandmother lived with them the years just before her death and when she died. She smoked a clay pipe and liked to light it with splinters from fence posts. Aunt Dessie got a scolding from Grandpa when he caught her crossing the road to gather splinters. She remembered her grandmother showing her things from her trunk which were of Indian origin. How I wish that the trunk had been preserved so that grandchildren and great-grandchildren could have shared in the treasure of history contained in its contents.

I remember making the trip from Beeson to the cemetery in a buggy with Grandma Mills. Grandma and Delmer sat up front on the high plank seat. Alastia and I sat in the back, usually with our legs dangling. The horses could not go very fast, so there was little danger of us being bumped out. Grandma sat up there, straight as a ramrod with her long dress covering her legs and her Sunday, wide-brimmed hat protecting her from the sun. I faintly remember one trip with Uncle Kelly doing the driving. He was shot and killed by Leslie Meadows in 1931 and is buried near his brother, Laurence, who was killed in a mining accident in the Springton mines in 1929. Both died at a young age. The stacked apple pies that Grandma made the night before got a good jolting, but they still tasted good when we got around to devouring them after grubbing, cutting and pulling weeds.

In those days, the Memorial Day reunion was a real work day. Men brought their axes, saws, scythes, and mattocks. Children and women pulled weeds and briars. When it came time to eat, tired workers were ready. Cousin Ray Rose, seventy-two years of age remembered these work sessions when he was a boy. This was quite a contrast to our later meetings, pleasantly held on the well-manicured grounds, just visiting, putting flowers on the graves and picnicing.

Aunt Lydia Rose made crepe-paper flowers during the summer when resting from garden work and during the winter months when snowed in. She would cut through several layers of paper for the petals and leaves. My cousin, Bernadine and my job was to take our thumbs and pull and shape the rose petals. The colors were so beautiful. There were flowers in every vase, on every table throughout the house. I used to walk through the house and just look at them, not daring to touch, afraid that I would get them out of shape. I just remembered, she laid the flowers all over the beds in the extra bedrooms. She worked until she was sure that she had a "bunch" of flowers for every grave. She knew which she made for each grave. These had to be packed and carried carefully, so that they would not get crushed. A few years ago, I tried my hand again to see if I remembered how to make them. I dipped mine in wax, so that they did last a little longer; however, at the first rain the colors ran and they had to be removed.

I am sure there are many cousins who have memories of going with their parents to the cemetery on Memorial Day. The only living aunt is Uncle Nathan Mills' widow, Aunt Versie. They lived in the Egeria area during much of their married life and cleared land near the cemetery.

The old fence was not so good. During the early thirties, Uncle Elmer Cole and Lundy Rose decided to put some barbed wire and new locust posts and build a better fence. Aunt Dessie told me that my father, Johnny Mills, donated five dollars. Others helped with the work. They went to Buford Foley and asked permission to fence a little more area. He told them that they could fence an acre if they wanted to. This is probably where we got the idea that there is an acre fenced; however, it is not that much. Buford confirmed that his father did tell them that they could fence an acre if they wanted to. The fence was erected with the gate being placed at the front on the main road. The bank was rather steep and this made it difficult to carry caskets into the cemetery. The gate was a regular, narrow, yard gate.

The first mower to be used at the cemetery was handmade by Elmo Dillon, husband of Bernadine Cole. He actually got parts from various pieces of machinery and built the mower.

This barbed-wire fence did not look so good, but it was durable and still standing in 1964, when Buford Foley called me and said that he would like to put a chain link fence around the cemetery and wanted me to help with the fund drive.

He contacted members of his family and I contacted ours and we started the fund drive in September 1964. The fence was completed in 1965, with lovely double gates. One of the gates had a little lamb on it. Buford and Shad Foley laid off and erected this fence with the help of Bennie Bowden. Shad brought his farm tractor and pulled the wire tight. At that time we were able to purchase from American Glass and Mirror Company 700 feet of wire, posts, two six foot gates, and all accessories needed for the sum of $535.59. We paid Bennie Bowden $460 for labor, O.S. Foley $60 for labor and Buford $41.34 for sand, gravel and tractor gas. (They really cemented the posts in. We had a job getting the blocks of cement out when we replaced the one knocked down by a car ramming into the fence.)

I herewith share with you a paragraph of a letter from Buford dated September 11, 1964: "Shad and I stepped off the fence and we came up with approximately 600' now fenced. I believe to extend the cemetery 50' South is all the additional room we will need. This will require 700' of fence we will need at $1.40 per lineal foot, will be $980.00 plus the gate".

We were able to do much better than that. The total cost of fence, gates, and labor was $696.93. I think that this was due to Buford's good bargaining.

In 1979, when we replaced just part of the fenceposts and bought new gates for the second time, it cost over $700. We had some materials donated and lots of labor. Larry Mills, Jesse Walker, Dale Walker, Scotty Hatcher, Ranie Hatcher, Donald Walker, Emogene Mills and I made up the work party and completed the fence repair in one day. Larry Mills welded it later. Basil Mills and Len Harmon came another day and cut some of the long tree limbs that were creating a hazard. Connie Walker, who lives at Egeria, brought his tractor up and removed the old damaged posts.

Looking over the cemetery, one can see some graves are mounded, others are flat with the ground. A boy from Pennsylvania who is married into the Oley Mills family was interested in this last year. He thought that is must be an English custom, since most of the cemeteries around the churches in England are kept this way. It probably is. I just know that my mother insisted that our close family graves be kept that way when it was decided by others to level them off. She did not like the flat ones and Aunt Dessie felt the same way. She and Uncle Elmer always kept their children's graves and also Grandma's and Grandpa's and others well-mounded.

My mother, who came across the mountain as a bride of fifteen years of age, contended until just a few years before her death that she wanted to be taken back and be buried in the McComas cemetery at Pinoak, changed her mind and is buried between Daddy and my sister, Lorena. In the years before her death, she made frequent trips to the cemetery, driving alone and sometimes picking up Ethel Mills at her home in Egeria, and the two of them would journey up to the cemetery, walking through, reading inscriptions and talking of times gone by. These were times that could be enjoyed in friendship and peace and not a time of sadness and grief as when there for a burial of a loved one. Buford Foley lived in his trailer on the farm in the summertime and would often invite them over for a cup of coffee or sometimes share the food and thermos for coffee that they had brought. He had a trailer set up in the field opposite the cemetery and spent several summers there. His sister, Ruth Rogers, and husband Rudy spent a couple of summers with him, escaping from the hot Florida summers to the mountain air. Buford enjoyed planting and working on his flower garden located in front of his family graves and kept colorful blossoms in bloom most of the year.

I remember when Mr. Foley died in 1939. He suffered a stroke. They brought a nurse from Beckley to take care of him. Mom spent most of the week there assisting the nurse. He was paralyzed and in a coma. I do not believe that he ever came out of it to speak. Their family cemetery was in a rather inaccessible place and they wanted to bury him near the farm. He was the first Foley to be buried in the Keaton Mills Cemetery. His wife, Mary Kelly Foley, sons, Croby Lee and Ohlen Shad joined him later and the most recent, James, was buried there this year (1981). James was the best basketball player Egeria High School ever had. He was tall, slim, and a good athlete. With better transportation to get to other schools to play and more exposure, I think he could have been a successful professional. Bodies wear out with time, and now his is resting in peace near his mother, father, and brothers.

The Foleys lost the farm during the terrible depression. They worked hard for years to redeem it. I believe that about all of them carried the mail. I remember Henry driving the mail truck up that terrible, rocky road. Mr. Butler was the postmaster and later, after he died, his daughter Anna Bell took over. Henry drove out in the morning and went to Odd and then Ghent, where he had a long, tiring wait for other mail to arrive and be transferred. He got back about the time we got out of school. He used to pass us on that rocky road as we headed for home.

The land was returned to the Foleys by deed dated March 8, 1951, H.H. Smallridge, widower to Mary K. Foley, widow. During the transfer by the Virginia Joint Stock Land Bank of Charleston, West Virginia, and the First Citizens Bank and Trust Company of Smithfield, North Carolina, they extracted the mineral. "There is excepted, however from this conveyance all of the coal, oil, and gas heretofore conveyed and there is also excepted from this conveyance the graveyard located on the said land above described."

The Harmon plots are near the Foley graves. Mary Harmon, who is related to Mr. Foley, was buried there in 1972 and her husband Ted was buried in 1974. Parthenia Foley Mitchem, Mr. Foley's sister, was buried in this area in 1947.

Great Aunt Nick Walker, who was Grandma Mills' sister, was buried in 1943. Her husband, Uncle German, was buried in 1966. Aunt Nick and Grandma Mills came from a family of eleven, and I did not realize until I started research that five of this family are buried in our family cemetery: Charles, Pyrus Ulla, Martha Ann, Nyanzi Nicti and Lydia Miranda.

There is a baby grave, name unknown, from the Blue Jay timbering camp. I believe that it was stillborn. I remember visiting the family in the two little cabins that the company transported in on the tiny railroad. They would hook two together for a family house. They had to set them off the railroad, just beside the tracks. They brought the groceries and supplies to the workers on this track. The mother of the baby was paralyzed and never left her bed. There were several children playing about, food on the table and pots and pans open on the stove. I especially remember corn on the cob scattered about the plates on the table, some eaten, some partially eaten. Flies were everywhere. I disengaged myself from playing with the children and picked up something to fan the flies away from the mother's bed. She smiled her thanks to me. She could not speak. The mother died sometime after the birth of the baby; however, I believe by that time they had moved on.

Near the baby, the Crouse family is buried. I believe Leeotery and Duffie Crouse hailed from North Carolina. He was a fiddler of considerable talent and his sons Coster and Delbert followed him in the musical field. I believe Bill, who lives in North Carolina now is also a good guitar player. Coster is buried near his father. Two daughters Noreen and Vodaleen, are also buried near. Delbert is active in church work and sings and plays hymns on the radio. He and his wife sang at Brother Corbit's funeral.

Bob Winston is buried in this area. He was gunned down on the schoolhouse grounds, and died under one of the pine trees. Kenneth Mills said that he and some others were with Bob at the time. There was either some kind of activity going on at the school or the boys had gathered there just to hang out, swap knives, watches, or listen to music when someone brought their guitar or harmonica. He was standing between the flagpole and tree when Jess Thacker drove up, stopped his car and asked Bob when he was going to pay him for the chickens that he had stolen. Bob answered, "Mr. Thacker, I just have not had the money." Jess then fired one shot which hit the French Harp that Bob carried in his shirt pocket and glanced off. Bob then ran to the tree for protection, but as he turned sideways, the next bullet got him through the neck. As Jess kept shooting, the boys in the car all managed to get out and run into the woods, except Merlin Mills. Oliver Mills told me that he never ran so fast in his life. I don't know Bob's age, but he was a young man. In our cemetery records, we have the year of his death as 1934.

The West Virginia State Police went to Jess' house and almost captured him, but he ran out the back door. He left the state and it was several years before he came back. His daughter-in-law informed the police of his whereabouts and he was arrested, tried and served five years. He died at Odd, West Virginia.

Charlie Gravely, who was a loner and seemed to have no family, was buried in 1969. He lived with various families in the Egeria area. He was living with Uncle Nathan Mills' family when he died. Corda Walker started a drive at our last meeting to raise funds to get a marker for Charlie. We hope to have it erected by next Memorial Day meeting. We had doubts about obtaining his birth date; however, Aunt Versie provided us with the necessary information. He was born July 1, 1892, and died November 2, 1969.

Buford has always said that the cemetery is made up of Mills, Walkers, Foleys, and odds and ends, and this just about covers it.

Of the thirteen children of Martha and Johnson Keaton Mills, ten are buried in the family cemetery. The three who are not are: Stella Mae, Lydia Anner and George Winfrey.

Trustees for our cemetery are on record in the clerks office at the Raleigh County Courthouse and have been since 1978.

I read a June 1995 newspaper article concerning a historic cemetery located on Santa Fe Springs, California, that made me thankful that Grandpa Mills started our family cemetery in 1890 and preserved it for future generations' use.

The owners of the cemetery in California uprooted remains and dumped bones in a dirt pile in order to resell the plots, sometimes over and over. This was also shown on television. They had carefully stacked hundreds of markers in a shed just in case relatives came looking for the grave of their loved one.

We have had some vandalism such as tearing down part of the fence and running vehicles into the fence, but we could never have anything like this since we do not sell plots and the family keeps a close watch.

Family Reunion
Held Every Memorial Day at the Cemetery Grounds

It is sometimes asked; Why not "Act in the living present," instead of giving so much attention to the history and genealogy of the past?

Daniel Webster's answer to this question is as follows: "It is wise for us to recur to the history of our ancestors. Those who do not look upon themselves as a link connecting the past with the future, do not perform their duty to the world".

A magazine of American History contained the following article entitled "Why Study Genealogy?" Because this study furnishes us one way of honoring "Thy Father and Thy Mother"; it broadens one's horizon; it links us to our kinsmen of the present and the past; it awakens and deepens an interest in history. It brings out family characteristics that may reappear, points out special talents that may well be cultivated and family failings that must be guarded against. It sometimes settles questions of heritage. It ministers to that honorable pride that all ought to feel in the grand accomplishments of one's ancestors. It is an incentive and an encouragement to the performance of similar deeds. The great historic events of the ages are personal matters to us, if someone of the same name took part in them. How delighted to find that one has kinsmen over all the land and even in foreign countries. When one comes of a long line of honorable ancestors, with what superb and "beautiful disdain" can he answer the implied challenge of "upstart wealth's averted eye!".

As one's interest in genealogy increases; as one goes from one's immediate family to other families connected by marriage, the interest grows so real and so great that the brotherhood of man and the fatherhood of God — the two cardinal doctorines of Christianity become instinct with life and beauty.

In Memoriam

WHEREAS: The Almighty in his wisdom has called many of our beloved kinsmen to the Great Reunion in that celestial home of the soul, and WHEREAS the Father designs to touch with Divine power the cold and pulseless heart of the buried acorn and make it burst forth from its prison wall, will He leave neglected in the earth the soul of man, made in the image of his Creator? And WHEREAS to every created thing God has given a tongue that proclaims a resurrection.

RESOLVED: That each and every kinsman, who has loved ones waiting in that blissful land where Jesus dwells so move through life dispensing rich values as we go along, realizing that we only become our own richest and fullest selves, as we entwine ourselves with the needs of others.

Be it further RESOLVED; that we walk uprightly and never fall by the way; with a hope we will all be reunited on that GREAT REUNION DAY.

Visits to cemeteries are a time of contemplation. They give one an opportunity to reflect on the meaning of life and the inevitability of death.

May 12, 1992

This article was written for the *Orlando Sentinel*, Orlando, Florida, in answer to the question, "What special person will you remember on Memorial Day?"

That is so easy — my mother, Thelma McComas Mills.

I will journey to the hills of West Virginia and the peaceful, quiet plot of land located at the foot of Bluff Mountain to the family cemetery. I will stand at the foot of Mom's grave and honor her with all thoughts that could be heaped upon a deserving, loving, hard working woman who raised five of us after Daddy's death and somehow hope that she is aware. I know that we did not tell her how much we appreciated her while living, but we did show it. I can remember an aunt telling me, when I came sobbing out of her hospital room, knowing there was no chance of recovery from the acute myocardial infarction she had suffered, that Mom was so proud of us, to the point of bragging. Guess that we really did not disappoint her, but she should have had more time for rest and enjoyment on this earth after she had to retire from the hospital where she worked and had the first heart attack, because she sure had worked all her life and had a hard time.

She married at the age of fifteen. Her parents did not approve of such an early marriage. She and her older sister had a double wedding ceremony and set out on horseback over the mountains to start a new life. She married into a family of thirteen, who lived and farmed a thousand or so acres. She and Daddy made their home with the family for a year. They moved into a log cabin with their own acreage and she often told me that these were the happiest years of her life, just cooking, cleaning and making her own home. My older sister did not come along until she was twenty, then me, then my brother, another sister, and another sister, average of two years between each.

Dad died when I was thirteen and Mom's father, who was a widower and alone at that time, wanted us to move in with him. He had a big house and I thought that it would be a good idea, more security for us and someone to "housekeep" for Grandpa McComas. Mom evidently thought that she could make it and had the courage to say "no." She not only managed to keep a roof over our heads, she built a new house.

When someone in the community needed a nurse, Mom was the one they called on. I remember her going every day for weeks to change the bandages for a man who had been severely burned in a sawmill accident.

Nieces and other young girls came to Mom with their problems. During the second world war, she managed an apartment house which was rented to girls working away from home. She was a mother to all of the girls, sewing for them, listening to their boy problems and keeping an eye on them for their parents.

My cousin Lila, who died at the age of seventy-two (in 1992) told me that Grandma Mills told her that, should she awaken some morning to find Grandma dead she was to go to Aunt Thelma's immediately. Mom was an "outsider" to the Mills clan, but she was always the one they turned to.

Mom got her driver's license when she was fifty-three. She drove over to visit her brother the week before she died. She had nerve.

Mom died at the age of sixty-seven. My husband said we were cheated. He wanted more time with her. He got along better with her than his own mother. He could call her from some distant city and she would pack a bag and be at the airport within an hour to fly with him anywhere. His mother would take two days and make a thousand excuses. Mom was a little nervous, flying in a small plane but, the chance for a trip would overcome.

Yes, I plan to return as usual to attend the family reunion at the cemetery. I will stand at the graves of my mother, father, grandmother, grandfather (who founded the cemetery in 1890), uncles, aunts and cousins.

I will pay tribute to the one hundred-plus buried there, most of whom are relatives. Most of all, I will honor my mother. I wonder if I would have had the courage to tackle the raising of five children alone. I will honor my mother for keeping us together as a family. She was some kind of woman!

My brother enlisted in the army at age sixteen. My older sister married at age sixteen, but we were still together as a family unit, not scattered to various adoptive families.

List of people buried in the Keaton Mills Family Cemetery

1. Kenneth B. McGlothlin (September 18, 1948 – February 26, 1979)
   Sp. 4 U.S. Army Vietnam
2. Bluejay Baby
3. Michael Lee Crouse (1972–1972)
4. Baby Crouse (1930 – Leeotery and Duffie, parents)
5. Vodaleen Crouse
6. Duffie W. Crouse (July 8, 1887 – May 21, 1951)
7. Baby Cochran (near fence – Freeman Cochran's baby)
8. Leeotery C. Crouse (March 10, 1897 – January 19, 1989)
9. Coster Crouse (January 9, 1913 –   )
10. Henry Winston (Son), (or Hobert Winston)?
11. Mrs. Ollie Winston (Husband buried in Virginia)
12. Bob Winston (Son) (Died 1934)
13. Amberus D. Redden (February 12, 1944 – October 22, 1967)
14. Norean G. Redden (November 30, 1917 – July 28, 1964)
15. Norman G. Redden (January 27, 1912 – April 8, 1970)
16. Clacy Meadows (1903 – 1943)
17. Myrtle Meadows (1900 – 1993)
18. Wilson T. Thompson (February 23, 1913 – March 15, 1969)
    West Virginia Sgt. Co. A. 4th Tank Bn. World War II
19. Corda Walker Thompson (January 22, 1902 – February 18, 1986)
20. Dallas Walker (February 11, 1915 – August 12, 1944)
21. Nyanzi Nicti Walker (April 1, 1879 – April 19, 1943)
22. German Christian Walker (April 14, 1877 – September 22, 1966)
23. Oda Oliver Walker (July 15, 1899 – March 15, 1971)
24. Karl Mason Walker (March 24, 1923 – October 16, 1975)
    Served in the U.S. Army in World War II

25. Connie G. Walker (Baby 1952)
26. Baby Laura Walker (Tilden Walker's baby)
27. Baby Walker ⎫
28. Baby Walker ⎬ (All babies of Lilly and Harrison Walker)
29. Baby Walker ⎪
30. Baby Walker ⎭
31. Baby Walker
32. Baby Woods (Elec Wood's baby)
33. Jim Robertson
34. Ma Robertson
35. Thomas A. Harris (1969) (Lived in Ada Butler's house – family unknown)
36. Benjamin David Mills (1860-1898)
37. Milton Clendenin
38. Mandy Mills
39. Martha Adeline Sizemore Walker (1835-1899)
   Numa Dink Walker, (d) November 21, 1884, age 55, Martha Adeline's husband is buried on a mountain side near his homeplace on Devils Fork close to Syd Place below German Walkers.
40. Charles Gideon Christian Walker (December 23, 1864 – May 23, 1892)
41. Pyrus Ulla Chananey Walker (April 9, 1867 – June 26, 1902)
42. Henry Simeon Walker (June 29, 1874 – June 24, 1926)
43. Lydia Miranda Walker (June 23, 1874 on tombstone – other records 1875 – February 23, 1923. *(grave far right – near woods)*
44. Tom Parker
45. Ivery Mae Mills (November 22, 1888 – June 15, 1890)
   (Beginning of cemetery)
46. Sara E. Walker (December 25, 1843 – December 16, 1934) Wife of Numa, C.C.
47. Numa C.C. Walker (May 22, 1857 – April 8, 1910)
48. Infant Caudill
49. Randolph W. Caudill (1937 – 1942)
50. Dora Hessie Sneed (April 8, 1890 – March 8, 1936)
51. Fred Sneed (January 14, 1893 – March 3, 1928)
52. Baby Sneed (Boy)
53. Baby Sneed (Boy) (stillborn)
54. Baby James Keaton (lived briefly)
55. Baby Sneed (Boy)

56. Autie Mills Cole (April 25, 1900 – December 20, 1921)
57. Rolland Darrel Walker (May 17, 1939 – July 20, 1937)
58. Lloyd A. Reed (June 21, 1940 – April 4, 1972)
59. Marsha E. Reed (1965 – Baby)
60. Della Dessie Cole (March 15, 1896 – March 4, 1980)
61. E. Elmer Cole (January 16, 1898 – September 3, 1969)
62. Lemma Lavada Cole (January 4, 1918 – February 27, 1923)
63. Beulah Lorado Cole (June 30, 1919 – February 26, 1923)
64. Nathan C. Mills (June 25, 1902 – July 4, 1967)
65. Kelly A. Mills (February 16, 1904 – November 26, 1931)
66. Laurence E. Mills (October 18, 1905 – October 25, 1927)
67. Johnson Keaton Mills (May 16, 1865 – July 15, 1924)
    "His toils are past – His work is done – He fought the fight – The victory won"
68. Martha Ann Charity Mills (February 25, 1865 – (1862?) – April 11, 1936)
69. Ella Graham Mills (September 22, 1897 – March 7, 1919)
70. Arbrie Mills (March 26, 1917 – September 17, 1942)
71. Michael Edward Mills (July 25, 1964 – August 3, 1964)
72. Eulalia Sneed Caudill (May 8, 1917 – April 3, 1977)
73. James V. Mallamas, Sr. (February 14, 1893 – July 23, 1970)
    West Virginia, Sgt. Co. B 59th Inf. 4th Div. World War I
74. Kerby L. Walker (September 16, 1917 – November 20, 1977)
75. Lorena Mills Walker (January 24, 1922, – January 3, 1964)
76. Thelma McComas Mills (April 25, 1903 – July 12, 1970)
77. Johnny Corbit Mills (March 17, 1898 – November 6, 1937)
78. Corbit Keaton Mills (November 1, 1924 – June 24, 1974)
    West Virginia 3rd U.S. Army – Pfc. World War II
79. Wayne Mills (Baby) (1956) (Ann and Corbit Mills, parents)
80. Barbara Gail Mills (September 21, 1951 – October 25, 1951)
81. Oley Dale Mills (February 4, 1928 – July 12, 1929)
82. Victoria E. Mills (1896 – August 8, 1939)
83. Oley J. Mills (August 26, 1894 – November 1, 1952)
84. Nina Mills Graham (November 28, 1921 – October 2, 1971)
85. Andrew Wesley Graham (1896 – 1977)
86. Charley Gravely (known also as Charlie Mank) (July 1, 1892 – November 2, 1969)
87. Alvirdie E. Allen (February 12, 1885 – February 19, 1965)
88. Archer T. Allen (August 30, 1887 – June 9, 1964) Virginia Sgt. U.S. Marine Corps.
89. Archie Lee Allen (December 31, 1921 – October 17, 1939)

90. Ernest D. Mills (December 17, 1929 – January 24, 1977)
91. Ted Harmon (April 19, 1902 – August 20, 1974)
92. Mary M. Harmon (November 28, 1905 – September 16, 1972)
93. Parthenia Foley Mitchem (Teney) (1884 – 1947)
94. James Noel Foley (April 20, 1940 – April 23, 1940)
95. Jack T. Harmon (February 28, 1932 – October 3, 1932)
96. Brian I. Reed (1974 – Baby)
97. James K. Foley, Sr. (December 27, 1919 – May 12, 1981)
    Tec. 4 U.S. Army World War II
98. Ohlen Shad Foley (1905 – 1970)
99. Croby Lee Foley (1903 – 1958)
100. Mary Kelly Foley (1887 – 1964)
101. Buford R. Foley (1880 – 1939)
102. Robert Lee Auer (November 9, 1929 – May 1, 1931)
103. Bucy Mitchem (January 31, 1928 – October 27, 1957)
104. Dallie Mitchem (July 15, 1917 – August, 26, 1934)
105. W.E. Mitchem (April 14, 1869 – November 27, 1945)
106. Manzie B. Mitchem (July 23, 1895 – June 12, 1976)
107. Sally Walker
108. Calvin Walker
109. Mary Agnes Mallamas (April 14, 1906 – August 19, 1989)
110. Kerby Randal Walker (February 26, 1945 – July 2, 1986)
     (U.S. Navy – Vietnam)
111. Renee' Mills (August 8, 1990 – August 8, 1990 (Daughter of Donna and Larry Mills)
112. Straley Walker
113. Dade Walker
114. Trema Cole

(Choice Walker (in his nineties) pointed out that these two were buried at the far right corner where Harris is buried before the old fence was removed, so if the fence was extended it would be on this side of Harris. He told me this in 1987 while at the cemetery. He was very positive.)

115. Hallie Foley (June 20, 1907 – May 15, 1984)
116. Charles David Robertson (April 16, 1928 – August 25, 1995)
117. Frank D. Combs, Jr. (April 5, 1971 – March 24, 1996)
     Desert Storm Veteran
118. Felicia Ann Marcum (1963 – 1997)
119. James Vincent Mallamas, Jr. (June 27, 1924 – February 13, 1997) (West Virginia, Sgt. U.S. Marine Corps, World War II) Co. B
120. Jason Anderson Jarrett (August 14, 1970– December 13, 1997)

121. Icy Emogene Mills (August 11, 1931–April 10, 1998)
122. Frankie Dale Combs (March 19, 1951-May 11, 1998)

We feel there are several sunken spots that may be graves. No records and no one now living to tell us.

I do not feel that this list is 100 percent correct. Information was taken from the headstones and Corda Walker Thompson personally walked the entire area with me and gave me names of some who did not have markers.

From my research, I filled in the day and month on some where the stones only gave the year.

Egeria Schoolhouse built in 1923. High school closed in 1960. Grade school closed in 1961. I graduated in the class of 1941. My niece, Linda Carol Walker (Jarrett) was in the last graduating class in 1960.

Noel Christian, our teacher and later the principal; Mr. Bryson, superintendent of schools; Mr. Wykle, principal, 1939.

John L. Hornbeck, the principal of the high school for several years.

Linda Carol Walker and Gloria Mills Mallamas. Puppy in left front "Button."Graduated Egeria High School 1941.

Graduated last class of 1960 Egeria school. Linda Carol Walker Jarrett, last of the Mohicans.

Egeria School

The schoolhouse and vast fenced yard was the hub of all social activity of the community. The gymnasium was the same size as the four-room school and was used for school activities such as basketball etc. It had a stage in front with a dressing room on each end. Christmas plays were held annually with a huge decorated tree which had been cut in the nearby woods. Halloween was always a big festive occasion. The corner and every post was decorated with cornstalks. There would be a fishing pond where one could pay their dime and throw a line and someone behind the cornstalks would tie a prize onto the line, cake walking, dancing and other games. Usually a pretty girl cake, where the boys would pay for points for their favorite girl. The girl getting the most points or votes would be given a cake.

The gymnasium building was used for all church services. There was plenty of wooden fold-up chairs stacked on the inside railing. There was a big burnside coal stove on either side. (It certainly did not heat up the building when the temperature was really cold).

Sometimes when there was a small congregation of twenty-five or so, the services would be held in one of the schoolrooms. I will always remember one Sunday when a couple wanted to be married after the services. The bride was a tiny little girl and the groom was about six feet tall. They had a couple to stand up with them. She placed a lace medallion on top of her head. I was spellbound and ever since I have loved to attend weddings.

When the school bell rang, one through fourth grades lined up on the left of the sidewalk, fifth, sixth, seventh, eighth, and high school students lined up on the right. We gave the pledge to the flag and then marched in. The left side turned left, the right side turned right and the high school marched down the hall. The narrow hall leading to the schoolroom had hooks on both sides to hang coats and toboggans on. Boots were lined up on the floor. Inside the room there was a small closet with shelves where lunch buckets were stored.

The hall to the high school rooms was wide and went all the way to the back door where you could step out and across to the gym. Metal lockers lined each side.

I wanted to obtain a list of all the teachers who taught at the Egeria school and perhaps the students, however, I couldn't get anyone from the school board or superintendent's office to return my calls. I did determine from other sources that Verlie Walker was the last teacher and that Ada Butler was the last principal.

The following list of 158 people who attended Egeria school reunion that James Foley put together in 1978 gives a pretty good sampling of students and teachers.

Egeria School Reunion
September 3, 1978
Held at the Foley Farm, opposite the Mills Cemetery

1. Rachel Walker Hatcher, 827 Longson, Ave., Elyria, Ohio, 1940
2. Dave (Walker) Lewis, Box 43A, Route 1, Millington, Maryland, 1931
3. Francis Hatcher Green, Route 1, Box 387, Saint Thomas, Pennsylvania 17252, 1921, 1922, 1923
4. Dola Walker Auer, Rich Creek, Virginia 24247, 1917
5. Zola Lewis Johns, Box 40B, Millington, Maryland 21651, 1934 and 1935
6. Pansy Harvey Wood, Route 1, Box 10, Odd, West Virginia 25902, taught 1913-1914, last 1946
7. Vicy V. Walker (Buster), 741 Tod Avenue, S.N. Warren, Ohio 44485, 1937
8. Kathleen Walker (wife)
9. Walter Reed
10. Edith Reed – 1926
11. James Mills, Olney, Maryland, 1945
12. Vessie Verco Walker, Midway, West Virginia, 1941
13. Delta Walker Mills, Sophia, West Virginia, 1935
14. O'Kee Dunn (DeHart) 311 Virginia Avenue, Saint Albans, West Virginia

15. Opal Dun (Hodges), Box 478, Coal City, West Virginia 25823
16. Arthur A. Lewis, 1045 B, Monmouth Court, Atlantic Beach, Florida
17. Drema Walker, Beaver, West Virginia
18. Verlin H. Walker, 504 North Kanawha, Beckley, West Virginia 25801, 1932
19. Arland Hatcher
20. R.W. Shrewsbery, Odd, West Virginia, 1939
21. Vannie Wood Shrewsbery, Odd, West Virginia, 1939
22. Vertie Mills Halsey, MacArthur, West Virginia, 1932
23. Cicki Mills Richards, Beckley, West Virginia
24. Arthur K. Walker, 834 Chapel Heights, Elkview, West Virginia, 1957
25. Rose E. Walker
26. Arthur E. Walker, Jr. (wife and children – Arthur Walker)
27. Denise E. Walker
28. Rhonda E. (Betsy) Walker
29. Opal G. Tormino, 1932
30. Sam A. Tormino
31. Charlie Teague, 107 E. Street, Southfield, Michigan 48076
32. Hazel Teague
33. Hobert L. Walker, Route 1, Odd, West Virginia, 1940
34. Penny Walker (Hobert's wife)
35. Tracy Shrewsbery, 103 Hargrove Street, Beckley, West Virginia, 1932
36. Waneta Walker Mitchem, Beckley, West Virginia, 1932
37. Rebecca Mitchem Hancock (Waneta's daughter) Beckley, West Virginia
38. Sherry Mitchem Halstead (Waneta's daughter) Beckley, West Virginia
39. Sonya Faye Hancock (granddaughter), Beckley, West Virginia
40. John Hancock (grandson), Beckley, West Virginia
41. Colston Walker, Berea, Ohio, 1938
42. Elizabeth Heath Walker (wife), Berea, Ohio
43. Kenneth Mills, Route 1, Box 52, Beckley, West Virginia 25801
44. Lowell Mills, Beckley, 1935
45. Lonnie Cooper, Beckley, West Virginia, 1933
46. Edith Fugate, Beckley
47. Dale Walker, North Ridgeville, Ohio
48. Jupe Walker (Dale's wife)

49. John Walker (Dale's son)
50. Macel Walker Mills, Route 1, Box 52, Beckley, West Virginia 25801, 1941
51. Harold Walker, Shady Spring, West Virginia, 1939
52. Ruth Reed Walker, Shady Spring, West Virginia, 1940
53. Harold Anthony Walker (Harold's son), 1954
54. Stephen Walker (Harold's son)
55. Rosemary Fara Walker (Harold's daugher-in-law)
56. Stephanie Walker (Harold's granddaughter)
57. Gene Humphrey Walker
58. Howard Walker
59. Lara Walker
60. Monica Matherly, Cool Ridge, West Virginia, first grade 1951
61. Jean Walker, Ghent, West Virginia
62. Gerry Walker, Ghent, West Virginia
63. Danny Armstrong
64. Tammy Armstrong
65. Mariah Armstrong, West Jefferson, North Carolina
66. Gloria Mills Mallamas, 138 Sunrise Avenue, Beckley, West Virginia, fourth grade to graduation, 1941
67. Beulah Mills Austin, 106 Quarry Street, Beckley, until 1944
68. James V. Mallamas, Jr., Beckley, West Virginia, (Gloria's husband)
69. Norma Walker Pegram, Barger Springs, West Virginia, 1927
70. Claire Walker
71. James K. Foley, Cool Ridge, West Virginia
72. Edith Foley
73. Randy Mullins (Foley's grandson)
74. Mike Heika (Foley's grandson)
75. Lillie Harvey Walker (1912), also taught four years at Egeria
76. Betty Foley Porter, 1885 Rosemary Lane, Chesapeake, Virginia 23321, 1941
77. Debra Porter (daughter)
78. Lota Walker Porter, Suffolk, Virginia, 1941
79. Thomas W. Porter
80. Roger E. Porter
81. Glenn Seay
82. Anne Porter Seay
83. Vannie Hatcher Collins, 1934
84. Archie Collins (husband)
85. Wana Mahaffey, 1944

86. Lendo Walker, 1947
87. Joyce Walker Mize, 1947
88. Benny Mize
89. Marie Mize
90. Melissa Mize
91. Howard Mize
92. Susan Mize
93. Bud (Owen) Lands
94. Roger Steele (Hilda Foley's son-in-law)
95. B.P. Steele II
96. Doris Foley Shrewsbury, 1936, 1937, 1938
97. Hallie Foley
98. Hilda Foley McKinney, 1934, 1935, 1936
99. Andy McKinney (son)
100. Fred Walker
101. Verlie Walker (student and teacher)
102. Noel Christian, Beckley, West Virginia 25801, 222 Vine Street, taught 1936-1941
103. Berkley Shrewsbury
104. Hester Foley Shrewsbury
105. Timmy Shrewsbury
106. Carson Walker, Beckley, 1937
107. Retha Walker
108. Atha Shrewsbury, 1926-1927
109. Loraine Walker Fletcher, 1960
110. Victor Fletcher
111. Melissa Fletcher
112. Marshall Fletcher
113. Bernard Mills, Beckley, 1949
114. Betty Mills, 1951
115. James R. Walker, 1946
116. Ellen O. Walker
117. Kenneth Walker
118. V.J. Walker
119. Robie E. Wallace, 1953
120. Dewey L. Wallace
121. Thomas Wallace
122. Leroy Walker, 1950s
123. Phyllis Walker
124. Donald Walker
125. Julia Walker

126. Gail Pegram Wallace, 1952
127. Barbara Wallace Hurst
128. Jason Allen Hurst
129. Connie Wallace
130. Kerby Randall Walker, 1960
131. Carolyn Walker (wife)
132. Lanny Walker (son)
133. Missy Walker (Randy's daughter)
134. Julie Walker
135. Sherman Lilly
136. Billy Lilly
137. Benji Lilly
138. Cressa Walker Fendley, 1927, 1930, 1931
139. Florence Harmon Neely, 411 Grafton Street, Beckley, West Virginia 25801, 1946
140. Dorothy Harmon Roles, Odd, West Virginia 25902, 1946
141. Frank Mills, Crab Orchard, West Virginia 25827
142. Ruby Mills
143. Russell Neely, Beckley, West Virginia (Florence's husband)
144. Lessie Thompson, 224 Beckley Avenue, Beckley, West Virginia 25801
145. Francis Thompson, 224 Beckley Avenue, Beckley, West Virginia 25801
146. Betty Thompson
147. Juanita Peregoy, Beckley
148. C.G. Peregoy, Beckley
149. Irene Mills Meadows, Egeria, 1947
150. Lacy Meadows
151. Donna Meadows
152. Walter L. (Scotty) Hatcher, Sr., 1921
153. Ranie Walker Hatcher, 504 North Kanawha Street, Beckley, West Virginia, 1932
154. Lenox R. Walker, 1946
155. Mary Elizabeth Auer, 110 Hedge Street, Princeton, West Virginia 24740
156. Inza Akers, Beckley, West Virginia, 1927
157. John McKinney (Hilda Foley's husband)

The Genealogy and History of the Mills Family

By Barton (Barty) Wyatt--Written in 1968

In searching the available records, I find that the Mills family hails from merry old England and it seems to be their ancestral home. Nugent's history of "Caveliers and Pioneers" gives John Mills and William Mills as the first of the Mills family to come to America in the year 1637.

John Mills came to America from England as a passenger on John Barker's ship, July 12, 1637.

William Mills came to America July 19, 1637, in his own ship. He received a land grant of 350 acres on the south side of the James River at Jamestown, recorded in patent Book No. 1 at page 443. He paid for this land by transporting seven persons, namely, William Burgess, William Godfrey, William Holiday, John Garret, Robert Bateman, John Grange and Nicholas Abdy.

Samuel Mills, Sr. had a large family of sons and daughters, as many as twelve children. We can only locate three of the sons, namely: Samuel Mills, Jr., William (Billy) Mills and Robert Mills. Samuel (Sam) Mills, Jr. had a large family but we are only able to locate one son, Samuel David, who married Mary Akers and were the parents of a son and two daughters, namely: Cinda who married Ballard Mills and they had the following children: Belle, Delbert, Etta and Carce Mills; Rosa, who married Arch Crough and Samuel Willie married Maude Walker, a daughter of Gaston P. Walker. They were the parents of a son, Earl Mills who is the father of a barber in Princeton.

William (Billy) Mills and his wife, Marilla Mills had a large family which was as follows: Jeremiah, Anderson, Hiram, Roday, Ellen and William F. Mills, Jr.

Anderson Mills, son of Billy and Marilla Mills had four

children, namely: Charley Mills (known as "Liquor Making Charley"). He married Nancy Wallace and they were the parents of Mary, Zack, and Rose. Anderson's other two children were Jacob Reley and Mary Susan Mills. Trifania was Anderson's wife's name.

Robert Mills, son of Samuel Mills and Rebecca Mills, his wife, were the parents of a large family of sons and daughters as follows: He had five children when the 1850 census was taken with ages given at that time. Miley E. Mills, sixteen, Emelia, fourteen, Green, eleven, Marella, seven, Tabitha, two, and the other children were born after 1850 census were John Mills, Henry Mills, Keaton Mills, Aden Mills, Enon Mills and Ben Mills.

John Mills married a Foley and they were the parents of the following children: Horace, Bobby, who married Jesten Bailey, Amanda, who married a Shrewsbury and she is the mother of Mack Shrewsbury, the town police of Matoaka; Nita, Loma and Dessie.

Henry Mills married a Shrewsbury and they were the parents of three children, namely: Robert, Braxton (Brack), who married Viola Bailey and they were the parents of Cammie, Raymond, Verda and Aubrey Mills, Gelva and Nova; Lesta Mills was the only daughter of Henry Mills and his wife. She married Edgar Parcell.

Keaton Mills married Martha Ann Charity Walker and they were the parents of a large family of sons and daughters, namely: Stella, Alvirdie, Lydia, Ivery May, Hessie Dora, George Winfrey, Oley Johnson, Dessie Destine, Autie Easter, Nathan Crandall, Kelly Alderman and Lawrence Evestus. Lydia married Lundy Rose and they had Ray Vernan and Roy Vardon. They raised Bernadine, daughter of Autie Mills and Dolphus Cole. Bernadine Cole married Elmo Dillon.

Aden Mills, son of Robert and his wife, Rebecca, had a large family of sons and daughters, namely: Mandy, Sianna, Hattie, Lula, Erastus, Numa, Okey, Charles Henry, John Calvin, Wather Dewey and Aubrey.

Wather Dewey, son of Aden and Hulda, married Agnes Gray Neal and they were the parents of the following children: Wather D. Mills, Jr., who married Lillian Marie Blankenship and their children are Brenda Gail, Wather Dewey III and Virginia Gray; Jerry C. Mills who married Hazel Jane White and they are the parents of one son Jerry C. Mills, Jr.; Charles J. Mills who married Sadie Ray Thompson and they have two sons, Charles Jr. and Ralph; James A. Mills who married Violet Horn and they are the parents of a daughter, Karen Lee Mills; Gail Mills, the only daughter was twice married. Her first husband was Bramwell Reed and they had a son Bramwell Reed, Jr. Her second husband was Carl Hare and they have a daughter, Faith Annette Hare; Numa Grover Mills was twice married. His first wife was Belle Walker and to this union were born four children, namely: Crancy Mills, who married Tressie McComas, son of Dennis McComas. Her husband has served a number of years as a deputy sheriff of Mercer County; Admer Ray Mills (deceased); Gilmer Fay Mills married Blevins and Fern Mills married Rutledge.

Numa's second marriage was to a daughter of Tildon Walker and they were the parents of seven children, namely: Numa Dale Mills, Billy Gail, Keith (deceased), Gene, David, Florence, who married Lawson and Louise who married Matherly. (We lack information on the rest of the Aden Mills family).

The Enon Mills family is one of the largest families in the nation, consisting of fifteen boys and two girls. Sixteen lived to the age of puberty and beyond, none died in infancy. Enon and his wife, Fannie McComas Mills were a hardworking couple and were proud of their family of seventeen children and gave them the best education possible in those early days. The names of this family are as follows: Emerson, Rozella, Rufus, Clayton, Howard, Baxter, Okley, Covel, Wilder, Ile S., Claren, Ofa, Tharwell, Bonnie, Burwin, Woodrow, Jimmie and Albert. This writer had eight members of this family in school in the year 1906 at Rich Creek Graded School.

Emerson Mills married Clarice White and unto them were born three daughters Lorine, Olga and Ama. Lorine married Fink, Olga married Kelly Brammer and Ama married Ralph Swim.

Rozella married first Giles Shrewsbury and they had a son, Kernsey Shrewsbury. Her second marriage was to Hayden Wimmer and they were the parents of Billy, Earl, Hayden Junior and Betty Grace Wimmer.

Rufus Clayton Mills married Dora Arizona Cook, a direct descendent of John Cook, the first settler at Oceana in Wyoming County. Rufus Clayton Mills was born May 2, 1891. His wife, Dora Arizona Cook Mills was born June 7, 1896. They are the parents of the following children: Okey Andrew Mills, who married Lettie Mae Neely. They have no children. Okey, is at present the sheriff of Releigh County. He is now serving his second term as sheriff, which speaks well for his popularity. (*Insert by Gloria - 1994--Okey Mills ended up by serving five terms as sheriff, the only man in the history of West Virginia to be elected sheriff five times*). Clayton's second son, Ordie Mills lives in Jacksonville, Florida. Orris C. Mills was killed in the coal mines in 1946. Vera Olive Mills married Jamison and Orpha Jean married Donahoe.

Elbert Baxter Mills married Onvie Lotie Lemon and they are the parents of the following children: Arless Monroe Mills who married Ellen Campbell; Elbert Curtis Mills who married Mae Spangler; Janet Lee Mills who married Jerry Stiles; Miranda Mills who married Howard Miller and they have a son, Scott Miller; Carla Mills who married William L. Ball and they have a son, Linn Ball.

Howard Mills married (unknown) and they have four children, namely Kenneth, Keeford, Wilma who married York, and Eugene Mills.

Okley Mills married Novie Shrewsbury and they are the parents of five children, namely: Arthur, Lila, Adrian and Monya, Covel Mills (deceased).

Wilder Mills married Delia Delp, a daughter of the late James Delp. Unto this union were born the following family of children: David Conard Mills who married Louise Davis and have no offspring; Glenn Mills at home, single; Christeen who married Othinel Vaught and are the parents of five children; Elma who married Glenn Bailey and they have an adopted son, Johnnie Mills who was killed by a sniper in Vietnam and one married daughter. Erma married Stanley Walker and they have two sons and one daughter, married.

Ile S. Mills married Okley Reid and unto this union were born the following children: Harold Mills, John Wallace Mills, Beverly Bowden Mills, Ilene Mills who married Warren P. Blake, Shelby Mills who married John Earnest Mason, Billy Ray Mills who married Mable Cottle, and Stanley Sheron Mills who married Martha Ann Warmanoven.

Claren Mills married Garnet Reid and they are the parents of four children, namely, Leroy Mills, Helen, Melva and

Gay Mills. Ofa Mills, a son is deceased.

Tharwell Mills married Clelie Ross and unto them were born a large family of sons and daughters, namely: Burnell Mills who married Audrey Ford, Drexel Mills who married Hildegard Leicht, Jacqueline Mills who married Herbert Harvey, Alva Mills who married Mary Farmer, Ima Jo Mills who married Freddy Williams, Mason Mills who married Carrie Cecil, Bobby Mills who married May Dean Hopper, Anna Mills who married Arnold Farley, Okley Ray Mills, who married Patricia Creech, Alma Fay Mills who married Albert Elliot, Rena Mills who married Larry Robert and Clinton Mills who married Jacquitta Muncy.

Bonnie Mills, the youngest daughter of Enon and Fannie Mills married David Leroy. Burwin Dale Mills married Ruby Lee White and unto this union were born nine sons and daughters, namely: Barbara Lee Mills who married Horace Darlow Setliff, Norman Burwin Mills who married Jo Ann Wells, Sandra Kay Mills who married Lanny Douglas White, Harry Wayne Mills who married Patricia Ellen James, Ray Olen Mills who married Donna Jean Bailey, Rex Wallace, Arlene Joyce, David Michael and Carol June Mills are all at home.

Woodrow Mills married Thelma Anderson and they are the parents of two sons and two daughters, namely: Yvonne Mills who married Onsby M. Hurst and they have a daughter, Jennifer; Dempsey Woodrow Mills, who married Sandra Tilley; Elaine Mills who married Kyle Kinzer and they are the parents of three sons, Douglas, Gregory and Steven; Darryl Lynn Mills who married Diane Spradlin and they have a son, Darryl Lynn Mills, Jr.

James Mills, Sr. married Erma Christian Vaught. To this union were born six children, namely: Jerry A. Mills (deceased), Larry Mills who married Eunice Burkett and they have two children; Judy Mills who married Blake Hurst, they have three children and live in Roanoke, Virginia; James B. Mills (divorced) who has two children, and lives at Lashmeet. Eanon and Rodney Mills live at home.

Albert Mills married Helen Syes and they have two children, Connie Mills who married Harvey, and Roger Mills who lives at home.

This ends the genealogy of one of Mercer County's most prolific families. Their foreparents knew the dint of hard labor and were acquainted with toil. Barty Wyatt was a retired school teacher at the time of this writing in 1968. He is deceased and has one living brother in 1994. While Barty Wyatt listed all the children as belonging to Rebecca, it seems that Lydia was the mother of John, Thompson, Dessie, Samuel, Aden, Francis, Ben, Keaton and Eanon. Rebecca was the mother of Miley, Ememlia, Green, Marella and Tabitha.

Family Pictures

Seated: Johnson Keaton Mills, Martha Ann Charity Mills, Lydia Anner Mills. *Standing – back row:* Oley Johnson Mills, Dessie Destine Mills, George Winfrey Mills. *Standing – second row:* Laurence Evestus Mills, Nathan Crandall Mills, Johnny Corbit Mills, Autie Easter Mills, Dora Hessie Mills, Kelly Alderman Mills.

Martha Adeline Sizemore Walker; (b) 1835, (d) 1899; Numa Dink Walker, (b) 1829, (d) Nov. 21, 1884, parents of Martha Ann Mills.

Front row – left to right: John Wise Council Walker (b) 05-23-1855, Numa Captain Calvin Walker (b) 05-22-1857 (d) 04-08-1918, Christopher George Columbus Walker (b) 07-29-1870 (d) 01-22-1941. *Back row – left to right*: Nyanzi Nicti Cerleon Walker (b) 04-01-1879 (d) 04-19-1943, Lydia Mirinda Cerdula Walker (b) 02-02-1872 (d) 07-30-1952, Martha Ann Charity Walker (b) 02-25-1865, Mahulda Elizabeth Caroline Walker (b) 12-18-1859 (d) 11-06-1934, Frankie Jane Ceberry Walker (b) 12-06-1854 (d) 08-08-1940.

Grandma Mills and Joel Tilley (3-24-1935), son of Lila Alastia Mills Tilley and Yule Tilley.

Lila Alastia Mills Tilley and son, Joel Tilley.

Certificate of Marriage

Book No. 1850-95   Page No. 40

STATE OF WEST VIRGINIA,
COUNTY OF RALEIGH, ss:

I, Elinor Hurt, Clerk of the County Commission in and for said county and state (the same being a court of record) and as such Clerk having the care and custody of the Records of Marriages, do certify that said records show that

Johnson K. Mills

and

M. A. C. Walker

were married on Sept. 9, 1886 at Raleigh Co., W. Va.,
by Charles Walker

(SEAL)

In testimony whereof, I have hereunto affixed my signature and official seal at Beckley, West Virginia, this 17th day of October, 19 79.

Elinor Hurt, Clerk.

By Betty Riffe, Deputy Clerk.

Keaton Mills

Are you destined to be unknown to your great-grandchildren? Do you know what their occupations and names were? In a national survey conducted February 13-19, 1995, by the Gallup organization 1,005 adults were asked if they knew the first names and occupations of their great-grandparents. More than 60 percent did not know the names of any of their great-grandparents, and only 8 percent knew their occupations.

It is harder to reconstruct than to just sit down and write something about your family now that you can pass on to your children. I cannot find much information on Grandpa Mills' sisters and brothers. The sisters seem to just have vanished as far as history is concerned and some of the brothers, we have names only.

In 1974, Doctor McGraw who was a pharmacist in a Beckley drugstore, called me. He told me that Mills, Vermillion and Strayley, with their families and belongings, were on a raft coming up the James River when Mills' wife fell overboard and was drowned and that two colored men were also drowned trying to save her. I did not ask Mills' first name. I did make a few notes, but not enough to get the whole story. He said that Vermillion, Strayley and Mills were aboard and that later Strayley bought Mills' and Vermillion's land grants. Vermillion settled in Bluefield and I think there was still a Doctor Vermillion in that area in 1992. He said that we could look into the Doctor Vermillion and Will Strayley properties in Wise or Russel counties. They came from England.

The records from the census of 1850 and 1880 are confusing. The 1880 census lists a Henry, and Henry was the second son of Robert, whose mother was a Gore, so they must have named another son Henry. On Saturday, July 29, 1995, I accidently stumbled into a Mills reunion while looking for the Foley reunion. I talked briefly with a young woman who did not know much of the family history. They were from the Zack Mills' family. Zack was the son of Anderson Mills, who was the son of William (Billy) Mills, who was Great-Grandfather Robert's brother. She said they were having trouble -- seemed they found two Henrys in the same family.

Gladys Walker Tilley's records show a Francis, however, the census of 1850 and of 1880 do not. She lists a Samuel, but the census does not.

Letter from Aunt Dessie Mills Cole dated November 15, 1974:

"Yes, I remember well Dad's two half brothers. Hugh lived between Egeria and Camp Creek and Uncle Henry lived at Pinoak not far from your grandparents McComas, back from Lundy and Lydia's farm, joined, I think and I know you must remember Uncle Henry's son Brack who was the father of Cammie and Virdie. Virdie married Millard McComas. I don't know how the half brothers came about. We treated them as full uncles, but I never was at Hugh's house, but I stayed at Uncle Henry's many a night. Lois Rose and I loved to visit them and was close friends with Cammie and Virdie Mills, Uncle Henry's grandchildren. Old Doctor Vermillion died near the time that my father died, but there was one younger in Princeton the last I knew. Willse Strayley got water, all he used to drink from the health spring, also many doctors and people from Princeton when Dad and family lived in Spanishburg. They had paid for it before Dad bought the place. They gave it to anyone who wanted the water and an awful lot of folks used that water. I just wish that I could get it to drink now. It sure was healthy water. People from Beckley, Bluefield and many places used that water. Grandpa Mills married a Swinny (Sweeney) who was Dad's mother. Some of her people live around Flat Top and Beckley."

* (Note) Grandpa Robert married Lydia Thompson who had previously been married to Green Swinney or Sweeney. Lydia was the mother of several children including Grandpa Keaton.

Since I can't remember my grandfather Mills and there is no one around now to tell me about him, very little is known. My cousin, Alastia told me what she remembered about Grandpa Mills before she died in 1992. She told me about growing up with Grandma, her brother, Delmer and Grandpa until she was eight years old. She could remember Uncle Kelly and Grandpa very well. In fact, she was the only living relative who could give me any history about Grandpa. She said that Grandma would say, "Keat is a hard working man." She remembered him as the only father she ever knew. She used to hate her father for "giving" her away, but when she was grown, she realized as a young man he was left with three small children and could not have gone to work to support them and take care of an eleven-day-old baby girl. She was taken by her maternal Grandmother Belle Graham for a few days, but her grandmother was crippled and practically bedfast and the two aunts living with her and taking care of her decided that they could not take care of a small baby so they sent word to Grandma Mills that she could have the baby and to come and get her. They lived on top of Bluff Mountain and Grandma told Alastia that she almost ran up the hill and had to slow down because she had chest pains. Alastia said that Grandma must have wanted her very much.

The day before Grandpa took to his bed to die, Alastia said they were working in the garden until almost dark when Grandpa said, "Alastia, I can't tell the weeds from the vegetables, so we will have to go in." He put a chew of tobacco in his mouth and got a tin cup to spit in and she sat on his knee. She said that she was very fond of him. While Grandpa was sick, Alastia broke out with German measles and they would not let her go into his room. The doctor finally told them to allow her to see him, that she could not hurt him and his illness would not hurt her.

It seems that Grandpa Mills was always a farmer, usually owned large acreage, worked hard, was a peaceful man and a good provider for his large family. My mother spoke highly of him and thought that he was a good man.

Reverend J.B. Mills who served as pastor having been ordained by the church. His faithful mule "Old Dick" who got him to his church services on time over rough, rocky, muddy roads from his Egeria home with "many a flat tire." In one pocket of the saddlebags was the servant's Holy Bible. The other pocket contained a feed bag with oats or corn for the faithful mule to munch on while his master preached a stirring message to the eager people inside the church.

Okey Mills, a cousin, told me about the Reverend John B. Mills, the born–again Baptist. When holding services, young men often got liquored up, riding their horses around the church, putting the horses head through the windows, shooting and even coming into the church, making loud noises and generally creating a disturbance. Reverend Mills would drop to his knees, pray and ask God's help in giving him strength and then, "Beat the hell out of them and throw them out". This is Okey's quote.

The Reverend would then go back in and continue his preaching of hellfire and brimstone.

He has been described as being tall, perhaps six feet two inches, a man of soldierly bearing, and straight as an arrow. Guess that he could "take care" of a few troublemakers.

The Reverend John B. Mills was the oldest son of Robert Mills and his wife Lydia Thompson Mills and he is my great uncle. My grandfather, Keaton was the eighth, according to records that I am able to find.

The Reverend John B. Mills — From Moonshiner to Minister

Shirley Donnelly

Raleigh County and adjacent territory has never had a more colorful character than the late Reverend John B. Mills (1856-1918). So many stories have been related about Mills that in 1950, I asked the late Reverend G.P. Goode, the eminent Wyoming County historian, who knew the Reverend Mills, to write me his recollections of that noted minister.

On April 22, 1950, Reverend Goode wrote out for me a long character sketch of Mills. John B. Mills hailed from Flat Top section of this area where he became noted. He was well-known to civil authorities because of his activities as an outlaw moonshiner, and bootlegger of the Devil's Fork and Flat Top Mountain region.

In 1899, Mills changed from being a moonshiner to become a minister in the Raleigh Baptist Association. Mills didn't mind telling of his life as an illicit distiller. For his offense in moonshining, Mills was arrested and hailed before Federal Judge Jackson, the "Iron Judge", who had been appointed by President Abraham Lincoln.

Mills was fined and sentenced to thirty days in jail. But Mills went back to making moonshine liquor. Coming before Judge Jackson a second time, Mills was fined five hundred dollars and given a year in jail. Out of the jail, Mills persisted in making and selling whiskey. When brought before Judge Jackson a third time, the long white-bearded judge walked the floor behind the bench at Parkersburg and sentenced Mills to two years at hard labor in Moundsville Penitentiary and warned him to "Never come back here again".

Mills, who said, "I've been in five of them there jail houses and slept on iron floors with no pillar to lay my head on," said to his wife, "Minerva, that whooped me." Mills said, "In the penitentiary I learned to make boots, and good ones, too."

As a minister he wore high-top boots and always stuffed the bottoms of his breeches in his boots. When he took up preaching he preached loud and long. When Mills attended the annual meetings of the Raleigh Baptist Association he was always on the program for a report on temperance. It was well known that the moderator always had to call time on Mills, who talked at great lengths against what he called "the damnable traffic," meaning the liquor industry.

Mills, who died at the age of seventy-two, is buried in a lonely graveyard near Egeria on Devil's Fork Mountain, some little distance from Beckley. He was a lurid character in his time.

In the course of his early life Mills was jailed five times for illicit liquoring, but eventually became a Baptist preacher. His experience from "moonshine to minister" is a long one.

According to the Reverend G.P. Goode, a Wyoming County historian, Mills was illiterate and unlearned. After he experienced the inner and divine call to preach the Gospel, Mills said, "I don't know just how the Lord is going to make me understand His book, for I don't know a letter in the Book." He later said his wife taught him the alphabet and how to spell out the sentences in the Bible. Mills took the Bible literally, every word of it. He said, "Way back in the morning of time, God said that 'who so sheddeth man's blood, by man shall his blood be shed.'"

Then Mills went on to show how that worked out literally in a given case. He said, "At a drunken dance on Devil's Fork, my brother Ben Mills killed a man. Years later, Ben Mills was shot and killed in a drunken row at Elkhorn".

"God said it should be so". In those tragedies Mills read the literal fulfillment of the Scripture about bloodshed crimes.

John B. Mills was converted in a protracted meeting at

Pleasant Home Church out Flat Top way. That night when Mills was converted about everybody in the church was shouting.

One thing for which the old fellow could never quite forgive himself was making his boy, Walter Mills, make, drink, and sell moonshine whiskey. Walter become a drunkard "and then took the gallopin' consumption and died in a few weeks" said his father. The memory of that haunted J.B. Mills to his dying day in late September 1918.

Mills liked to preach. Mills and John W. Gunnoe, another preacher, went around together. Once at a meeting they contested as to which of them would get to preach when both were ambitious to hold forth. Gunnoe argued that he should be allowed to preach because he hadn't preached a sermon in three months. Mills rejoined that was exactly the reason why Gunnoe shouldn't preach, because "a man who hasn't preached in three months is too cold to preach! I am going to preach the sermon myself." And Mills did. He went on to preach like the Bible admonishes men to pray – "without ceasing".

Try to picture this. A grown man, who has married, raised a family and well past "school age"; he could not read or write and did not know his ABCs. How would he preach and understand the Bible if he could not even read it? His wife taught him the alphabet and taught him to read, using the Bible. I would not want to be put in charge of teaching a child (who can learn much easier and faster than an adult) to read. There are words that are hard to pronounce and names that I would have no idea as to the pronunciation unless I had heard Bible scholars pronounce them.

This man was under the firm conviction that he had received from God a calling to go forth and preach His word. This would make one believe that there is such a thing as "divine" calling.

Will of Robert Mills

Dated March 30, 1870
Devils' Fork

BE IT <u>REMEMBERT</u> THAT I ROBERT MILLS OF THE County of Wyoming and State of West Virginia being weak in body but of sound mind and perfect memory blessed be almighty God for the same do make this my last will and Testament, in manner and form following that is to say First, I give and <u>declair</u> that son, Hugh G. Mills be made an equal heir with my last wifes children and also to Milley E. McKinney my oldest daughter I <u>bequath</u> one dollar and to Emily McKinney, my second daughter I <u>bequath</u> one dollar and to Marilla Mills, my third daughter, I bequath one dollar and to Tabitha J. Mills I beqauth one dollar and I <u>allso</u> hereby appoint William T. Sarver Benjamin Mills, Aden Thompson and John Howerton, Esq. executors of this my last will and testament hereby revoking all former wills by me made in witness whereof I have hereunto set my hand and seal the 11th day of December 1869.

Robert Mills, mark.

N.B. Wheras I stated above that I declared that Hugh J. Mills be made <u>and</u> equal heir with my last wifes children, that is be it understood from John B. Mills down to the youngest, and I <u>allso</u> further <u>declair</u> that if any of said <u>legatees</u>, beginning with John B. downwards should prove incoragible while under age and not under due obedience to their mother I hereby declair they shall be disinherited according to Justice and I further declair that my wife Lydia Mills is in free and full possession of all my property so long as she remains my widow and allso <u>se</u> that my children is fairley <u>deset</u> by after my decease.

In 1860 Census the Mills Family included Robert Mills, 48, farmer; Lydia, 35; Hugh G., 20; Marilla, 16; Jane, 12; Henry G., 11; John B., 10; William F., 9; Rewe D., 8; Samuel O., 7; Frances, 4, and Aden, 1.

Will of William Mills

Recorded June 2nd 1872
Written 26th Day of April 1871

BE IT remembered that I William Mills of the County of Wyoming and State of West Virginia being weak in body but of sound and blessed be Almight God, for the same, do make and publish my last will and testament in manner and form following.
That is to say I give and bequeath to my oldest son, Jeremiah Mills one dollar above what I have already given him. And to my second son, Anderson Mills I give and bequeath one dollar above what I have given him. And to Rhoda Wimmer, my oldest daughter, I give and bequeath one dollar above what I have given her. And to my second daughter, Ellen Mills, I give and bequeath one dollar for the same reason as above. And to my third son, John Mills, I give and bequeath one dollar same reason above. And to my fourth son, David Mills, I give and bequeath one dollar same reason above and to my fifth son, Henry Mills, I give and bequeath one dollar for the same reason as above and to my third daughter, Victoria Mills and Joseph Mills, my sixth son I give and bequeath my Ring Land to be equally divided among them and that Marilla Mills have a home on said land her lifetime and the balance of my estate I give and bequeath to my beloved wife both real and personal after my just debts is paid to her sole use and disposal forever and to the heirs of my son, William F. Mills, deceased, and bequeath one dollar above what I have already given them.
And I hereby appoint my beloved wife, Marilla Mills my sole executrix of this my last will and testament hereby revoking all former wills by me made in witness in whereof

I have hereunto set my hand and seal the 26th day of April in the year of our Lord, 1871.

Signed, sealed and published and declared by the above named William Mills to be his last will and testament in presence of us who at his request and in his presence hath herein to subscribed our names this 26th day of April 1871.

William Mills, (his mark)

John T. Ring
Richard Pate

ROBERT MILLS' WILL

-MARCH 3, 1870

Be it Remembered that I Robert Mills of the County of Wyoming and State of West Virginia being weak in body but of Sound mind and perfect memory blessed be almighty God for the same do make this my last will and Testament, in manner and form following that is to say first I will and declair that my Son Hugh J. Mills be made an Equal heir with my last wifes Children, and also to Milley E. McKiney my oldest Daughter I Bequeath one Dollar and to Emly McKiney my Second Daughter I Bequeath one Dollar and to Mariller Mills my third Daughter I Bequeath one dollar and to Tabitha J. Mills I Bequath one dollar and I also hereby appoint William T. Sarver Benjamin Mills Adm Thompson and John Howerton Esq executors, of this my Last Will and Testament hereby revoking all former wills by me made in witness whereof I have hereunto set my hand & Seal the 11th day of December 1869

Robert X Mills

Signed Sealed and Published & declared by the above Named Robert Mills to be his last will and Testament in the presence of us who at his request and in his presence have hereunto Subscribed our Names the day and date above written

George P. Peters
Thompson H. Alvis

N.B. Whereas I Stated above that I declared that Hugh J. Mills be made an Equal heir with my last wifes Children, that is be it Remembered understood from John B. Mills down to the youngest. and I, also further declair that if any of Said Legattes beginning from John B downwards should prove incoragible while under age and not render due obedience to their Mother I hereby declair they shall be disinherited acording to Justice and I further declair that my wife Syda Mills remain in free and full possession of all my property avery

53

so long as she remain my widow and also be that my Children is shering decent by & c. after my Decease

Signed Robert his mark Mills

State of West Virginia

In the Recorders office of Wyoming County the last Will and Testament of Robert Mills Dec'd was this day presented before me in this office proven by the oath of Thompson H. Peters one of the Subscribing Witnesses thereto and was Continued for the other Witness

Teste James Cook Recorder

Recorders Office of Said County the 30th day of March 1871 George P. Peters the other Subscribing witness to the annexed will of Robert Mills dec'd this day appeared before me in said office and the said Will Signature and acknowledgement was also duly and properly proven by said George P. Peters to be the last Will and Testament of Robert Mills Dec'd and the same being fully proven acording to law is admitted to Record in Said office

Teste Jas Cook Recorder

State of West Virginia

In the Recorders office of Wyoming County the 30th day of March 1870 On motion of Benjamin Mills and John Howerton two of the Executors named in the will of Robert Mills dec'd and who made oath thirdto together with Mr T. Sarver their Surety, Entered into and acknowledged a bond in the penalty of Two Thousand dollars Conditioned as the law requires Certificate is Granted them for obtaining probate of said will in due form, where upon the s'd Executors took the several oaths prescribed by law

A Copy

Teste James Cook Rec

FAMILY GROUP SHEET

Husband's Code ....
Wife's Code ....

HUSBAND'S NAME "Keaton" JOHNSON Joseph Keaton MILLS
Date of Birth 16 May 1865 (5c) (7) Place Wyoming Co.? WV
Date of Death 15 July 1924 (7) Place Raleigh Co.? WV
Present Address (or) Place of Burial Keaton Mills Cem - Egeria, Raleigh Co., WV
His Father Robert MILLS His Mother's Maiden Name Lydia THOMPSON (?)
Date of Marriage of HUSBAND and WIFE on this sheet 1880 Place Wyoming Co, WV
Check here if there was another marriage: By husband ☐ By Wife ☐ Was this couple divorced? Yes ☐ No ☐ When?____

WIFE'S MAIDEN NAME Martha Ann Charity WALKER (Use separate sheet for each marriage)
Date of Birth 25 Feb 1865 Place Wyoming Co. WV
Date of Death 11 April 1936 Place ____ Co.? WV
Present Address (or) Place of Burial With her husband
Her Father ____ Her Mother's Maiden Name ____

Items of interest about the above couple (occupations, hobbies, achievements; social, civil, and political activities; physical descriptions—include photos possible; military service; cause of death): Keaton bought the farm in Egeria, Raleigh Co. WV on 14 December 1890 (recording date) (7)

Use reverse side for additional information

Have family sheet		CHILDREN (Arrange in order of birth)	Code	Birth Information	Death Information	Marriage Information
	1	Stella Mae	(7)	ON 3 June 1881 AT	ON 5 May 1913 AT (7)	ON ____ TO ____
	2	Alverdie Elizabeth	(7)	ON 12 Feb 1885 AT	ON 19 Feb 1965 AT (7)	ON ____ TO ____
	3	Lydia Anner	(7)	ON 1 Mar. 1887 AT	ON 9 Mar 1972 AT (7)(5)	ON ____ TO Sundy ROSE
	4	Ivery Mae	(7)	ON 22 Nov 1888 AT	ON 15 June 1890 AT (7)(6)	ON ____ TO ____
	5	"Henie" Dora Henie	(7)	ON 8 Apr. 1890 AT	ON 8 Mar. 1936 AT (7)	ON ____ TO Fred SPEED b 1893

Check here if there are additional children ☒

Footnoting. To substantiate the information recorded on this page, please use the footnotes listed below. One of these numbers should be placed in the circle provided next to each answer on the questionnaire. If you got the information from a source not listed, place that source on a vacant line and use the number next to which it has been placed as your footnote number.

Use ① only if you have filled in the blank from personal knowledge (such as the name of your brother). If you must look up his marriage date, give the source wherever you looked it up. If you asked him, give him as the source.

① Name and address of person filling in this sheet. P. C. SCHAFFER Gloria C. Date 6 October 1994
453 Greencastle Lane Malamer
Virginia Beach, VA 23452

②
③
④
⑤ CENSUS of Wyoming Co. W.V.: (5c) 1870 (5J) 1880 (5c) 1900 (5J) 1860
⑥ "The Genealogy and History of the MILLS FAMILY" by Peyton Wyatt, 1968 (from Gloria C. Malamer
⑦ "The History of the Keaton Mills Cemetery" by Gloria C. Malamer, September 17, 1981
⑧

FAMILY GROUP SHEET
PAGE 2

HUSBAND'S NAME: Johnson Keaton MILLS   Code: ____

WIFE'S MAIDEN NAME: Martha Ann Charity WALKER   Code: ____

Have family sheet	#	CHILDREN (Arrange in order of birth)	Code	Birth Information	Death Information	Marriage Information
	6	George Winfrey	(7)	5 June 1892 (10) (1)	27 Nov 1948 (7)	
	7	Oley Johnson	(7)	26 Aug 1894 (7)	1 Nov 1952 (7)	"Ella" _____ (7)
	8	"Dessie" Della Bessie	(7)	16 Mar 1896 (7)	4 Mar 1980 (7)	10 Dec 1916 (7) E. Elmer COLE b 1898 d 1969
	9	"Johnny" (11) (9)(7) John Corbit Keaton		17 Mar 1898 (7)	6 Nov 1937 (7)	2 Thelma McCOMAS
	10	"Auntie" Auntie Easter Anthrim	(7)	25 Apr 1900 (7)	29 Dec 1967 (7)	Dolphus COLE
	11	Nathan Crankall	(7)	25 June 1902 (7)	4 July 1967 (7)	
	12	Kelly Alderman	(7)	16 Feb 1904 (7)	26 Nov 1931 (7)	
	13	Lawrence Everture	(7)	18 Oct 1905 (7)	25 Oct 1929 (7)	
	14					
	15					
	16					

FOOTNOTES:

(9) "World War II - hired Army veteran Corbit Keaton Mills... served in France and Germany under Gen. P..
(10) These three are the only ones of this family not buried in the cemetery (7)
(11) Parents of Gloria Catherine (MILLS) 7/7/23 MALAMAS and Corbit (1924-1974)

EXTRACT FROM 1870 CENSUS

State: W. Virginia **County or Parish:** Wyoming **Township/Ward/Beat:** Barkers Ridge **Person No.:**
Extracted by: Patty SCHAFFER **Date of Enumeration:** 11 Sept 1870 **Street:** **Microfilm reel No.** M593 #1702
504/1854

Page	Dwelling No.	Family No.	Names	Age	Sex	Color	Occupation, etc.	Value of real estate	Value of personal property	Birthplace	Father foreign born	Mother foreign born	Month born in year	Month married in year	School in year	Cannot read	Cannot write	Impairment	Males eligible to vote	Males ineligible to vote
564 A	68	68	MILLS, Robert (1911) *Last door came 1872 / 1st this direction + east C of 5 gdn*	59	M	W	farmer	$1000	—	Virginia										
			Sidney (Sydar?)	48	F		Keeping House													
			John? (Wilson?)	19	M		Works on farm									—	—			
			William F.G.?	18	M		Works on farm									—	—			
			Emila I.	17	F		at home									—	—			
			✓ Samuel? I.	15	M		Works a farm									—	—			
			? James (cer)	14	F		at home									—	—			
			? William (Allen?)	13	M		Works on farm									—	—			
			✓ Benjamin	8	M		at home		1862											
			✓ Johnson K	6	M		at home		1864		West Virginia									
			Willis Edwin	4	M		at home		1866		West Virginia			(?) Oct 6 24, 1865 probably Sept 26, 1865 Benjamin Linder McCarger (?) Oct 5 17 Children 1870							

*I put the age as 69, but Andex gives it as 59.

Please, I plan to look at this one again — but I was surprised that "Sidney" was a female. Therefore checked it. The name pretty carefully. But the mother of the children are TOO close to the ages ... Could Wilson, Rebecca or Sydna there a middle name: Sidney? Or the enumerator misunderstand the nomenclature?

FAMILY GROUP SHEET
Based on 1870

Husband's Code: _____
Wife's Code: _____

HUSBAND'S NAME Robert MILLS
Date of Birth c1811?, 1801? (5a)(5c) Place Virginia
Date of Death _____ Place _____
Present Address (or) Place of Burial _____
His Father Samuel MILLS? (6) His Mother's Maiden Name _____
Date of Marriage of HUSBAND and WIFE on this sheet: ?186_ Place _____
Check here if there was another marriage: By husband ☐ By Wife ☐ Was this couple divorced? Yes ☐ No ☐ When? _____

WIFE'S MAIDEN NAME Julia? Sidney (Use separate sheet for each marriage)
Date of Birth c1822 (6c) Place Virginia
Date of Death Oct 25, 1885 (63 yrs old) Place _____
Present Address (or) Place of Burial _____
Her Father _____ Her Mother's Maiden Name _____

Items of interest about the above couple (occupations, hobbies, achievements; social, civil, and political activities; physical descriptions—include photos if possible; military service; cause of death): "Aunt Bessie Mills Cole wrote me ... she remembered Grandpa Mills (child #8) "having two half-brothers." who may have been from 1st marriage. Sidney may be mother of #7, 8, + 9 (5 year break after #6)

Use reverse side for additional information

Have family sheet		CHILDREN (Arrange in order of birth)	Code	Birth Information	Death Information	Marriage Information
✓	1	John C (-19)		ON c1851 (6c) AT VA	ON ___ AT ___	ON ___ TO ___
-	2	William F? (67,19) ("Billy")		ON c1852 (6c) AT VA		
	3	Emila (17)		ON c1853 (6c) AT VA		
	4	Samuel? (15)		ON c1855 AT VA		
	5	Francis (me) 14 Jerrold		ON c1856 (6c) AT VA		

Check here if there are additional children ☒

Footnoting. To substantiate the information recorded on this page, please use the footnotes listed below. One of these numbers should be placed in the circle provided next to each answer on the questionnaire. If you got the information from a source not listed, place that source on a vacant line and use the number next to which it has been placed as your footnote number.

Use ① only if you have filled in the blank from personal knowledge (such as the name of your brother). If you must look up his marriage date, give as the source wherever you looked it up. If you asked him, give his name as the source.

① Name and address of person filling in this sheet. P. C. SCHAFFER + Gloria C. Malamar Date 6 October 1994
453 Greencastle Lane
Virginia Beach, Va 23452

②
③
④
⑤ Census of Wyoming Co WV: (5a) 1850 (5b) 1860 (5c) 1870 (5d) 1880
⑥ "The Genealogy and History of the Mills Family" by Barton Wyatt, 1968 (from Gloria C. Malamar
⑦ "The History of the Keaton Mills Cemetery" by Gloria C. Malamar, September 17, 1981
⑧ Corr: Gloria C. Malamar - Sept 12th, 1994 to PCS

FAMILY GROUP SHEET
PAGE 2

HUSBAND'S NAME: Robert MILLS Code: _____
WIFE'S MAIDEN NAME: Sidney Code: _____

Have family sheet	#	CHILDREN (Arrange in order of birth)	Code	Birth Information	Death Information	Marriage Information
	6	Aaron/Aden © (3)		c 1857 VA		
	7	Benjamin (7)		c 1862 VA	(M), Moreclose 26 acres sister to	Irvin Cooper CB? Feb. 2, 1872 Manuda who—
	8	Johnson Keaton (5)		16 May 1865 WYOMING CO WV	15 July 1924	married ather Martha Ann Chart, WALKS ©
	9	Walter/Wallace? E? ENON (4)		c 1866		
	10					
	11					
	12					
	13					
	14					
	15					
	16					

FOOTNOTES:
⑨
⑩
⑪
⑫
⑬
⑭
⑮
⑯
⑰
⑱
⑲

EXTRACT FROM 1850 OR 1860 CENSUS

State: VA (WV) County or Parish: Wyoming Township/Ward/Beat: ___
Extracted by: Patty SCHAFFER Date of Enumeration: 5/21 1860 / 1860
Person No.: ___ Street: ___ Microfilm reel No. 653 / 1355

Note at top: "Muere to June / at"

Page	Dwelling No	Family No	Names	Age	Sex	Color	Occupation, etc.	Value of real estate	Value of personal property	Birthplace	Married in year	School in year	Cannot read or write
679/A	193	166	MILLS, Anderson	20	M	W	farmer	300?/200?	60	VA			
p5	JohBranch		Sophia	16	F	"				"			
680/A	205	178	MILLS, Robert	48	M		farmer	2000	1000 (?)	VA			1
			Sophia	35	F								1
			? Hugh 91(?)	20	M		farm laborer						
			V Marella	16	F								
			? Jane / June ? (Joliff.)	12	F								
			Levin 19(?)	11	M								
			John 13 ?	10	M								
			William + T.	9	M								
			Reex ?? B ?	8	M								
			Samuel O	7	M								
			James	4	M								
			Eileen (1859)	1	M								

Notes:
J.B. (Julia?) Mills
(M) Prisoner Surley
Rev. Buy Mills 45
Mr E. MERITHA 09:33

quick check this census M420 Soundex for Allen's information

EXTRACT Fr. M 1880 CENSUS SOUNDEX

State: **WV**
County or Parish: **Stevens**
Extracted by: **Patty SCHAFFER**
Township/Ward/Beat: _____
Date of Enumeration: **5 Oct 94**
Street: _____
Person No.: _____
Microfilm reel No.: _____

Page	Dwelling No.	Family No.	Names	Color	Sex	Age prior to June 1st	Born in census year	Relationship to head of house	Single	Married	W-dowed/Divorced	Married in census year	Occupation	Cannot read	Cannot write	Place of birth	Place of birth of mother	Place of birth of father
			MILLS, Abram	W	M	33		Head		not recorded						WV		
			Laura			22		"								"		
			Mary A			1		Dau(?)		not recorded						"		
			Thompson, Walter			5		"								"		
			Moenhill, John			51		not recorded								VA		
			MILLS, Henry G. (B.1850)	W	M	30		Head								WV		
			Clara C. *(not recorded)*					Wife								"		
			Robert W.					Son								"		
			Dolores P.													"		
			Laura R.													"		
			MILLS, Hugh G. (B.1840)	W	M	40											WV		
			Elizabeth M.	W		40											VA		
			Robert B.			12										WV		
			Jeremiah J.			11												
			Hugh B. G.?			9												
			Elizabeth M.			4												
			William J.			1		Son										
			MILLS, Lidde		F	57													

see other sheet

No Robert, Johnson, Keaton, or JK in Soundex — may/will fit in dwelling proper

Morris Co: SE 8T - Morris Co: 56 84 - Mud 33 P 14 - Mud 14, C 24 - Mud 45 P 11 - Payette G.

Family Group Sheet

Husband's Full Name Robert Mills   **Chart No.**

	Day Month Year	City, Town or Place	County or Province, etc.	State or Country	Add. Info. on Hu
Birth					
Chr'nd					
Marr.	28 Apr 1832		Giles Co.	Va	
Death	1 Dec. 1869		Mercer Co.	NY	
Burial					

Places of Residence

Occupation   Church Affiliation   Military Rec.

2d: Lydia

His Father Samuel Mills   Mother's Maiden Name Rachel Prince

Wife's Full Maiden Name Rebecca Rinehart

	Day Month Year	City, Town or Place	County or Province, etc.	State or Country	Add. Info. on Wif
Birth	1814				
Chr'nd					
Death					
Burial					

Places of Residence

Occupation   Church Affiliation   Military Rec.

Her Father   Mother's Maiden Name

Sex	Children's Names in Full	Christening Date	Day Month Year	City, Town or Place	County or Province, etc.	State or Country	Add. info on Childre
	1 Milly Ellen Mills	Birth	1834				
		Marr.					
	Full Name of Spouse Joseph McKinney	Death					
		Burial					
	2 Emelia Mills	Birth	1836				
		Marr.					
	Full Name of Spouse Jessie Green McKinney 185-	Death					
		Burial					
	3 Hugh Green Mills	Birth	1838				
		Marr.					
	Full Name of Spouse Catherine Neely	Death					
		Burial					
	4 Marilla Mills	Birth	1843				
		Marr.					
	Full Name of Spouse	Death					
		Burial					
	5 Tabitha June Mills	Birth	1848				
		Marr.					
	Full Name of Spouse John Morgan -1876-	Death					
		Burial					
	6 Henry G. Mills	Birth	1849				
		Marr.					
	Full Name of Spouse Clara Shrewsbury 1873	Death					
		Burial					
	7 Zurah D. Mills	Birth					
		Marr.					
	Full Name of Spouse Tom White	Death					
		Burial					
	8	Birth					
		Marr.					
	Full Name of Spouse	Death					
		Burial					

Compiler   Notes:

Address

City, State, Zip

Date

Family Group Sheet

Husband's Full Name Robert Mills **Chart No.** ____

Husband's Data	Day Month Year	City, Town or Place	County or Province, etc.	State or Country	Add. Info. on Husb
Birth					
Chr'nd					
Marr					
Death					
Burial					

Places of Residence

Occupation ____ Church Affiliation ____ Military Rec. ____

Other Husbands: 1st: Rebecca Rinehart

His Father Samuel Mills   Mother's Maiden Name Rachel Prince

Wife's Full Maiden Name Lydia THOMPSON

Wife's Data	Day Month Year	City, Town or Place	County or Province, etc.	State or Country	Add. Info. on Wife
Birth					
Chr'nd					
Death					
Burial					

Places of Residence

Occupation ____ Church Affiliation ____ Military Rec. ____

Her Father ____ Mother's Maiden Name ____

Children

Sex	Children's Names in Full	Children's Data	Day Month Year	City, Town or Place	County or Province, etc.	State or Country	Add. Info on Children
	1 John B. Mills	Birth	1850				
		Marr.					
	Full Name of Spouse: Minerva Elizabeth Farley	Death					
		Burial					
	2 William F. Mills 1871	Birth	1851				
		Marr.					
	Full Name of Spouse: Marilla Perdue	Death					
		Burial					
	3 Rewe D. Mills	Birth	1852	This name keeps showing up, but no record of marriage that I can find and no family member remembers.			
		Marr.					
	Full Name of Spouse	Death					
		Burial					
	4 Samuel O. Mills	Birth	1853	Samuel listed Aug. 24th, 1856. Martha Mills, female died 30th July 1855. Cause unknown. Age 15 days. (Robert and Lyda Mills) Informant, father.			
		Marr.					
	Full Name of Spouse: Martha Ann Cook	Death					
		Burial					
	5 Frances Mills	Birth	1856	Frances listed Wyoming county births Nov. 24 1857, Robert and Lyda Mills.			
		Marr.					
	Full Name of Spouse: Jesse Keon	Death					
		Burial					
	6 Aden Mills	Birth	1859				
		Marr.					
	Full Name of Spouse: Mahulda Walker	Death					
		Burial					
	7 Benjamin (Ben) Mills	Birth					
		Marr.	1864				
	Full Name of Spouse: Narcissa Walker	Death					
		Burial					
	8 Johnson Keaton	Birth	1865				
		Marr.		Married Martha Ann Charity Walker			1886
	Full Name of Spouse: Wallis Eanon	Death					
		Burial	1868	Married Servilla Francis McComas 1888			

Compiler ____ Address ____ City, State, Zip ____ Date ____

FAMILY GROUP SHEET

Based on 1860 census

Husband's Code ....
Wife's Code ....

HUSBAND'S NAME Robert MILLS
Date of Birth ±1812   Place VA
Date of Death ___   Place ___
Present Address (or) Place of Burial ___
His Father ___   His Mother's Maiden Name ___
Date of Marriage of HUSBAND and WIFE on this sheet ___   Place ___
Check here if there was another marriage: By husband ☐ By Wife ☐ Was this couple divorced? Yes ☐ No ☐ When? ___

WIFE'S MAIDEN NAME 2nd. Sydra THOMPSON (?⊙) (Use separate sheet for each marriage)
Date of Birth ±1825   Place VA
Date of Death ___   Place ___
Present Address (or) Place of Burial ___
Her Father ___   Her Mother's Maiden Name ___

Items of interest about the above couple (occupations, hobbies, achievements; social, civil, and political activities; physical descriptions—include photos if possible; military service; cause of death):

Use reverse side for additional information

Have family sheet	#	CHILDREN (Arrange in order of birth)	Code	Birth Information	Death Information	Marriage Information
	1	Hugh M(?) 20		ON ±1840 AT VA	ON 1936 AT	ON TO
	2	Manilla 16		ON ±1844 AT VA		
	3	Jane/Jane? 12 / JANE		ON ±1848 AT VA		
	4	Henry M(?) 11		ON ±1849 AT VA		
	5	John B 10		ON ±1850 AT VA		

Check here if there are additional children ☒

Footnoting. To substantiate the information recorded on this page, please use the footnotes listed below. One of these numbers should be placed in the circle provided next to each answer on the questionnaire. If you got the information from a source not listed, place that source on a vacant line and use the number next to which it has been placed as your footnote number.

Use ① only if you have filled in the blank from personal knowledge (such as the name of your brother). If you must look up his marriage date, give as the source wherever you looked it up. If you asked him, give his name as the source.

① Name and address of person filling in this sheet. P.C. SCHAFFER + Glorva C. Date 6 October 1994
453 Greencastle Lane   Malaman
Virginia Beach, Va 23452

②
③
④
⑤ CENSUS of Wyoming Co VA/WV: (5a) 1850 (5b) 1860 (5c) 1870
⑥ "The Genealogy and History of the Mills family" by Barton Wyatt, 1968 (from Glorva C. Malaman)
⑦ "The History of the Keaton Mills Cemetery" by Glorva C. Malaman, September 17, 1981
⑧ Conv. Glorva C Malaman — Sept 17 & 1994 to P.C.S.

FAMILY GROUP SHEET — PAGE 2

HUSBAND'S NAME: Robert Mills Code: ____
WIFE'S MAIDEN NAME: Lydia Thompson (?(3)) Code: ____

Have family sheet	#	CHILDREN (Arrange in order of birth)	Code	Birth Information	Death Information	Marriage Information
○	6	William T. 9		c 1851 VA		
○	7	Brewer D. 8		c 1852 VA	Birth needs Wyoming Co	
○	8	Samuel O. 7		c 1853 aug 24 1856 VA		
○	9	Frances 4		c 1856 Nov. 24 1957 VA	Two listed Dec. 15, 1858	
○	10	Aden 1		c 1857 D' 1933 VA	Bailey Cemetery on Diastrows Ridge, McDowell	on Diastrows-Crimpler, County 26, VA.
○	11	CM1 Malinda Elizabeth Caroline Hacker CB1 Dec. 18, 1859		Hacker CD7/1934		
○	12					
○	13					
○	14					
○	15					
○	16					

FOOTNOTES:

⑨
⑩
⑪
⑫
⑬
⑭
⑮
⑯
⑰
⑱
⑲

Census List

1. Milly (Miley) Ellen Mills, 1834, married Joseph McKinney; 2. Emelia Mills, 1836, married Jesse Green McKinney, June 28, 1856; 3. Hugh Green Mills, 1839, married Catherine Neely, June 5, 1884, Mercer County; 4. Marilla Mills, 1843; 5. Tabitha Jane Mills, 1848, married John Morgan; 6. Henry G. Mills, 1849, married Clara C. Shrewsbury in 1873, Mercer County; 7. John B. Mills, 1850, married Minerva Farley, December 21, 1871; 8. William T. Mills, 1851, married Victora Jane Clendinin, March 8, 1877; 9. Rewe D. Mills, 1852; 10. Samuel O. Mills, 1853, married Martha Feazell; 11. Frances Mills, 1856, married Jess Monk; 12. Zurah Dessie Mills, married Thomas H. White; 13. Aden Mills, 1859, married Mahulda Elizabeth Caroline Walker; 14. Benjamin (Ben) Mills, 1864, married Narcissa Emily Caspen Walker; 15. Johnson Keaton, 1865, married Martha Ann Charity Walker; 16. Wallis Eanon Mills, 1866, married Fannie McComas.

Martha Mills, female, died July 30, 1855, cause unknown, age fifteen days. (Robert and Lydda Mills) Informant, father.

Wallis Eanon, born in 1866 or 1868, the youngest of Lydia and Robert Mills married Servilla Francis McComas and they were the parents of a large family, fifteen boys and two girls: 1. Rozella, 2. Emerson, 3. Clayton, 4. Baxter, 5. Okley, 6. Jimmie, 7. Bonnie, 8. Howard, 9. Wilder, 10. Burwin, 11. Tharwell, 12. Woodrow, 13. Claren, 14. Albert, 15. Ofa, 16. Ile, 17. Covel.

John and Minerva Mills are both buried in the John Mills cemetery located on the Babbington place, Egeria, West Virginia, near Willie Mills place: Minerva Farley Mills (1951 – 1907), John B. Mills (1850 – 1918).

Benjamin and Johnson Keaton buried in the Keaton Mills cemetery, Egeria. Tomp buried in the Willie Mills cemetery, Egeria.

While doing research at the library, I found some interesting information, which I am passing on as it is all family. **1850 Census, Mercer County**: Samuel Mills, 30, Lerna, 30 — 1. Nathaniel, 16, 2. Priscilla, 13, 3. Francis, 11 (male), 4. Charlotte, 9, 5. John P., 6, 6. Ballard, 3.

1860 Census - Mercer County: William Mills,48, Emaritha, 33 — 1. Rhoda, 14, 2. Ellen, 13, 3. William F., 12, 4. John, 10, 5. Samuel D., 7, 6. Henry A., 4, Joseph W. and Priscilla, both 3 1/2.

1860 - Mercer County: Samuel Mills, 46, Zeniah, 46, wife — 1. Nathaniel R., 26, 2. Frances (female), 18, 3. Charlotte, 15, 4. John P., 14, 5. Electa, 12, 6. Robert W., 10.

Henry G. Mills, age 23, married Clara C. Shrewsbury, age 27, in 1873, Mercer County, West Virginia – Rev. Elias Reed; William T. Mills, 25, married Victoria Jane Clendinin, 18, March 8, 1877, Mercer County – Rev. Elias Reed; Robert Mills (Preacher), 19, married Jeston Bailey, 18, October 19, 1899, Mercer County, West Virginia – Rev. Wm. A. Bailey, (Father John Mills); S.W. Mills, 19, married Mandy L. Walker, 16, September 16, 1899, Mercer County, West Virginia – Rev. Jas. W. Lilly; Samuel B. Mills, 22, married Nectaie Nicholas, 22, December 26, 1898, Mercer County, West Virginia – Rev. J.A. Cassaday; John D. Mills, 20, married Minerva Farley, 16, December 21, 1871, Mercer County, West Virginia – Rev. Charles W. Walker; John Mills, 20, married Jane Sizemore, 18, August 29, 1865, Mercer County, West Virginia – Rev. Charles Walker; Nathaniel Mills, 26, married Julia Karnes, 19, September 13, 1860, Mercer County; Samuel Mills, 52, married Martha J. Brown, 31, November 25, 1867, Mercer County; Samuel O. Mills married Martha Feazell; Samuel D. Mills, Jr. married Mary Akers; Ballard W. Mills married Cinda Mills, 1. Belle, 2. Delbert, 3. Etta, 4. Carse; Benjamin Mills married Sarah Hatcher November 15, 1885; Anderson Mills married Trifonie, Hugh Mills' children, 1. Robert, 2. Jasper, 3. Sophia, 4. Hugh Green; Anderson Mills died June 29, 1875; John D. (Preacher) Mills married Minerva Elizabeth Farley December 21, 1871, children, 1. Vessie, 2. Loma, 3. Nita, 4. Oley, 5. Aden, 6. Robert; Dessie Mills married Tom White, children, 1. Delbert (Peg) White, 2. Pearl White; Rhoda J. Mills daughter of William and Emmarila married Samuel Wimmer, June 27, 1867; Lectory J. Mills, son of James and Mary Mills married R.A. Lipford (no date); Wallis E. Mills, son of Robert and Lydia married Servilla F. McComas, September 16, 1888; Robert Benjamin Mills, 22, son of Hugh and Catherine, married Sarah J. Hatcher, 19, November 11, 1888; Jeremiah J. Mills, son of Green and Catherine, married Eliza J.E. McBride, November 21, 1888; John Mills, 27, son of John and Jane, Staffordshire, England married Rhoda Shrewsbury October 28, 1889; Sallie A. Mills, daughter of John and Elizabeth married K.W. Bailey, January 29, 1890; Elizabeth M. Mills, 14, daughter of H.G. and Amanda, married Mack H. Shroder, 20, September 4, 1890; William B. Mills, 22, married Sarah E. Graham, 18, August 18, 1892, married by E. Howerton, Raleigh County.

Marriage records of Wyoming County 1854 – 1910:
Anderson Mills, 20, son of William and Emarilla married Adaline L. Thompson, 16, May 3, 1859; Anderson Mills, widower, son of William and Marilla married Trifhana Akers, 22, June 18, 1869; E.L. Mills, 18, daughter of Robert and Rebecca, married Jessie Green McKinney, 18, June 28, 1856; Jane Mills, 28, married John Morgan, 31, February 24, 1876; Notie Mills, 18, married Andrew Jackson Laxton, 19, August 31, 1907; Zurah Mills, 17, daughter of Robert and Lydia married Thomas H. White, 17. (I believe this is Zurah D. Mills and that the D. is for Dessie as she was known later).

Francis Mills married Jesse Monk, children, 1. Minnie, 2. Ocie, 3. Allie (or Ollie), 4. Kelly; Henry Mills married Clara C. Shrewsbury, children, 1. Verdie Elizabeth, 2. Connie Monk, 3. Lestie Parcell; Thompson (Tomp) Mills married _____ _____, children, 1. Willie, 2. Maggie, 3. James, 4. Cleve, 5. Mary, 6. Avery, 7. Mack, 8. George Oley; Samuel Mills married Martha Ann Cook (previously married to Richard Mitchell), one child, Katherine Mitchell; children, 1. Gennie, 2. Armintha Frances, 3. Ira, 4. Willie, 5. John Riley, 6. Nellie; William (Billy) Mills married Marilla Perdue, children, 1. Jeremiah, 2. Anderson, 3. Rhoda, 4. Ellen, 5. John, 6. David, 7. Henry, 8. Victoria, 9. Joseph, 10. William F.; John Mills married Minerva Foley, children, 1. Horace, 2. Bobby, 3. Amanda, 4. Nita, 5. Loma, 6. Dessie; Henry Mills, 23, married Clara Shrewsbury, 27, February 20, 1873, children, 1. Robert, 2. Braxton, 3. Lesta.

Brothers married sisters:
Aden Mills married Mahulda Elizabeth Caroline Walker. She was born December 18, 1859, on Meadow Fork of Devils

Fork, Slab Fork District, Wyoming County, West Virginia and died November 6, 1935. Known as "Hulda" she was the fourth child of Numa Dink and Martha Sizemore Walker. They were married September 13, 1887, by Elder Charles Walker in Raleigh County, West Virginia. Aden was born May 12, 1859, and died February 3, 1936. They are buried in Bailey Cemetery on Beartown Ridge at Crumpler, McDowell County, West Virginia. Their gravestones show Mahulda 1858-1934 and Aden 1859-1935. They were the parents of eleven children: 1. Martha Sianna "Anner" Mills, 2. Amanda Elizabeth Mills, 3. Erastus Granger "Ras" Mills, 4. Numa Grover Mills, 5. Benjamin Okey Mills, 6. Hattie Clementine Mills, 7. Lula Caroline Mills, 8. Charles Henry Mills, 9. John Calvin Mills, 10. Wather Dewey Mills, 11. Aubrey Crandell Mills.

Benjamin Mills married Narcissa Emily Caspen Walker. She was born February 2, 1872, on Devils Fork, Slab Fork District, Wyoming County, West Virginia. (This district was very soon thereafter annexed by Raleigh County). Narcissa was known as "Sis" and was the ninth child of Numa Dink and Martha Adeline Sizemore Walker. She married at age sixteen. Benjamin David Mills was age twenty-two when he was married on August 17, 1886, by Elder Charles Walker in Raleigh County, West Virginia. They first lived on Devils Fork near Egeria, West Virginia. Narcissa and Benjamin were the parents of six children, 1. Roxie Mills, 2. Nota "Notie" Mills, 3. Lois Mills, 4. Pina "Piney" Mills, 5. Pearlie Mills, 6. Estel "Tub" Mills. Barty Wyatt, a school teacher and historian from Princeton, West Virginia, gives the following: Five children when the 1850 census was taken, 1. Miley E. Mills, 16, 2. Emelia, 14, 3. Green, 11, 4. Marella, 7, 5. Tabitha, 2.

After 1850 census, 1. John Mills, 2. Henry Mills, 3. Keaton Mills, 4. Aden Mills, 5. Enon Mills, 6. Ben Mills, (Aunt Dessie Mills Cole added), 7. Francis Mills, 8. Dessie Mills.

Cousin Delmer Mills (age eighty-one) told me there were sixteen children. After the 1850 census, Rebecca was no longer listed. I thought that she had died between the 1850 and 1860 census, as divorce was not so common then. Delmer said that they were divorced and that she was living with her oldest daughter, Ellen at Gauley Bridge. I found a Rebecca Mills listed in the census as fifty-six, F. Falls of Kanawha, Fayette County and Robert Mills listed as fifty-nine, Barkers Ridge, Wyoming

County and was confused until Delmer cleared it up. Benjamin Mills, fifty-three, Beaverpond TWP, Mercer County and William Mills, sixty-two, Rock Township, Mercer County were also listed.

Mercer County was formed in 1837 from parts of Tazewell and Giles County, Virginia. The first census was taken in 1840 with only names of the householder listed: Samuel Mills, Rachel Prince, – married May 6, 1807, parents of twelve children. Only able to locate three, 1. Samuel Mills, Jr., married Nancy Rheinhart in 1833; 2. William (Billy) Mills, married Emmarila (or Marilla) Perdue; 3. Robert Mills, married Rebecca Rinehart, May 3, 1832 – Giles County, Virginia.

Robert Mills, (b) 1811, first wife, Rebecca Rhinehart, first son, Hugh, second son, Henry, (mother, Gore), second wife, Lydia Walker Thompson (Sweeney).

1850 Census: Robert Mills, (b) 1811, Rebecca Rhinehart, (b) 1820, 1. Miley E., (b) 1834, 2. Emelia, (b) 1836, 3. Green, (b) 1839, 4. Marella, (b) 1843, 5. Tabitha, (b) 1849.

1860 Census: Robert Mills, (b) 1812, 48 years old in 1860, married Lydia Thompson in 1861; Lydia Thompson Mills, (b) 1825, 35 years old in 1860, (d) October 25, 1885, 1. Hugh G., (b) 1840, 20 years old in 1860, 2. Marella, (b) 1844, 16 years old in 1860, 3. Jane, (b) 1848, 12 years old in 1860, 4. Henry G., (b) 1849, 11 years old in 1860, 5. John B., (b) 1850, 10 years old in 1860, 6. William F., (b) 1851, 9 years old in 1860, 7. Reewe D., (b) 1852, 8 years old in 1860, 8. Samuel O., (b) 1856, 4 years old in 1860, 9. Frances B., (b) 1858, 2 years old in 1860, (born November 24, 1857 to Robert and Lydia Mills, also listed December 15, 1858 at Flat Top, according to Wyoming County births 1853-1884, 10. Aden, (b) 1859, 1 year old in 1860.

1870 Census: Mercer County, Jumping Branch District, Hugh G. Mills, 30, Elizabeth M., 31, 1. Robert B., 3, 2. Jeremiah J., 2.

1880 Census: Mercer County, Hugh G. Mills, 40, 1. Robert B., 12, 2. Jeremiah J., 11, 3. Hugh G., 9, 4. Elizabeth M., 4, 5. William J. Merilla Mills, 59, keeping house, 1. Joseph Mills, 18, 2. Trifenia Mills, 18. Daniel Mills, 25, Mary Mills, 27, 1. Lewis H., 9, 2. Mary L., 7, 3. Sarah V.,4, 4. Samuel, 3 1/2.

Wyoming County death records 1853-1890, Martha Mills, female, died July 30, 1855. Cause unknown, age fifteen days. (Robert and Lydia Mills) informant, father. No deaths recorded between 1867-1875, marriages, Eleanor P. Mills, daughter of Samuel and Zeurah Mills, married George P. Miller July 22, 1859.

Priscilla Mills, daughter of Samuel and Nancy Mills married David Russell, February 4, 1860. Nathaniel R. Mills, son of Samuel and Zeurah married Julia A. Karnes, September 13, 1860. James R. Mills, son of D. and Nancy Mills married Nancy R. Cooper, August 8, 1865. William F. Mills, son of William and Emmarilla married Sarah E. Shrewsbury, February 24, 1867.

1870 Census, Robert Mills, (b) 1811, Lydia, (b) 1822 (d) October 25, 1885, 63 year old, date of marriage 1861, Wyoming County. 1. John B., (b) 1851, 19 years old, 2. William F., (b) 1852, 18 years old, 3. Emila, (b) 1853, 17 years old, 4. Samuel, (b) 1855, 15 years old, 5. Francis (female), (b) 1856, 14 years old, 6. Adran/Aden, (b) 1857, 13 years old, 7. Benjamin, (b) 1862, 8 years old, 8. Johnson Keaton, (b) 1865, 5 years old, 9. Walis/Wallace, (Enon) (b) 1866, 4 years old.

1880 Census, Lidda Mills, age 57, 1. Samuel O., son, 23, 2. Aden, son, 21, 3. Benjamin K., son, 18, 4. Johnson K., son, 15.

Age listed prior to June 1. Grandpa Keaton is sometimes listed as born in 1864.

Gladys Walker Tilley, who compiled extensive records lists the children of Robert and Lydia Thompson as follows: 1. John Mills, 2. Thompson (Tomp) Mills, 3. Dessie Mills, 4. Samuel Mills, 5. Aden Mills, 6. Francis Mills, 7. Ben Mills, 8. Keaton Mills, 9. Eanon Mills.

Thompson (Tomp) Mills does not show up in any census. Gladys Walker Tilley has him listed in her records. It seems logical that Lydia Thompson would name one of her sons Thompson since it was her maiden name. I have the names of his eight children.

I knew Oley since he was a magistrate here in Beckley for many years. I was told as a child that Uncle Tomp left his family and spent most of his younger years in Texas. Lowell Mills, son of Willie tells me that when he was a boy that Uncle Tomp stayed with them at times and he talked about his motel in Florida and his Indian wife and baby.

I know that he existed because I went to his funeral. I was attending Beckley College in 1942 when I heard of his death. I broke a date and went home to Egeria for the weekend. I was not able to contact the date but left word with my girlfriend.

When I returned, he made another date and then did not show up. He called me long distance and said that he had been called out of town. I found out later from my girlfriend that the "long distance" consisted of him climbing a telephone pole and connecting his working phone which sounded like long distance. Guess he thought that he was getting even with me, but I didn't mind at all.

I remember that my Uncle Oley Mills and others built the casket for Uncle Tomp. Brammer's store stocked the hardware and cotton lining for caskets. You could get black or bronze hinges, handles, etc. This was the only homemade casket that I ever saw. He was buried in the Ethel and Willie Mills Cemetery on their farm on top of a little hill in Egeria.

When visiting us for a few weeks, I can remember him sitting on the porch helping us string green beans to dry into "leatherbritches". I can't remember him telling any stories about his travels so I did not learn much about him.

Beulah located the children in the Charleston Archives, but it did not give the name of his wife, 1. Willie, 2. Maggie, 3. James, 4. Cleve, 5. Mary, 6. Avery, 7. Mack, 8. George Oley.

July 15, 1997

I called Connie Walker in Egeria and he was kind enough to go down to the Willie Mills place and look up the dates on the stone for Uncle Tomp. He found William Tomp Mills, 1842-1936.

Some of the census records have William F. born in 1852. Some have 1851. I find in the marriage records that William T. Mills, age 25, married Victoria Jane Clendinin, 18, March 8, 1877, Mercer County, Rev. Elias Reed.

Since Thompson or Tomp never showed up in any census, I am inclined to believe that William F. should have been William T. for Tomp since this is the only gravestone in the cemetery with the name Tomp. I believe that the date 1842 is in error and should be 1852. The stone was placed at his grave many years after his burial.

If he was buried in 1936, then my memory is faulty as to whose burial that I attended in 1942. Lowell Mills seemed to think that he was buried in 1942.

Perhaps Uncle Thomp was not Robert's son. I know that Daddy called him uncle and that he stayed with Willie, and John Riley Mills and us in his later years.

Deed of Reverend J.B. Mills
Deed of the last 102 acres of land Keaton Mills owned in Egeria, and where our cemetery is located

J.B. Mills, wife and others
To deed B. and S., J.K. Mills and al
This deed delivered to Enon Mills
this April 25, 1889

      This deed made this 7th day of November in the year 1885, by and between John B. Mills and Manerva, his wife, William T. Mills and Electra J., his wife, T.H. White and Z.D. White, his wife, Samuel C. Mills, Aden Mills, Benjamin D. Mills, Eliza J., his wife of the county of Raleigh, State of West Virginia and Henry J. Mills and Clara C. Mills, his wife, Jesse Monk and Francis, his wife of the county of Mercer and state aforesaid, party of the first part and Johnson K. Mills and Walace E. Mills of the county of Raleigh and state aforesaid of the second part, witnesseth that for and in consideration of the sum of one hundred seventy dollars paid in hand, the receipt of which is hereby acknowledged, the parties of the first part doth sell, grant and convey into the said Johnson K. Mills and Walace E. Mills of the second part their entire interest, claim and title in and into a certain tract of land lying in the counties of Raleigh and Mercer on the Flat Top Mountain containing 102 acres, be the same more or less, being the same land conveyed by William H. Snider and wife on the 26th day of September 1853 to Robert Mills, their father and bounded as follows, to wit:

      Beginning at an Indian cucumber on the bank of a hill and near a trace leading from the Bluff Springs to a place known by the name of Charyspyanos improvement and running N 80 E 89 pole to a cucumber and white oak (the same for several more paragraphs – will spare you).

To have and to hold with all the appertenances situte thereon.

The parties of the first part doth covenant with the parties of the second part that they will warrant specially the title to the property hereby conveyed, to them, theirs and assigns forever. Witness the following witnesses and seals: John B. Mills, Manerva Mills, William T. Mills, Electra J. Mills, T.H. White, Z.D. White, Samuel O. Mills, Aden Mills, Benjamin D. Mills, Eliza J. Mills, Jesse Monk, Francis Monk, Henry G. Mills, Clara C. Mills.

I have found records of many transfers of land between the Mills family. Grandpa Mills evidently bought his brother Enon's share later.

Benjamin (Ben) Mills - Glennis Walker

Grandpa Keaton Mills' brother Ben married Narcissa Emily Caspen Walker. She was born February 2, 1872, on Devils Fork, Slab Fork District, Wyoming County. (This district was soon annexed by Raleigh County). Narcissa was known as "Sis" and was the ninth child of Numa Dink and Martha Adeline Sizemore Walker. She was sixteen years old when married to Benjamin David Mills, age twenty-two, on August 17, 1886, by Elder Charles Walker in Raleigh County, West Virginia. They first lived on Devils Fork near Egeria.

Egeria was used as a shortcut for people from the settlements of Mercer County, West Virginia, who went into the Guyandotte River area seeking employment. On one occasion several black people passing through were caught up in bad winter weather. They took refuge in an empty house, but were soon after frozen and starved out of the house. They made their way to the home of Narcissa and Benjamin and were taken in. Narcissa had a huge pot of leather britches beans (dried green beans) cooked and wanted to warm them up, but the starving blacks could not wait and just dived into the cold pot. They slept on the floor two nights and when they left the Mills family soon learned they had been left with a seige of head lice.

The Narcissa and Ben Mills' family some years later lived in one half of a large double house in the Ashland coal mining community of McDowell County, West Virginia. The other half of the large structure was occupied by the family of Aden and Mahulda Mills. Aden was a brother to Ben and Mahulda was a sister to Narcissa. These Mills brothers worked in the coal mining industry.

August 15, 1898 - Narcissa and Ben journeyed to Keystone, McDowell County, West Virginia, to do some shopping in preparation of an upcoming Primitive Baptist Association. Following some shopping, Ben entered a bar or restaurant, where trouble erupted between him and a black police officer named Cobb, with whom previous trouble had occurred. Following some conversation and some physical encounter, the police officer is said to have swiveled his undrawn revolver, firing on Ben and killing him instantly.

Narcissa still shopping in Keystone upon receiving word of the shooting went directly to the establishment, where excitement and uneasiness was at a high pitch. It was some time before Narcissa was permitted entrance to ascertain just what had befallen Ben. (I thought when I was a child that it was Indians who had kept her out.) Women working in the establishment told Narcissa that Ben had covered the police officer for a time with a pistol, and no doubt could have shot him at will.

It is said on good authority at the time of the tragedy Nardissa had only five dollars left to her name. On the fateful day Ben had looked at a hat for himself, but declined to buy it due to their limited amount of money. In her sentimental mood, she bought the hat and buried it with Ben in the Keaton Mills Cemetery at the foot of Bluff Mountain at Egeria, West Virginia. (The next time that I am at the cemetery, I will visit Great Uncle Ben's grave and try to picture the hat.)

Learning of the tragic death of a relative, the Mills' clan allegedly converged on Keystone. That "nigger" will never see the sun come up tomorrow was the order of the day. As might be expected Cobb did not see the sun come up the next morning. Silence enshrouded the identity of the person responsible for the demise of Officer Cobb.

Following the death of Ben, Narcissa was left with several small children to raise, the oldest daughter being less than ten years old. Narcissa later married James Alfred Farley. She died July 30, 1952.

When Glennis Walker visited Notie Mills Laxton, daughter of Ben Mills at a nursing home in 1978, she was almost eighty-eight years old, very alert and possessing a very good memory. She related the gun her father, Ben Mills was carrying on the fateful day in Keystone wasn't loaded. The gun belonged to Pyruss Ulla Chennany Walker, who was a brother to Narcissa and had been picked up for him by Ben at a repair shop in Keystone. It is unknown if the gun was ever returned to Ulla following the fatal shooting of Ben.

When Glennis again visited Notie when she was about eighty-nine years old, she still had a good memory. She mentioned the Mills family living at Ashland, West Virginia, with a creek dividing the community. White families lived on one side and black families on the other. Notie said that when the news came of her father, Ben Mills' death a middle-aged black couple named Fran and Grif came to their home to console and care for the grief-stricken children. She had a high regard for the couple.

For many years Benjamin David Mills' grave was marked by a native stone, but in 1984 or 1985, Corda Walker Thompson had a proper tombstone erected with name and dates inscribed (1860-1898).

Pioneer Mills Family
The New River Heritage Volume IV
by William Sanders

The only cemetery located on the four-mile-long, four-thousand-feet-high Bluff Mountain of Flat Top Range is that of Billy Mills, with the only readable gravestone on the many fieldstones being that of a woman. The cemetery is located on a beautiful high point of the east edge of the flat land overlooking all of Mercer County, up the New River and beyond and through the Narrows. As were many of the early Mills, Billy Mills was a mountain preacher. He established his school and church not far from the cemetery point. That school later become known as the Cunningham school, and is now part of the home of Robert Bailey and Shirley Shrewsbury, his wife and their young family, who leased the mine out and reclaimed approximately a two-hundred fifty acre southward portion of the bluff from Pocahontas Land Company of Norfolk Southern Railway. Shirley used to walk to the school from her home in Wyoming County several miles. The church operated alternately as Primitive Baptist and Dunkard (German) Baptist. The church was dismantled and some parts reassembled elsewhere.

John "Booge" Harmon is buried on a bench off the east side of the bluff on the portion of his land that he gave to his son, Amaziah. Other members of the family are buried there, but Aunt Bet Harmon is buried with other members of the family at the Shrewsbury graveyard at the Shrewsbury Chapel at nearby Beeson. Amaziah is buried in the Crews Cemetery on Sand Knob of Jumping Branch where he later moved and lived along the ancient Giles-Fayette-Kanawha Turnpike at the border of present Bluestone Park on Sand Knob of Bluestone Mountain.

* Note: Burnell Mills, a family historian later brought the following information to the office of William Sanders. He had been able to decipher two gravestones which he found lying face down in the Billy Mills Bluff Mountain Cemetery.

"To the memory of Ellinor Perdue – Death March 16, 1869 – age 72 Y 10M," (This was the mother-in-law of Billy Mills.)

"Lydia Mills died October 25, 1885. Note: This was the wife of Robert Mills, and had been previously married to Green Sweeney (Swinney). I had found the information as to Lydia Mills' death, but not where she was buried. Also this solved the mystery as to Aunt Dessie Mills Cole remembering that her father's mother was a Swinney when records showed that she was a Thompson. I also located the handwritten will of William (Billy) Mills and a typed copy which I am including.

In his book *A New River Heritage, Volume IV*, William Sanders of Princeton, West Virginia, tells of a famous lawsuit Robert Mills' widow and heirs brought against an out-of-state purchaser Robert McCulluck.

The Mills family is set forth in a deed of October 3, 1906, from B.W. Pendleton, special commissioner to Hugh G. Mills, John B. Mills, Aden Mills, Samuel O. Mills, William T. Mills, J.K. Mills, Zeruah D. White, M.F. Cunningham, Oscie Reed, Alice Monk, Roxie Smith, Notie Mills, Locie Mills, Pinie Mills and Perly Mills, the children of Robert Mills, deceased (all of these were not Robert's children. Some were children of Benjamin Mills, deceased, which made them heirs). (*This had me confused and I had to do a lot of research to locate marriages and names – Gloria*).

A famous lawsuit was waged against this family to oust them from the possession of one thousand acres, which land, as shown by deed description, was part of an original thirty-five thousand acre tract land grant of Robert McCulloch. The deed shows the one thousand acres was bounded by Robert James' three thousand acre tract and by the Brammer's line and with the line of Massie and a corner to Jeremiah Ferguson.

The final Supreme Court decision is dated February 1912, in favor of the Mills' heirs and against McLanahan and others representing the interest that was later owned by Pocahontas Land Company and the Blue Jay Lumber Company.

Robert Mills (deceased) had a contract to purchase the one thousand acres for one thousand dollars by paying four hundred dollars down and six hundred dollars at a later date. This contract was dated 1866, and the land was surveyed for the seller by L.M. Stinson and the Mills family on the property. Several of their children and relatives also moved on the property and lived there for a period of years in various homes and on various tracts of the one thousand acre parcel. They had never recorded their contract, and the parties seeking to oust them from possession challenged the sufficiency of the deed description and also claimed they had sold the same property later to other purchasers, representatives of the coal and timber interests, who were innocent purchasers, without knowledge of the prior conveyance to the Mills. The Supreme Court held that living on the land over a long period of years was notice enough.

There was evidence of six improvements from the tract surveyed by Stinson and known as the "Sneed Place, Clark Place, Halstead Place, Little John Sneed Place, Doc White Place and the Hubble Place," all occupied and cultivated continuously, with many improvements. The party who claimed he was an innocent purchaser, without knowledge of the prior deed to Mills was a Pennsylvanian. The court held that the notorious possession was enough notice to him and all others the land was owned by others than his grantor, McLanahan and Company.

This lawsuit lasted many years. The trouble began when Robert Mills' widow Lydia Mills gave the title bond and receipt for four hundred dollars, which she claimed was the residue of the purchase price of $1,000.00 for this 1000 acres of land to an attorney for him to bring suit. John R. Dunlap, the administrator of the estate of Robert McCulluck had died in the meantime and the attorney failed to ascertain who his personal representative was in the commonwealth of Virginia. Soon thereafter the attorney himself moved to Virginia and just forgot to bring the suit.

I would like to add that "the trouble" began when Robert failed to record the contract for the land at the time that he purchased it. All ended well with the Mills' heirs getting a good deed to the property. This is the land that was divided, traded, carved into parcels to brothers and family members and finally my grandfather, Keaton ended up with it. It began with the Brammer line in Barn and ended up in the Egeria area.

Grandma Mills – Five Generations Indian Ancestry

1. "Old Ned" Sizemore and Cherokee Indian wife; 2. George Sizemore, married Annie Hart; 3. Edward B. Sizemore, married Anne B. Blevins; 4. John Sizemore, married Virginia "Jenny" Arms; 5. Martha Adeline Sizemore, married Numa Dink Walker.

Chrispi Anos Walker, (b) March 14, 1782, (d) February 14, 1876, Frances "Frankey Jane" Peters, (b) 1794, (d) April 7, 1884, 1. Council Walker, married Nancy D. Bailey, 2. Emily Walker, married Green W. Meador, 3. Marinda Walker, married Andrew H. Lilly, 4. Mahulda Walker, married Gordon Lambert, 5. Christian Walker, married Mahalia Manus, 6. Narcissa Walker, married Josiah Cooper, 7. Valoris Walker, died at a young age, 8. Numa Walker, married Martha Adeline Sizemore, 9. Underwood Walker, married Louisa Bailey, 10. Francis Walker, married Lewis Lilly, 11. Valeria Walker, married William P. Lilly.

Numa Dink Walker, (b) 1829, (d) November 21, 1884, Martha Adeline Sizemore, (b) 1835, (d) 1899, their children were: 1. Frankie Jane Ceberry Walker, (m) Charles Bailey, 2. John Wise Council Walker, (m) Nancy Bailey, 3. Mahulda Elizabeth Walker, (m) Aden Mills (he was born 1859, died 1935), 4. Martha Ann Charity Walker, (m) Johnson Keaton Mills, 5. Numa Captain Calvin Walker, (m) Sallie Wood, 6. Charles Gideon Christian Walker, (never married), 7. Purvis Ulley Chananey Walker, (m) Hickok, (buried Keaton Mills Cemetery), 8. Narcissis Emily Caspin Walker, (m) first Ben Mills (buried Keaton Mills Cemetery), second, Alfred Farley, 9. Christopher George Columbus Walker, (m) Josephine Shrewsberry, 10. Lydia Merinda Cerdula Walker, (b) 1874, (d) February 23, 1823, (m) Henry Walker, (buried Keaton Mills Cemetery), 11. Nyanzi Nicti Ceruleon Walker, (b) April 1, 1879, (d) April 19, 1943, (m) German Christian Walker. (They are both buried in the Keaton Mills Cemetery).

Indian Claims

The following information was obtained with the help of Chief Robert S. Youngdeer, who was elected principal chief, Eastern Band of Cherokee Indians in 1987. This is a full-time position with 9,000 tribal members and 58,000 acres of land to oversee.

He served in the marine corps and belonged to Edson's Raiders. My husband Jimmie and I regularly attend the Edson's Raiders annual reunion in February at Quantico, Virginia. I did not know that Robert was an Indian until the year he was elected president of Edson's Raiders Association. The marines used the Indians in the communications systems however, I do not think this was Chief Youngdeer's job during the war.

Navajo Indians used their native language to transmit information on tactics and troop movements, orders and other vital battlefield communications over telephones and radios for the marine corps during World War II. Native Americans worked as messengers and performed general marine duties. On September 17, 1992, the Navajo code talkers of World War II were honored for their contributions to defense at the Pentagon. The Japanese, who were skilled code breakers, were baffled by the language.

I told him that I was trying to trace our Cherokee Indian blood, and asked him how to go about it. He told me to send twenty-five dollars to Enrollment, Qualla Boundary, Cherokee, North Carolina, and provide the names to research. I requested Sizemore and Arms or Armes, because I had the idea that Jenny Armes was Indian. A search of records showed no enrollment for these names. Chief Youngdeer then sent my request and other information to a woman in Tennessee, who he said had spent a large part of her life researching Indian families. She called me in Florida and then sent pages of testimony for the Sizemore

Clan when descendents of Ned Sizemore filed their claims for money which the government finally paid generations later, money promised when the treaty was signed and they were relocated in Oklahoma.

Chief Youngdeer served his term as chief of the Eastern Band of the Cherokee Nations and he and his wife, Aline, retired to Oklahoma, where two of their children live. When I talked with him, he said that he had always thought that Jimmie was Indian because of his dark complexion and always wearing an Indian Thunderbird tie. Our nephew, Jeffrey Walker, sent Jimmie this tie from Tucson, Arizona, many years ago and it is the only tie that he wears.

There were five pages of the application for claims by Grandma Mills for herself and children, but the copy was so bad that I could not make out all of it.

The application was completed by Clouney Harvey and it seemed that Grandma appointed Belva Lockwood of Washington, D.C. as her "true and lawful attorney and in her nameplace to allow Belve Lockwood ten percent of commissions for said services in said case." This was filed on the fifth day of January 1907. This application stated that Ned Sizemore was a Cherokee Indian and that his wife was also a Cherokee Indian. It was sent to the commissioner of Indian Affairs, Washington, D.C., as follows:

Sir:

I hereby make application for such share as may be due me of the fund appropriated by the Act of Congress approved June 30th, 1906 in accordance with the decrees of the Court of Claims of May 18th, 1905, and May 28th, 1906, in favor of the Eastern Cherokees. The evidence of identity is hereby subjoined.

State full name —
English name: Martha A.C. Mills.
Indian Name: Sizemore.
2. Residence: Egeria, West Virginia.
3. Town and post office: Egeria.
4. County: Raleigh.
5. State: West Virginia.
6. Date and place of birth: Feb. 25th, 1862, Raleigh County, West Virginia.

7. By what right do you claim to share? If you claim through more than one relative living in 1851, set forth each claim separately: Through my mother who was a daughter of John Sizemore and wife of Numa Walker. John was son of Ned Sizemore, Jr., who was son of George Sizemore and George was son of old Ned Sizemore, who was the Cherokee Indian.

8. Are you married? Yes.

9. Name and age of wife or husband: J.K. Mills age 42 years old.

10. Give names of your father and mother, and your mother's name before marriage:

    Father: English name: Numa Walker.

    Indian name: Martha A. Sizemore.

    Maiden name: Martha A. Sizemore.

11. Where were they born:

    Father: In Giles County, Virginia, now Mercer County, West Virginia.

    Mother: In Giles Co., VA, now Wyoming Co. W.Va.

12. Where did they reside in 1851, if living at that time?

    Father: In Raleigh Co., W.Va.

    Mother: In Wyoming Co., W.Va.

13. Date of death of your father and mother:

    Father: Nov. 21st, 1884. Mother: Dec. 24th, 1899.

14. Names of all your children who were living on May 28, 1906:

    1. Lydia Mills, age 20, born March 6, 1887.

    2. Hessie Mills, age 17, born April 8, 1890.

    3. G.W. Mills, age 15, born June 5, 1892.

    4. Oley J. Mills, age 12, born Aug. 25, 1894.

    5. Dessie Mills, age 11, born March 15, 1896.

    6. John Mills, age 9, born March 17, 1898.

    7. Autie Mills, age 7, born April 25, 1900.

    8. Nathan Mills, age 5, born June 25, 1902.

    9. Kelly Mills, age 3, born Feb. 16, 1904.

    10. Laurence Mills, age 1, born Oct. 18, 1905.

15. Were they ever enrolled for money, annuities, land, or other benefits? If so, state when and where, and with what tribe of Indians: I sent in a blank claim January, 1907, just after I sent my claim, as claimant E.C.T. (Under that head the applicant may give additional facts which will

assist in proving his claim).

I filled out a blank in January, 1907 and sent to Belva Lockwood and received a card later that it had been filed and would be considered later. Following Affidavit accompanying claim papers:

Personally appearing before me, H.G. Mills and J.G. Shrewsberry, who being duly sworn, on oath depose and say that they are well acquainted with Martha A.C. Mills, who makes the foregoing application and statements, and have known her for 10 years and 20 years, respectively, and know her to be the identical person she represents herself to be, and that the statements made by them are true, to the best of their knowledge and belief and they have in interest whatsoever in said claim.

This was signed by H.G. Mills and J.G. Shrewsberry and notarized by C.L. Harvey on the 5th day of January, 1907.

An interesting note at the bottom: Affidavits should be made, whenever practicable, before a notary public, clerk of the court, or before a person having a seal. If sworn to before an Indian agent or disbursing agent of the Indian service, it need not be executed before a notary, etc.

Grandma Mills was given Claim #10123.

Glennis Walker in *The History of the Walker Family* tells of his grandfather George Walker making application through the Cherokee Indian Ancestory of his mother, Adeline, for a portion of the Cherokee Indian money (promised by President Jackson) which was to be paid per capita. He also made an additional Application July 30, 1907, and was assigned Claim #10125, just two numbers higher than Grandma Mills. The Sizemore claims were probably all processed about the same time. His claim was also defended by Belva Lockwood, who had on March 3, 1879, become the first woman attorney to practice before the United States Supreme Court.

Elizabeth Ramsey and two children. Swain Ark. 415
Rejected: Applicant nor ancestors ever enrolled. Does not establish fact of descent from a person who was ever a party to the treaty of 1835-1836 and 1846. Applicant's ancestors through whom she claims left the Cherokee in about 1825 and lived with white people ever afterward.

Mareyan Ramsey and 4 children, Swain Ark. 416
Rejected. Claims through same source as #415.

Geo Washington Plummer, Saratoga, Wyo. 417
Rejected. Applicant is one of the Sizemore claimants. These applicants claim through Ned (or Edward), John (or Doctor Johnny Gourd), Joseph Sizemore and William Sizemore, and for convenience, they are designated the Sizemore claims. These applications number about 2,000, representing approximately 5,000 individuals. The claimants reside chiefly in northwestern North Carolina, northeastern Tennessee, southwestern Virginia, and southern West Virginia and northwestern and western Alabama. The statements in the applications and affidavits filed in support of the same and in the testimony taken are not entirely consistent but substantially the same claim is made for all of these individuals. More than 80 witnesses were examined in the field and their testimony will be found in Sizemore testimony, pages 1 to 75. It does not appear that any of the claimants or any one of the ancestors of any of the claimants were ever enrolled with the eastern Cherokees, nor does it appear that any of these claimants or their immediate ancestors ever lived as Indians with the Cherokee Nation or with the eastern Cherokees. None of them appear to have been living with the Cherokee domain at the date of the treaty of 1835-1836, but, on the contrary, most of these claimants or their immediate ancestors were living from 150 to 300 miles from the Cherokee domain at that time. From the applications, affidavits and testimony, it appears that Ned Sizemore, John Sizemore, and Joseph Sizemore were brothers, but the exact date or place of birth could not be definitely determined. It is probable, however, that they were born somewhere between 1740 and 1760. Some accounts fix the place of birth as Halifax County, Virginia, while others say it was Halifax County, North Carolina, while still another account states that Ned Sizemore "was duly enrolled upon the rolls of Cherokee Nation, taken and made in the year 1749, in the Catawba Reservation," and William H. Blevins, a prominent man among the claimants and one who has been largely instrumental in prosecuting this claim, testified (Sizemore testimony, page 56): "I remember one Elisha Blevins who said that old Ned Sizemore came from the Catawba River,

or the Catawba Reservation as he called it. Elisha Blevins has been dead some time. Wesley Blevins also testified that in 1893 to the same effect, "This would seem to indicate that Ned Sizemore came from South Carolina, but in any event, none of the accounts places their origin within the territory of the Cherokee Indians. The claimants were examined as witnesses were nearly all well advanced in years and testified almost without exception that they and their parents were generally recognized as white people, that neither they or their parents had ever received any money from the government as Indians and had never been enrolled as such. Many of them stated that until this enrollment had been agitated they had never heard of what tribe of Indians they belonged but only that they had Indian blood. Henry A. Holland testified at Pilot Mountain, North Carolina (Sizemore testimony, page 1) that he was sixty-three years of age, and that he knew John Sizemore, (or Doctor Gourd) and Joseph Sizemore: that he never heard either of them state where they were born, and that: "I never heard either of them say that they were Indians. I heard they were kin to them. I never heard either of them say they were kin to the Indians. I don't remember hearing it said to what Indians they were kin. There were no bands of Indians living in Stokes County in my life time, as Indians. I never heard them spoken of as Cherokees. I am not a claimant myself; I was asked to come here by Mr. Whittaker, as agent for Mrs. Belva A. Lockwood". Morgan D. Sizemore testified at Pilot Mountain, North Carolina (Sizemore testimony, page 2), that he is forty-six years of age, and that: "So far as I can say, I have no Indian blood. I do not know whether there is any tradition in my family that we have Indian blood. I have never heard my father, Atha Sizemore, say that he was of Indian blood". Benjamin F. King testified at Pilot Mountain, North Carolina (Sizemore testimony, page 3) that he is fifty-three years of age and that "I claim Indian blood from having heard my mother I am kin to the Indians. I remember my grandmother quite well. I do not remember ever hearing her say anything about the Indians. Neither my mother or my grandmother ever lived with the Indians. My mother never said to what tribe of Indians she belonged – simply said she was kin to the Indians. I never heard her mention the Cherokees. Neither my mother or grandmother were ever enrolled with the Indians. I have never enrolled". Tandy Bennett testified at Pilot Mountain, North Carolina

(Sizemore testimony, pages 4 and 5) that he is sixty-seven years of age and has Indian blood in his veins through his mother who is a Sizemore; that his mother died in 1893, at the age of eighty-two; that she was born in Halifax County, Virginia; that she got her Indian blood through her father, Joseph Sizemore who died in Halifax County, Virginia; that his understanding was that he was born there and that he (Joseph Sizemore) was born here when the war broke out; he must have come to Stokes County about 1821 or 1823, but Doctor Johnny Gourd came out here several years before he did. Doctor Johnny Gourd died and was buried in Stokes County. I have seen him thousands of times and he was a very old man. I could not say that I have heard him say that he was Indian. He resembled an Indian right smart; I don't recollect his saying that he was an Indian. I remember Joseph Sizemore. I don't remember hearing him say he was an Indian. I was in the twenties when he died. I saw him frequently in my lifetime and have talked some to him. He was pretty dark-skinned, but he passed as a white man. I never heard of Joseph Sizemore or Doctor Gourd receiving any money from the government as Indians nor my mother, Rebecca Bennett; if she had gotten it, I would have known it. My mother lived in Stokes County, North Carolina in 1851. I never heard her say anything about any enrollment of Indians by the government. I have heard Doctor Gourd called an old Indian doctor. I never was enrolled for any benefits as an Indian. I have heard of there being Indians ever since I can recollect. I know they have been called Cherokees. When people would get mad, they would call them Cherokee Indians. They would not take it very well. I have been called a Cherokee Indian but of course I did not like it. I have always lived as a white man and have tried to fill a white man's place. There are none of our family who claim Indian blood other than through Joseph Sizemore". James Sizemore testified at East Bend, North Carolina (Sizemore testimony, pages 7 and 8) that he is sixty-seven years of age and was born and raised in Yadin County, North Carolina, that he has never lived with the Indians and never received any money from the government on account of his Indian blood; that his father was Ison Sizemore who was born in Halifax County, Virginia – that his father never received any money from the government on account of his Indian blood, and that: "I never heard him say of what tribe of Indians he belonged. In 1851 he lived in Stokes County and lived there in 1885 also. Doctor Johnny Gourd had fair skin and dark eyes and light hair. I remember him. He lived with my father right smart while before he died. I have heard my grandmother say that he was an Indian, but I don't recollect him telling of what Indian he was, but he said he was from Cherokee. My father voted and was mustered. My great grandfather lived in Virginia, but was born and married in Cherokee, and then he moved to Virginia when my grandfather was a small boy. My grandfather, John, told me this. I have heard it said that my great-grandfather, John Sizemore, was a Captain in the Revolutionary War, fighting with the Colonies". John R. Stallings testified at Yadkinville, North Carolina (Sizemore testimony, page 13) that he was fifty-five years of age and that : "I have always been a voter and my grandfather, Isom Sizemore was a voter. I have always been considered a white man in this community". Leah M. Harris also testified at Yadkinville, North Carolina (Sizemore testimony, page 14) that she is sixty-nine years of age and that her father was Isom Sizemore, and that he died twenty-three years ago at the age of ninety-two, and that he was born in Virginia and that she knew Doctor Johnny Sizemore, and that; "he was born in Cherokee; I don't recollect in which Cherokee he was born; he just said he was born in Cherokee. I have always passed as a white woman and my father as a white man. I have heard Doctor John Sizemore say that he was an Indian. He said that he belonged to the white complexion Indians. I never heard him say any other tribe of Indians than that. I never paid much attention to him. He was a good looking old man and was light complexioned. I made him a suit of clothes, got him a new hat, and he shaved up and looked like another man. I have heard my father say he was kin to the Indians. I never heard him say to what tribe of Indians he was kin. When grandfather came to our house, he wore his hair down to his shoulders, his beard down on his chest and wore a little old green cap." John Henry Sizemore testified at Wilkesboro, North Carolina (Sizemore testimony, page 16) that he is sixty-one years of age and had heard his father speak of having Indian blood; that: "he said his father was kin to the Indians. He did not say to what tribe of Indians. We always passed in the community as white people". James Woody, eighty-four years of age, who is not a claimant but was produced as a witness on behalf of these claimants, in speaking of Ned Sizemore (Sizemore testimony page 20) states that he has seen old Ned Sizemore. "I do not know what descent he originated from, but he was represented to be somewhat Indian". He also states that he never knew Owen Sizemore and that: "I did not hear it talked when I first knew them what they were or what they originated from. Ned Sizemore was here in this country when I was a boy. Owen Sizemore was regarded as a white man but he had a little grain of Indian in him. Before this present money question came up, I never heard that the Sizemores were Cherokee Indians. They used to meet on the hills and muster. I do not know whether Ned Sizemore mustered or not, but the younger men did". Catharine Petty, sixty-four years of age (Sizemore testimony page 21) testified that she was born and always lived in Ashe County, North Carolina, and claims Cherokee blood through her father, David Osborne; that her father was ninety-two or ninety-three years of age at the time of his death, which took place in 1903, and that: "I have heard my father say that he was kin to the Indians. He never said what kin we were. He never received any money from the government on account of his Indian blood that I know of. I never knew of my father visiting the Indians. He was recognized as a white man in the community in which he lived. My father always voted". Jesse D. Osborne, a brother of Catharine Petty, testified (Sizemore testimony page 23) that his grandfather, Jesse Osborne, lived and died in Ashe County, North Carolina, and that: "I have been a voter all my life. I have never heard that the Indians visited my father or grandfather or that they ever visited the Indians: Francis M. Woody, eighty-two years of age and brother of James Woody referred to above, testified (Sizemore testimony page 26) that he knew old Ned Sizemore when affiant was seventeen or sixteen years of age, and that Ned Sizemore was about sixty or seventy years of age and claimed to be a full-blood Cherokee Indian. He testified that: "I have heard old Ned say that he was an Indian many a time. He used to brag of being a Cherokee Indian. He never spoke of having received any money from the government on account of his Indian blood that I ever heard. He went backward and forward to Cherokee to visit the tribe many a time. He died in Allegheny County, to the best of my recollect – that he was probably in his fifties". If the Ned Sizemore referred to was the one referred to as the ancestor of so many of these claimants, he certainly must have been more than sixty or seventy years of age when this affiant was sixteen years old, and if he lived in the fifties; he must have been considerably over a hundred years of age at the time of his death. This witness testified: "Ned Sizemore's beard was not gray when I first saw him. I never knew any Indians living in this country except the Sizemores". This is the most direct testimony connecting the Sizemores with the Cherokee people and is not consistent with the testimony of his brother, James Woody, above referred to, nor with the testimony of other witnesses and claimants that Ned Sizemore came from Halifax County, or from the Catawa Reservation. Eli J. Phipps testified at Jefferson, North Carolina (Sizemore testimony, page 30) and that he is sixty-four years of age and lived in Ashe County all his life, and that; "I have always been a recognized white man in the community and have always voted. I have always been taught that I am a descendant of an Eastern Cherokee Indian" Nancy E. Porter testified at Jefferson, North Carolina (Sizemore testimony, page 31) that she was born in Grayson County, Virginia and that: "I have always been taught that I have Indian blood by my father and mother and have always heard others say the same thing. I do not remember what kind of Indian they said I was descended from. My father lived with white people all his life. I did not know of any Indians living in Grayson County, with the exception of my father and his connections". John A. Peck testified at Grassy Creek, North Carolina (Sizemore testimony, page 33) that he is sixty-one years of age and that: "I claim my Indian blood through my mother and the Sizemores only. My mother and her ancestors were recognized as white people, but it was claimed through the country that we had Indian blood". Claban H. Pennington testified at Grassy Creek, North Carolina (Sizemore testimony, page 36) that he is seventy-seven years of age and claims his Indian blood from the Sizemore race; that "Old Ned Sizemore lived on a creek called Blackwater that ran into Clinch River right at where he lived in Lee County, Virginia . Old man Owen lived up on Clinch River on the Virginia side. I suppose they were recognized white people, for there was nothing said about Indian or Negro in those days. I do not recollect hearing anything mentioned about their being Indians – I cannot remember. I did not apply because I thought I was Indian, for I did not know, but I am kin to the Sizemores". Owen Blevins testified at Grassy Creek, North Carolina (Sizemore testimony, page 37) that he is sixty-two years of age and claims Indian blood through his father. "I heard that Sizemore was a full blood Cherokee. I have been taught that all my life. My father was a recognized white man in the community in which he lived. My father's Indian blood came through his mother, Lydia Blevins, who was a daughter of Owen Sizemore". George Blevins testified at Grassy Creek, North Carolina (Sizemore testimony, page 39) that he was born and raised in Ashe County and is seventy-nine years of age, and that; "I have been a voter and was always recognized as a white man with the exception of the Indian blood in my life. I have never heard that the Indians visited my father or grandfather or that they ever visited the Indians". Francis M. Woody, eighty-two years of age and brother of James Woody referred to above, testified (Sizemore testimony, page 86) that he knew old Ned Sizemore when affiant was seventeen or sixteen years of age, and that Ned Sizemore was about sixty or seventy years of age and claimed to be a full-blood Cherokee Indian. He testified that: "I have heard old Ned say that he was an Indian many a time. He used to brag of being a Cherokee Indian. He never spoke of having received any money from the government on account of his Indian blood that I ever heard. He went backwards and forwards to Cherokee to visit the tribe many a time. He died in Allegheny County, to the best of my recollect – that was probably in the fifties". If the Ned Sizemore referred to was the one referred to as the ancestor of so many of these claimants, he certainly must have been more than sixty or seventy years of age when the affiant was sixteen years old, and if he lived in the fifties, he must have been considerably over a hundred years of age at the time of his death. This witness testified: "Ned Sizemore's beard was not gray when I first saw him. I never knew any Indians living in this country except the Sizemores". This is the most direct testimony connecting the Sizemores with the Cherokee people and is not consistent with the testimony of other witnesses and claimants that Ned Sizemore came from Halifax County, or from the Catawa Reservation. Eli J. Phipps testified at Jefferson, North Carolina (Sizemore testimony, page 80) and that he is sixty-four years of age and lived in Ashe County all his life, and that: "I have always been a recognized white man in the community and have always voted. I have always been taught that I am a descendent of an eastern Cherokee Indian". Nancy E. Porter testified at Jefferson, North Carolina (Sizemore testimony, page 31) that she was born in Grayson County, Virginia and that: "I have always been taught that I have Indian blood by my father and mother and have always heard others say the same thing. I do not remember what kind of Indian they said I was descended from. My father lived with white people all his life. I did not know of any Indians living in Grayson Co., with the exception of my father and his connections". John A. Peck testified at Grassy Creek, North Carolina (Sizemore testimony, page 33) that he is sixty-one years of age and that: "I claim my Indian blood through my mother and the Sizemores only. My mother and her ancestors were recognized as white people but it was claimed through the country that we had Indian blood". I never received any money from the Government on account of my Indian blood nor did my father. I claim Indian blood through my father's side only. He claimed to be of Cherokee Indian blood." John Baldwin also testified at Grassy Creek, North Carolina (Sizemore testimony, page 40) that he is seventy years of age and was born in Ashe County, North Carolina, and that; "I have always been taught that I had Cherokee Indian ancestors. My father lived in Grayson Co., Va. He was a very old man when he died". His father died in 1898. He claimed through his father's mother, Catherine Hart. He further testified that his grandmother, Catherine Hart, lived in Ashe County, and that: "My grandmother, father and I were considered white people, but when people got mad with us they would throw up the Indian". In this connection, it may be well to note that the Cherokee Nation surrendered all claim to the territory that now constitutes Ashe County, North Carolina by the Treaty of 1777, and no portion of Ashe County is within a hundred miles of what constituted the Cherokee domain in 1835-1836. Mary A. Sullivan testified at Weasels, North Carolina (Sizemore testimony, page 44) that she claims through her mother, Louisa Baldwin, who is seventy-seven years of age, who was born and raised in Grayson County, Virginia, and that her mother's Indian blood came through her father, William Baldwin, who was also born in Grayson County, Virginia. This is likewise in territory which was surrendered by the Cherokees as early as 1768 and is still further removed from the Cherokee domain in 1835-1836. Matilda Davis testified at Weasels, North Carolina (Sizemore testimony, page 47) that she is sixty-eight years of age, was born in Ashe County, North Carolina and that: "I do not know what kind of Indians the Sizemores were thought to be. My Indian blood comes through my mother who was a Blevins. I have heard my mother say that her grandfather was full-blood Indian. His name was Neddie Sizemore. I reckon she was born in Ashe County and lived there most of her life". David Tucker who lives near Weasels, North Carolina and who is not a claimant, testified (Sizemore testimony, page 40) that he is eighty-seven years of age and moved to Ashe County when he was ten years old; that he had seen Ned Sizemore many times, that he was an old man and claimed to be Cherokee; that his acquaintance with him terminated when affiant was about grown; that he believed he went west; that the people in the neighborhood recognized Ned Sizemore as an Indian, and that: "I have heard it said he took part in the war of 1818, but I do not know. Old Ned Sizemore was a preacher. I have heard him preach. He talked english very well. He did not show any sings of white blood. I have heard all through my life that old Ned ought to have a claim, although the Sizemores I have known have not talked a great deal about their Indian blood until the time of the land matters in the Indian territory". Byron Sturgill testified at Weasels, North Carolina (Sizemore testimony, page 49) that he is sixty-two years and claims his Indian blood through his mother only: that she had been dead about thirty years, and that "She never spoke to me about her Indian blood. Cicero Price, up in the mountains, told me about my Indian blood since this Cherokee judgment. Before that I had not heard that I was related to the Cherokees". William H. Blevins, sixty-seven years of age, testified at Marion, Virginia. (Sizemore testimony, page 56) that he was born in Ashe County, North Carolina and claims through his father who lived and died in Ashe County, North Carolina that he never received any money from the government on account of his Indian blood and that: "I have heard my father say that old Ned Sizemore lived in what is now Allegheny Co., N.C., but was then Ashe Co. I have heard that old man Ned Sizemore's father was John Sizemore and he lived in Stokes Co., N.C. and had a son, Dr. Johnny Gourd Sizemore who was a brother of old Ned. I remember one Elisha Blevins, who said that old Ned Sizemore came from the Catawa River or Catawa Reservation, as he called it. Elisha Blevins has been dead some time. Wesley Blevins also testified in 1896 to the same effect. I never heard that any of the Sizemores ever received any money from the Government on account of their Indian blood. If they did, I think I should have known it. That since I was old enough to recollect. I was not enrolled on the Census of Eastern Cherokee Indians in 1885 and never heard of it before. I was not enrolled in 1851 by the Government. I did not receive any of the money paid in 1851 and none of the Sizemore family did as I know of. I have heard my father and his brothers talk something about the enrollment of 1851. They were afraid of the enrollment, were afraid they would be carried to the Territory and scattered on that account. I do not think my father was enrolled in 1835 or any of the Sizemores that I know anything of. They were afraid of enrollment. My father, Armstrong Blevins, I do not think was a party to the treaty of 1836 and 1848. Elisha Blevins who gave testimony in 1886 and 1896 before me, was not a party to the treaty of 1833 and 1836, and did not claim to be an Indian at all. I suppose Wells Blevins was living in 1835 and 1836. He lived in Ashe Co., N.C. I do not know that he was a party to the treaty of 1835-36. I do not know that any of the descendents of the Sizemores, or old Ned himself, ever lived with the Cherokee Indians". While it seems certain that there has been a tradition in this family that they had a certain degree of Indian blood, the testimony is entirely too indefinite to establish a connection with the Eastern Cherokee Indians at the time of the Treaty of 1835. The locality where these claimants and their ancestors are shown to have been living from a period considerably prior to 1800 up to the present time, is a territory that, during this time, has not been frequented by Cherokee Indians. It is a region much more likely to have been occupied by Indians from Virginia or by the Catawa Indians, who ranged from South Carolina up through North Carolina into Virginia. It is also significant that the name of Sizemore does not appear upon any of the Cherokee rolls. For the foregoing reasons, all the Sizemore claims have been rejected.

Rachel Thompson, Eucha, Oklahoma
Admitted. Applicant enrolled in 1851 by Drennen, Del. 738.

Jenni Starry, Eucha, Oklahoma
Admitted. Applicant's parents enrolled in 1851 by Drennen, Del. 890. (Miscel. Test. P. 3405 and 3180).

James Turner and five children, Eucha, Oklahoma
Admitted. Applicant's father and grandfather enrolled in 1851 by Drennen Del. 685

Jennie Oldfield and 3 children, Eucha, Oklahoma Admitted. Sister of #420 and claim through the same source.

Custis Harnago, Talala, Oklahoma
Admitted. Applicant's mother, Emily Harnago, enrolled in 1851 by Drennen, 420.

John M. Tucker, Cherry Log, Georgia
Admitted. Applicant enrolled in 1851 by Chapman #1895. Also by Hester #1923. (Miscel. Test. P. 1401).

William P. Tucker, Cherry Log, Georgia
Admitted. Son of #435 and claims through same source. Applicant enrolled by Hester.

Laura J. Cornett and 4 children, Cherry Log, Georgia
Admitted. Daughter of #423 and claims through same source. Applicant enrolled by Hester.

The Cherokee is Promised $5,000,000

In 1829, gold was discovered on Cherokee Land in the southeastern United States. President Andrew Jackson feeling the Indians would be overrun by superior numbers of white people, promised the Indians $5,000,000 if they would allow themselves to be relocated on a reservation in Oklahoma.

December 29, 1835 — A Treaty at New Echota, Georgia consumated Jackson's promise and the United States Government invested $5,000,000 for the Cherokee. "WHY DID THEY NOT GIVE IT TO THE INDIANS?" For years and years small amounts of money was dribbled to The Indians occasionally as they became aroused. Seventy-two years later, by 1907, the original amount invested by the government had grown to $6,000,000.

The Cherokee Indians were not paid the majority of the money for over 140 years, several generations were born and expired before on September 11, 1972 the final award for the Eastern Band of Cherokee in North Carolina was said to be $1,855,254.50, and was paid primarily to enrolled members living in Graham and Cherokee counties, North Carolina. The Eastern Band of Cherokee hold about 12,000 acres in the Great Smoky Mountains, known as the Qualla Boundary.

May 30, 1974 — The final award for the Western Band of Cherokee in Oklahoma was said to be $3,887,557.07. The difference in the awards of the two groups was perhaps justified according to population, and after all, the Eastern Band had defied the western migration move.

By the 1970s when the money promised the Cherokee was finally awarded, seven generations had made appearances. It is needless to say the descendents of Great-grandmother Adeline Sizemore of her brothers and sisters, Calvin, John, Franklin, Gideon, Carolina, Elizabeth, Jane and Lydia Sizemore.

I am indebted to Glennis Walker for the foregoing article. He graciously gave me permission to use any material in his book *The History of the Walker Family 1734-1990*.

This ties in with the application forms that Grandma Martha Ann Charity made through her connection with the Sizemore Clan, of which I was able to obtain with the help of a real Cherokee Chief of the Qualla boundary. I notice this report gives the figure of 12,000 acres of land in this boundary. When Robert S. Youngdeer was elected Principal Chief in 1987, there were 9,000 tribal members and 58,000 acres of land.

After reading the above report and the denial of Grandma Mills' claim, I believe the government deliberately paid only Indians who had enrolled and remained on the reservations. I am sure there was enough proof from Indians who had scattered to support their claim. They listened to the testimony, wrote it down for the records, but they had their guidelines, and that was what they went by. When people testified that "Old Ned Sizemore" told people that he was Indian and several people testified that he made frequent trips back to the reservation for visits and that he looked Indian — that should have been enough.
Glennis Walker Book

Great-grandmother Martha Adeline Sizemore Walker was born in 1835 in North Carolina. She was the daughter of "Little

John" Sizemore and Virginia "Jenny" Arms, who was born in 1807 in North Carolina. John was born Jan. 22, 1810 in Hawkins County, Tennessee, and was the son of Edward B. and Ann B. Baldwin Sizemore. John later became a Primitive Baptist Preacher of the Mate Creek Association in Wyoming County, Virginia (now West Virginia). He died February 27, 1853 of tuberculosis at the comparatively young age of 43Y 1M 5D while living at Pinnacle Fork, Wyoming County, Virginia.

Saturday, September 4, 1852. 9th Annual Session of the Indian Creek District Primitive Baptist Association convened with the Camp Creek Primitive Baptist Church at Flat Top, Mercer County, Virginia. The Elder John Sizemore was present and chosen as a Sunday speaker, however on Sunday, he was replaced, perhaps due to his respiratory conjection. Less than six months later he had expired of tuberculosis. His daughter, Martha Adeline Sizemore was the great-great-granddaughter of "Old Ned" Sizemore, a Cherokee Indian. Five generations of Sizemores shown here:

1. "Old Ned" Sizemore and Cherokee Indian wife.
2. George Sizemore – Married Annie Hart.
3. Edward B. Sizemore – Married Anne B. Blevins.
4. John Sizemore – Married Virginia "Jenny" Arms.
5. Martha Adeline Sizemore – Married Numa Dink Walker.

The Sizemore Tribe prior to the division of the Cherokee Indians in 1838 was quite large at times and appointed their own chief. "Old Ned" Sizemore was chief for a number of years. His grandson, Edward B. Sizemore, known as "Ned Jr." was in charge of the Sizemore wagon caravan, which was assembled in the vicinity of Jefferson, North Carolina about 1835, and migrated into Wyoming County, Virginia, later West Virginia. This wagon caravan was made up mostly of persons from Cherokee Indian ancestry, still possessing some tribal customs, various relics and many primitive artifacts.

Great-grandmother Martha Adeline Sizemore was a small child at the time and was taken on this northwestern migration by her parents, John and Virginia Arms Sizemore. This was just prior to the movement from which came the Cherokee Indian Trail of Tears, resulting from the U.S. Government forcing a relocation of the Indians from the southeastern United States to eastern Oklahoma. The Indians who survived the move came to be known as the Western Band of Cherokee.

The winter of 1838-1839 was the period of forced exodus of the Cherokee Indians to Oklahoma, in which they were escorted by U.S. soldiers. The Indians were assembled in groups of approximately 1,000 and pressured westward. The last of 14 groups arrived in Oklahoma in late March 1839. An estimated 4,000 Cherokee died enroute from exposure, exhaustion, starvation freezing and drownings before they were resettled in Cherokee County, Oklahoma. Lots of soldiers also died on the way.

The segment of Cherokee who more or less defied the U.S. Government and soldiers receded into the Great Smoky Mountains and came to be known as the Eastern Band of Cherokee. They refer to their home as "Land of Big Smoke". They now inhabit the most part of Graham and Cherokee counties, North Carolina. They are unrestricted and living conditions are steadily improving for most of the Indians.

Following Numa Walker's death in 1884, Martha Adeline Walker and heirs sold ten separate tracts of land on Devils Fork between 1885 and 1890, with the combined total being almost 1,400 acres. The total amount received for this vast amount of land averaged 50 cents per acre. Martha Adeline suffered from a terrible case of asthma from which she found very little relief. She last lived with the Keaton Mills Family (a daughter and son-in-law) at Egeria, West Virginia. Dessie Mills Cole, a young girl at that time told me Great-grandmother had a trunk which contained some Confederate money and quite a collection of Indian relics and artifacts.

The 1860 census of Wyoming County, Virginia, listed John Sizemore, 18, and Franklin Sizemore, age 13, as being members of the Numa Walker household on Devils Fork. They were the brothers of Martha Adeline, and were very young children at the death of their father, Preacher John Sizemore in 1853.

"Great Grandmother Killed a Bear"

As unusual as it might appear Great-grandmother Martha Adeline Sizemore Walker killed a bear while living on Devils Fork. She heard a commotion one night at the hog pen. Taking a butcher knife she went to investigate. She found a bear among the hogs. She wielded the knife fortunately striking the bear in a vital spot and killed it.

With the assistance of her children she proceeded to dress

out the bear and had a portion of it cooked and ready to serve Great-grandfather Numa when he returned at a late hour that night. He had probably gone to Beckley the county seat of Raleigh where he periodically auctioned off delinquent land with the proceeds going into school fund.

(This is an interesting "tale". Thanks Glennis.)

Indian Trails

Among the most historic places for which we have data today, and important to early pioneers, are old Indian trails. Many buffalo and Indian trails led from the Ohio River into our region over the Elk, Kanawha and New rivers, Indian and Muddy creeks, up the Greenbrier and across Jackson and James rivers. Indians in quest of food first followed old buffalo trails. Then came Indians on raid and war expeditions.

The trails were traveled by pioneers across the Allegheny Mountains into what was then known as Western Virginia. Some of the fiercest Indian raiding parties of the Eighteenth Century came across these old trails and rivers in 1740 to 1780.

One of the heavily-traveled trails was from the Kanawha and Gauley up Paint Creek and over Ellison Ridge to the New River, on to the Draper Meadows section of Virginia. Ellison Ridge extends from the west side of Big Bluestone River to the crest of Flat Mountain. The Indian trail crossed Ellison Ridge, down New River to the mouth of Indian Creek, then along the west side of New River to the mouth of Big Bluestone, up Big Bluestone to the mouth of Little Bluestone River, following it to the mouth of Suck Creek, along it across Ellison Ridge and Flat Top Mountain to where the Raleigh Courthouse is now located, to the head of Paint Creek and down the Paint to Kanawha River.

Two other trails joined the main route on top of Ellison Ridge, one from New River over Talley Mountain, crossing Big Bluestone River and up Ellison Ridge on the main trail. The other crossed Little Bluestone River near Fall Rock, up the ridge by way of Panther Knob to join the main trail. Panther Knob, the highest peak, was named by early settlers who killed panthers there.

Indians would raid early settlements and use the Bluestone and Paint Creek Indian trail to escape. This was a puzzling and misleading trail which delayed the posse from overtaking Indian raiders. Shawnee Indians used this trail across Ellison Ridge and the Flat Top Mountains in 1755 with prisoners and spoils taken from the Draper Meadows massacre. Among the prisoners were Mary Draper Ingles and an old Dutch woman, the first white women to have crossed Ellison Ridge.

Years later a student of the land, my nephew, Kerby Randal (Randy) Walker, avidly studied the Southern West Virginia trails, Indians who had roamed the hills and history of the area. His expertise led to his selection in 1980 to guide an archaeological team on a study of the New River Gorge National River for the National Park Service. He was credited with charting 248 previously undocumented Indian sites and confirming others already recorded. Randy died unexpectedly in 1986 at the age of 41 years. He was buried in our family cemetery, and the Randy Walker Memorial was established in his honor for cemetery maintenance funds.

The Trail of Tears

Now I'll tell the poignant story
    of that awful Trail of Tears,
The Cherokee won't be forgetting
    even for ten thousand years.
Now in the Great Smokey Mountains
    they would not hunt or roam,
For here President Andrew Jackson
    decided wasn't to be their home.

Now in eighteen and twenty-nine
    there was discovered gold.
It was found on the Cherokee land
    and was theirs since days of old.
Since Jackson knew the Cherokee
    could not stand up to the white,
The Indians were made an offer
    and some finally said alright.

Gathered in groups of one thousand
    with possessions ever so meager,
When pressured by U.S. soldiers
    the Indians were not too eager.
They were to receive five million,
    which did not quiet their fears,
Then in eighteen and thirty-eight
    came that awful Trail of Tears.

Imagine the severe grueling agony
    with the weak paying a high toll,
Starvation, freezing and sickness —
    drowning in rivers we are told,
Columns of Indians struggled onward

   toward an Oklahoma Reservation,
And far behind they were leaving
   a Great Cherokee Civilization.

To our graves we would be haunted
   by the Cherokees' forlorn wail,
Whose heartbreak never diminished
   on that crucifying trail,
Their sad dark eyes reflecting
   pain and age beyond their years,
As some abandoned all hope of life
   upon that awful Trail of Tears

Not all the Cherokees moved westward,
   safety in mountains some did find,
Among these were the Sizemore family
   and Great-grandmother Adeline,
Who later migrated in a wagon caravan,
   lived in Wyoming County many years,
For the thing we are most thankful,
   they escaped an awful Trail of Tears.

Glennis Walker

Martha Ann Charity Walker, (b) February 25, 1865, (d) April 11, 1936; Johnson Keaton Mills, (b) May 16, 1865, (d) July 15, 1924, 1. Stella Mae, (b) June 3, 1881, (d) May 5, 1913, 2. Alvirdie Elizabeth, (b) February 12, 1885, (d) February 19, 1965, 3. Lydia Anner, (b) March 1, 1887, (d) March 9, 1972, 4. Ivory Mae, (b) November 22, 1888, (d) June 15, 1890, 5. Dora Hessie, (b) April 8, 1890, (d) March 8, 1936, 6. George Winfrey, (b) June 5, 1892, (d) November 27, 1948, 7. Oley Johnson, (b) August 26, 1894, (d) November 1, 1952, 8. Della Dessie, (b) March 16, 1896, (d) March 4, 1980, 9. John Corbit Keaton, (b) March 17, 1898, (d) November 6, 1937, 10. Autie Easter Anthrim, (b) April 25, 1900, (d) December 23, 1921, 11. Nathan Crandall, (b) June 25, 1902, (d) July 4, 1967, 12. Kelly Alderman, (b) February 16, 1904, (d) November 26, 1931, 13. Laurence Evestus, (b) October 18, 1905, (d) October 25, 1929.

All the Mills children were born either in Wyoming or Mercer County and mostly raised in the Egeria area. Grandpa Mills sold the home place, 106 acres in 1923. His land holdings had dwindled from 1 to 2 thousand acres to 106.

They bought a place at Spanishburg and resided there until his death in 1924. After his death, they lost the place due to a "lost" note that Grandma thought had been paid off, however the court held that it had not. She then rented a small house on the upper bank of the road near the grocery store and road entrance from the bridge located in Spanishburg.

I remember an incident there when visiting one Sunday. The boys were playing in a sawdust pile at a sawmill in the bottom on the other side of the road. They did not want us girls to follow, but that was just the place we wanted to be, so we tagged along behind. They held us and put sawdust in our eyes. We scrambled across the road screaming and rubbing our eyes to Grandma's house to have the sawdust washed out.

They learned of a few acres of land at Beeson that was for sale. Grandma, Uncle Laurence and Uncle Kelly bought it. Grandma lived there until her death and later Uncle Nathan's family lived there. That is where he died. Since then, Basil, Oma and Aunt Versie have lived there.

Uncle Laurence was killed in the Springton mines in 1929 at the age of twenty-four. Uncle Kelly was shot and killed by

Leslie Meadows at Egeria in 1931 at the age of twenty-seven. Grandma, Delmer and Alastia continued to make their home at the Beeson place.

Grandma died in 1936. She died of a broken hip, cancer of the liver, complications from the broken hip and age. Surely, she must have been worn out. She raised ten children of her own to maturity and two grandchildren.

1. Children of Martha and Keaton

Descendants of Stella Mae Mills   21 Aug. 1996

```
Stella Mae Mills (1881-1913)
sp: William Henry Harrison O'Bryan (1871-1925)
    ├── Icye India O'Bryan (1900-1944)
    │   sp: David Alton Dick (-1944)
    │       ├── Devanna Herlock Dick (1921-)
    │       │   sp: Gloria Joyce Walker (-)
    │       │       ├── David Ralph Dick (1952-)
    │       │       └── April Gail Dick (1954-)
    │       │           sp: Ronald F. Wilson (-)
    │       ├── Normandia Dore Dick (1926-)
    │       │   sp: Jolete Deeds (-)
    │       │       └── Timothy Adrian Deeds (1959-)
    │       ├── Vilma Nimo Dick (1928-)
    │       │   sp: Artie Edward Morgan (1928-)
    │       │       ├── Arnetta Nimo Morgan (1954-)
    │       │       │   sp: Loyd Gene (Bimbo) McKinney (1954-)
    │       │       ├── Vonne O'Dell Morgan (1956-)
    │       │       ├── Milton Edward Morgan (1960-)
    │       │       ├── Calvin Dwain Morgan (1951-)
    │       │       ├── Myrna Elvira Morgan (1966-)
    │       │       └── Andra Lynn Morgan (1969-)
    │       ├── India Crystal Dick (1930-)
    │       │   sp: Andrew G. Saintsing (-)
    │       │       ├── David Saintsing (1954-)
    │       │       ├── Charles Saintsing (1955-)
    │       │       └── Marty Saintsing (1957-)
    │       ├── Darold Ninan Dick (1932-)
    │       │   sp: Louise Marie Weakley (-)
    │       │       ├── Donald Ninan, Jr. Dick (1971-)
    │       │       └── Dane Lillian Dick (1972-)
    │       └── Kerryold Ninan Dick (1934-)
```

```
            sp: Astrid Brier (-)
                ├── Cynthia Marie Dick (1961-)
                ├── Edger Verne Dick (1962-)
                └── David Wayne Dick (1963-)
            Albra Kirtel Dick (1937-)
            sp: James Donald Young (-)
                ├── Kelly Louis Young (1961-)
                ├── Lance Kerry Young (1965-)
                └── Shane Lee Young (1971-)
            Deanna O'Dell Dick (1939-)
            sp: Bobby Joe Young (-)
                ├── Derrick Egan Young (1965-)
                ├── Gavin Eric Young (1968-)
                ├── Darold Sean Young (1969-)
                └── Darren Kenneth Young (1971-)
            Orvis Colin Kelly Dick (1942-)
            sp: Linda Susan Geadd (-)
                ├── Milissa Lynn Dick (1970-)
                ├── Heather Denise Dick (1973-)
                └── Bryan Kelly Dick (1979-)
    ├── Infant Son O'Bryan (1902-1902)
    ├── James Rathburn O'Bryan (1903-1966)
    │   sp: Vera Mae Adkins (-)
    ├── Keaton Carson O'Bryan (1905-)
    │   sp: Elmo Toogood (-)
    ├── Voy Travis O'Bryan (1907-)
    │   sp: Oma Bragg (-)
    │       ├── Elizabeth O'Bryan (1945-)
    │       │   sp: James E. Coffin (-)
    │       │       └── Chester Travis Coffin (1974-)
    │       └── Sandra O'Bryan (1951-)
    ├── John Dee O'Bryan (1909-1970)
    │   sp: Helen Carpenter (-)
    │       ├── Loretta O'Bryan (1937-)
    │       ├── Patricia O'Bryan (1940-)
    │       ├── Barbara O'Bryan (1949-)
    │       └── Larry O'Bryan (1950-)
    └── Annie Alice O'Bryan (1911-)
        sp: Roy Lenwood Hutcherson (-1963)
            ├── Nancy Lee Hutcherson (1933-)
            │   sp: Richard Lauzier (-)
```

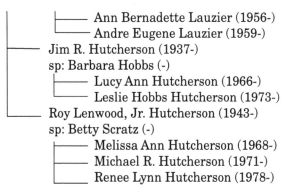

```
        ├── Ann Bernadette Lauzier (1956-)
        └── Andre Eugene Lauzier (1959-)
    ├── Jim R. Hutcherson (1937-)
    │   sp: Barbara Hobbs (-)
        ├── Lucy Ann Hutcherson (1966-)
        └── Leslie Hobbs Hutcherson (1973-)
    └── Roy Lenwood, Jr. Hutcherson (1943-)
        sp: Betty Scratz (-)
            ├── Melissa Ann Hutcherson (1968-)
            ├── Michael R. Hutcherson (1971-)
            └── Renee Lynn Hutcherson (1978-)
```

Standing, Johnie, three years old, *sitting*; Travis, five years old. This photo taken late in 1912 or early 1913. Stella died a few months after this was taken.

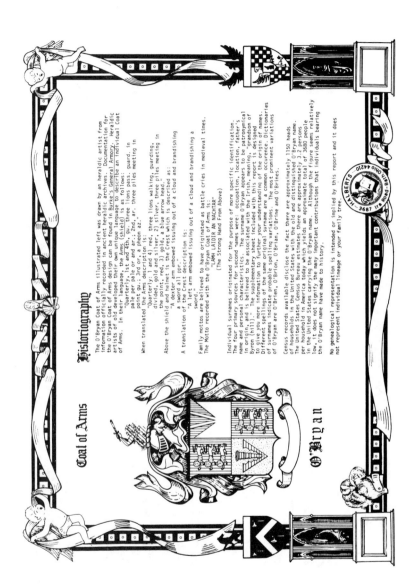

Coat of Arms

Historiography

The O'Bryan Coat of Arms illustrated left was drawn by an heraldic artist from information officially recorded in ancient heraldic archives. Documentation for the O'Bryan Coat of Arms design can be found in Burke's General Armory. Heraldic artists of old developed their own unique language to describe an Individual Coat of Arms. In their language, the Arms (shield) is as follows:

"Quarterly, 1st and 4th, gu. three lions pass. guard. in pale per pale or and ar.; 2nd, ar. three piles meeting in point, gu.; 3rd or, a pheon az."

When translated the Arms description is:

"Quarterly: 1 and 4) red, three lions walking, guarding, divided, gold and silver, 2) silver, three piles meeting in the point, red, 3) gold, a blue arrow head."

Above the shield and helmet is the Crest which is described as:

"A dexter arm embowed issuing out of a cloud and brandishing a sword all ppr."

A translation of the Crest description is:

"A left arm embowed issuing out of a cloud and brandishing a sword."

Family mottos are believed to have originated as battle cries in medieval times. The Motto recorded with the O'Bryan Coat of Arms is:

"LAMH LAIDIR AN NACHTAR".
(The Strong Hand From Above)

Individual surnames originated for the purpose of more specific identification. The four primary sources for second names were: occupation, location, father's name and personal characteristics. The surname O'Bryan appears to be patronymical in origin, and is believed to be associated with the Irish, meaning, "grandson of Byron (hill)." The supplementary sheet included with this report is designed to give you more information to further your understanding of the origin of names. Different spellings of the same original surname are a common occurence. Dictionaries of surnames indicate probable spelling variations. The most prominent variations of O'Bryan are O'Brien, O'Brion, O'Brian, O'Brine and O'Brines.

Census records available disclose the fact there are approximately 1150 heads of households in the United States with the old Arms distinguished O'Bryan name. The United States Census Bureau estimates there are an average of 2 persons per household in America today which yields an approximate total of 3680 people in the United States carrying the O'Bryan name. Although the figure seems relatively low, it does not signify the many important contributions that individuals bearing the O'Bryan name have made to history.

No genealogical representation is intended or implied by this report and it does not represent individual lineage or your family tree.

O'Bryan

YOUR NAME AND YOUR COAT OF ARMS --- Priceless Gifts From History

Until about 1100 A.D. most people in Europe had only one name (this is still true in some primitive countries today). As the population increased it became awkward to live in a village wherein perhaps 1/3 of the males were named John, another sizable percentage named William, and so forth.

And so, to distinguish one John from another a second name was needed. There were four primary sources for these second names. They were: a man's occupation, his location, his father's name or some peculiar characteristic of his. Here are some examples.

Occupation: The local house builder, food preparer, grain grinder and suit maker would be named respectively: John Carpenter, John Cook, John Miller, and John Taylor.

Location: The John who lived over the hill became known as John Overhill, the one who dwelled near a stream might be dubbed John Brook or perhaps John Atbrook.

Patronymical: (father's name): Many of these surnames can be recognized by the termination--son, such as Williamson, Jackson, etc. Some endings used by other countries to indicate "son" are: Armenian's---ian; Dane and Norwegian's ---sen, Finn's---nen, Greek's---pulos, Spaniard's---ez, and Pole's---wiecz. Prefixes denoting "son" are the Welsh---

Ap, the Scot's and Irish---Mac, and the Norman's--Fitz. The Irish O' incidentally denotes grandfather.

Characteristic: An unusually small person might be labeled Small, Short, Little or Lyttle. A large man might be named Longfellow, Large, Lang, or Long. Many persons having characteristics of a certain animal would be given the animal's name. Examples: a sly person might be named Fox, a good swimmer, Fish; a quiet man, Dove; etc.

In addition to needing an extra name for identification, one occupational group found it necessary to go a step further. The fighting man: The fighting man of the Middle Ages wore a metal suit of armor for protection. Since this suit of armor included a helmet that completely covered the head, a knight in full battle dress was unrecognizable. To prevent friend from attacking friend during the heat of battle, it became necessary for each knight to somehow identify himself. Many knights accomplished this by painting colorful patterns on their battle shields. These patterns were also woven into cloth surcoats which were worn over a suit of armor. Thus was born the term, "Coat of Arms."

As this practice grew more popular, it became more and more likely that two knights unknown to each other might be using the same insignia. To prevent this, records were kept that granted the right to a particular pattern to a particular knight. His family also shared his right to display these arms. In some instances, these records have been preserved and/or compiled into book form. The records list the family name and an exact description of the "Coat of Arms" granted to that family.

Interest in heraldry is increasing daily. This is especially true among people who have a measure of family pride and who resent attempts of our society to reduce each individual to a series of numbers stored somewhere in a computer. In our matter-of-fact day and age, a "Coat of Arms" is one of the rare devices remaining that can provide an incentive to preserve our heritage. We hope you will agree that it is much more than just a wall decoration.

If you are interested in a more in-depth study of the subject of this paper, may we suggest you contact this genealogical department of your fair-sized public library. We especially recommend the "Dictionary of American Family Names" published by Harper & Row and also "The Surnames of Scotland" available from the New York Public Library as excellent sources on the meaning of surnames.

Nancy L. Halbert

Nancy L. Halbert

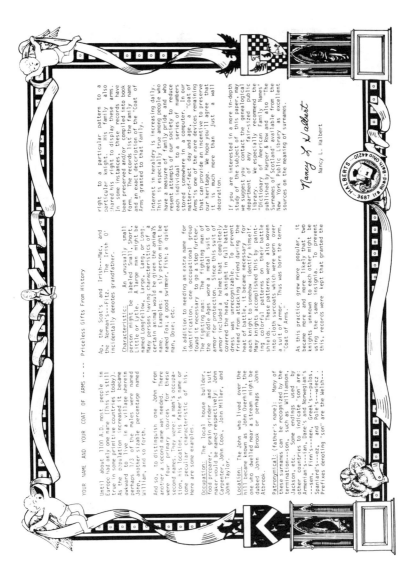

William Henry Harrison O'Bryan (Bud)
08/10/1871-03/04/1925
Stella Mae Mills O'Bryan
06/03/1881-05/05/1913

Stella Mae Mills, (b) 6-3-1881, (d) 5-5-1913; William Henry, (Bud) O'Bryan (b) 8-10-1871, (d) 11-21-1899; married November 21, 1899 at Aden Mills home by Henry Smith; 1. Icye India O'Bryan, (b) 11-7-1900, (d) 12-4-1944; 2. Infant Boy, (b) 5-1-1902, (d) 5-10-1902; 3. James Rathburn O'Bryan, (b) 6-11-1903, (d) 3-4-1966; 4. Keaton Carson O'Bryan, (b) 4-15-1905, (d)_____; 5. Voy Travis O'Bryan, (b) 7-14-1907, (d)_____; 6. John O'Bryan, (b) 5-4-1909, (d) 8-12-1970: 7. Annie Alice O'Bryan, (b) 3-3-1911, (d) 4-1-1960.

Henry spent his early years on a farm in Floyd County, Virginia. Stella and Henry lived at Tarpon, Virginia, for a time, and were living at Crumpler, McDowell County, West Virginia, at the time of Stella's death.

I met a daughter of Icye, Velma Nimo Dick, who would be my second cousin, at Aunt Dessie Cole's funeral. Velma married Artie Edward Morgan. She wanted us to make the trip to Hinton so that she could take us to the cemetery where Stella and Bud are buried, but we never got to make the trip. I did correspond with her and she sent me a record of births and deaths in the family, I will share a letter that I received from her dated, March 29,1980.

"Dear Gloria, I only regret I've never got to meet any of the Mills. Until the past 3 or 4 years, I didn't know Aunt Dessie was a close relative. As you probably know my mother died several years ago, so that left us kids to learn nothing of her family. Would love to visit you sometimes and get to know you.

"Enclosed is some of the information you wanted. Do you have the rest of my uncles and aunts names? Uncle Travis, Carson, etc. If not, I could get them for you. I am so anxious to have a copy of the genealogy of the Mills-Walker.

"I live on a farm about 14 miles from Hinton. My children go into Hinton to school. I have three already finished High School. One will graduate this spring. Both of the older girls graduated from college. One boy is in second year college. I guess the other one will go this fall. They soon grow up. Let me hear from you as to when you have the Mills-Walker reunion in the summers. Let me know when and where. Uncle Travis and us started one Sunday and I guess he got mixed up on the date or place because we missed it.

"If I can locate a picture of Mother, I'll send you one later. My homeplace burned a few years back, burning a lot of treasured pictures.

"Hope to hear from you and we can get to know one another. I have heard so much of Corda Walker. I'd love to meet her.

"A Cousin, Vilma D. Morgan."

This June 1995, I read of Vilma's death. "Mrs. Velma Nimo Dick Morgan, 66, died Thursday, June 29th, 1995, at her home, following a short illness." This is one thing that makes me very sad and regretful that I did not finish the Mills Family history several years ago. She was buried in the O'Bryan Cemetery, Hix, West Virginia. In 1978, Travis and Carson moved their mothers remains from Crumpler to a grave beside their fathers in the O'Bryan cemetery at Hix. I did send Vilma a copy of the history that I wrote of the Keaton Mills Cemetery, which gave her some family information.

The fourth son, Carson wrote a very interesting history of the O'Bryan family. He obtained a copy of the O'Bryan Coat of Arms, which was two pages and reproduced very well. The preface to his book is so interesting that I am going to copy parts of it, just to show you what our people were made of.

"The writer was born at Crumpler, West Virginia (a small coal mining town,) located in the southern part of the state.

"My father migrated to West Virginia in the late 1890s, after spending his early years on a farm in Floyd County, Virginia. Shortly after arriving in West Virginia, he met Stella Mae Mills of Egeria, West Virginia, (who was reared on a farm) and on November 21st, 1899, they were married and settled at Crumpler, until her death May 5th, 1913. To this union, there were seven children, five sons and two daughters. At this writing, they are still living, Travis of Lake City, Florida and the writer of Wynnewood, Pa. and Marco Island, Florida.

"Three years after mother's death, father remarried. This

time to Maggie Adkins. This marriage (after two years) terminated in divorce. The latter part of 1919, father again remarried to a very fine woman, Mary Ellen Puckett, of Cleveland, Virginia. To this union there was born one daughter, Evelyn, who at this writing is living in Wood River, Illinois.

"Father passed away March 4th, 1925. Mary Ellen followed him in death December 2nd, 1965.

"My father spent most of his adult life as a coal miner and as a farmer during his last few years.

"My early life until age 8 (at my mother's death) was spent at Crumpler, West Virginia with the family. From age 8 until 15, I lived with several different relatives and close friends, to whom I am very grateful for their help and guidance.

"Due to circumstances, my education terminated at the 8th grade level. Schools attended were a total of seven, all one room, except one with two rooms.

"At the age of 15, my first paying job was in a coal mine at Tarpon, Virginia (name later changed to Steinman), where father at the time was mine foreman. During the next five years, most of my time was spent working in several different coal mining towns, plus going back to school for one term, and helping on the farm periodically.

"In July, 1925, I left the coal mines and a couple of months later, September 9th of the same year, started to work for the F. W. Woolworth Co., in the Charleston, West Virginia, store at a salary of $18.00 per week (six days, 56 hours).

"I am very grateful to William R. McGinnis (one of my former school teachers, as well as a first cousin through his marriage to Delola O'Bryan) for his influence in getting the job for me with Woolworth. It turned out to be a tremendously successful break in my life. My career with the company covered a span of 45-1/3 years.

"From Trainee, Asst. Store Manager, Store Manager, Supt. Pittsburgh District, Merchandising Manager, Mid Atlantic Regional Office, Philadelphia, Pa and then retirement in 1970."

(I think that he did "ok" with his eighth grade education!- Gloria.)

I am going to share with you a letter that I received from Carson in 1979 and one in 1981. (*Very good handwriting for an eighth grader.*)

"April 25th, 1979.

"Dear Gloria,

"This is in reply to your most interesting letter which was accompanied with many interesting articles, as well as a number of photographs. All the information was very much appreciated, especially the list of those attending the Egeria School reunion. I remembered quite a number of those present.

"The writer, along with brother Rathburn attended the Egeria school during the 1914-1915 term. Lilly Harvey was our teacher. During this period, we were staying with Uncle Cal and Aunt Sally. Also, brother Johnnie was with us, however he was not of school age at the time.

"Sorry to hear that your husband has had a health problem during the past few years. Hope he is somewhere near normal again.

"Since my retirement (Dec. 1970) the wife and I have our summers in Wynnewood, Pa. and winters in Florida. We plan to go back to Wynnewood within the next three weeks. The yearly trip is becoming more of a chore every year. At this point, we are considering settling down, either here in the south or up north.

"I am so glad that you are near Aunt Dessie and in a position to see her often and give her a helping hand.

"Enclosed is a copy of the O'Bryan History for you. Found the Mills history (which you sent) very interesting.

"It would be nice to attend the forthcoming reunion at Egeria, however due to Elmo's health she is not able to do any extra traveling. She suffered a mild stroke nine years ago and is on heavy medication, which pretty well saps up most of her strength.

"Travis and the writer had mother's remains removed from Crumpler last year to a grave beside fathers in the O'Bryan Cemetery, near Hinton and our old homeplace.

"Give my regards to all the folks.

"With love to all-Carson and Elmo"

"Oct. 15, 1981.

"Dear Gloria,

"Thank you very much for sending a copy of the *History of the Keaton Mills Cemetery*. You undoubtedly spent a tremendous amount of time and research to come up with such a complete document. I have read it several times and filed it with all my other family history papers.

"I remember a great many of those included in the Keaton Mills Cemetery History. I recall my first visit to Grandpa and Grandma's home. The year was probably 1910. Dad, Mother, Icie, Rathburn, myself, Travis and Johnnie made the trip from Crumpler. The youngest, Annie was born in 1911. She was 2 years old at the time of mothers death. After mother's funeral, we children were separated as follows: Icie, 12 and Annie 2 went to Floyd Virginia and lived with a childless couple by the name of Lee. After a couple years, Icie came back to West Virginia and lived for a period of about 4 years with one of fathers brothers, Uncle Ross and Aunt Annie. The Lees raised Annie until she married when 18 years old. Rathburn was taken in by Aunt Verdie where he stayed a year or so. Aunt Verdie's first husband, Uncle Ed Ratliff died with T.B. a few months before mother died.

"I lived with Uncle Lundy and Aunt Lydia 6 or 8 months and then I lived with Uncle Aden and Aunt Hulda Mills for a year or so. Rathburn also joined me there. Travis went to live with one of dad's brothers and his wife. He was raised by them. Johnnie went to live with Grandpa and Grandma Mills for the next 2 years.

"After the above, Johnnie, Rathburn and I were taken in by Uncle Cal and Aunt Sallie. Where we lived for about 2 years. Rathburn and I attended two terms at the Egeria school. Our school teacher was Lillie Harvey.

"At this point, Dad took us three to Ramp, West Virginia near Hinton where he had bought before Mother died 104 acres of woodland, where we cleared a few acres and built a small house where we 4 lived for the next four years. Dad did the cooking. We then with the help of Dad's four brothers built a four room house. Dad remarried a year or so later. This union didn't last more than a couple of years. It ended in divorce. I won't burden you with any more of what happened after the above. Believe you have a copy of the O'Bryan History which goes into some details that happened after Dad remarried where we lived in a small coal town in western part of Virginia until 1921 and then back to the West Virginia farm.

"During the next four years, Rathburn and I worked most of the time in the coal mines which included Pickshin, Besoco, Lillybrook. During the period, I boarded with Alfred Farley's family, Uncle George's family and for several months at the Pickshin Company boarding house which during that period, managed by Piney (Am not sure of her married name), however she was one of Aunt Sis's daughters by her first Husband, a Mills).

"After Father's death 3/4/25, Rathburn, Johnnie and I lived together in what we called a shanty near the company store in Pickshin. We did our own cooking and house keeping. I quit my job of running a motor in the Pickshin mine in July 1925 and in July, 1925 started to work at the Charleston Woolworth store. The O'Bryan history covers the balance of my career, retiring Dec. 31, 1970, after almost 46 years with Woolworth.

"When Rathburn, Johnnie and I were staying with Uncle Cal and Aunt Sally, Grandpa, Grandma, and the following were still living in the old house across the road from where they later built a new house, which I believe was near where the Keaton Mills cemetery was established.

"The children at home were: Dessie, Autie, Johnnie, Nathan, Kelly and Laurence.

"As to the photos. I remember when the photo of myself was taken and where. I was probably 3 or 4 years old. It was taken during a day that Mother and Jeston Mills were doing their weekly clothes washing in a nearby creek where we lived at Crumpler. Am returning the preprint photo of Mother, Dad and two of the children. Note complete details on back of photo. The photo of Grandma, her sisters and brothers was appreciated. I recognized most of them.

"We will probably go to Florida sometime in December. We fly to and from Orlando. We leave one car down there to use while there. For a number of years we made the trip by car. However it would be too tiresome at this stage to drive. It's only a two-hour flight to Orlando. I think I have rambled enough for now. Hope you and Jimmie are well. The best of luck to you both, With Love--Carson and Elmo."

Carson was seventy-six at the time of writing the above letter.

I have a letter from Evelyn O'Bryan Sowers, who is the daughter of Bud O'Bryan and his third wife, Mary Ellen Puckett, dated March 9, 1983.

"Dear Gloria, What a pleasant surprise and many thanks for the information you sent me. I have nieces and nephews who will welcome the information.

"Larry O'Bryan, thats John's son once asked me how his Indian blood came about. The pictures are nice. After your Aunt Stella Mae Mills O'Bryan died, my father married 2 other women. He was divorced from number 2. My mother was number 3. I was born May 7, 1924. My father died 10 months later, when I was ten months old. My half brother and sisters were very good to me. Thats why I am delighted to pass family history on to my nieces and nephews.

"I have often pictured in my mind how sad it must have been at Stella's funeral. Icye (Vilmo's mother was not quite 13 years old), Rathburn near 10, Carson near 8, Travis near 6, John just 4 and Annie 2 years old.

"I have been told Travis and Carson moved Stella to the O'Bryan cemetery just a few years ago. I was happy to hear this as neither of my fathers' 3 wives were buried beside him. His five brothers in the same cemetery have their wives buried beside them.

"Carson will be 78 years old in April. Travis will be 76 in July, if he lives until then. I hear he is very ill.

"Both the Mills and the O'Bryan cemeteries are well tended and both are lovely resting places.

"During World War II, I worked in Maryland. Two of Arthur Mills' daughters worked there, Arvella and Othella. Arvella married Frances Moses from New York State. I've often wondered about them. Arvella really had Indian features. Do you know how Arthur fits into the picture? Whose son is he?

"A couple of my great nieces have Indian features also.

"In your information, there is a statement of how the doctor didn't treat Aunt Dessie's Children I have often wondered if maybe anyone really had what treatment that was available at the time.

"How my father was able to save enough money to buy a farm I'll never know. He and Stella went and looked at the place, as it was near his brothers' farms. Stella died before the place was bought. She was not well when they went to look at the place.

"Yes, I have a copy of the O'Bryan history, Carson wrote. In some of the information, I see where the Walkers and Lilly families were related. My ex-husband was related to the Lillys.

Also, I told my daughter besides being her Uncle Carson, he might be about her fifty-seventh cousin. Family histories are so interesting. Many thanks for all the information--Evelyn O'Bryan Sowers". *I can find no record of an Arthur Mills--Gloria.*

2. Descendants of Alvirdie Elizabeth Mills
21 Aug. 1996

1 Alvirdie Elizabeth Mills (1885-1965)
sp: Edd Ratcliff (-)
— James Jackson Ratcliff (1911-)
— Wauther Jerome Ratcliff (1913-1913)
sp: Archer Tarpley Allen (1888-1964)
— Weldon Tapley Allen (1915-1996)
  sp: Ethel White (-)
— John Keaton Allen (1917-1943)
  sp: Opal Foley (-)
— Virdie Ann Allen (1919-)
  sp: Ernest Jackson Dunford (1917-)
    Judith Ann Dunford (1941-)
    sp: Edward Joseph Marreno (-)
      — Rebecca Lynn Marreno (1961-)
      — Edward Joseph, Jr. Marreno (1964-)
      — Cathy Ernestine (Twin) Marreno (1968-)
      — Mary Christine (Twin) Marreno (1968-)
    Ronald Jackson (Twin) Dunford (1942-)
    sp: Grace Annette Bosswell (-)
    Donald Archer (Twin) Dunford (1942-)
    sp: Sandra Annette Ramos (-)
      — Dinna Carol Dunford (1968-)
    Carolyn Elizabeth Dunford (1944-)
    sp: Curtis Hershal Arnold (-)
      — Kristie Lynn Arnold (1967-)
      — Curtis Hershal, Jr. Arnold (1967-)
      — Elizabeth Ann Arnold (-)
    Virginia Lee Dunford (1945-)
    sp: William Henry Lowder (-)
      — William Henry, Jr. Lowder (-)
    Nina Ernestine Dunford (1948-)
    sp: Gene Junior Jowers (-)
      — Cynthia Jowers (-)
      — Scott Jowers (-)
    Mary Roberta Dunford (1949-)
    sp: William Humbert, Jr. Dew (-)
      — William Adam Dew (1971-)
      — Alan Dew (-)
    John Allen Dunford (1955-)

```
├──── Archie Lee Allen (1921-1939)
├──── Paul Woodrow W. Allen (1924-1994)
│     sp: Paula Maxine Sullivant (-)
│     ├──── Paul Douglas Allen (1946-)
│     │     sp: Jean Stratton (-)
│     ├──── Paulette Ann Allen (1948-)
│     │     sp: Henry Albert Wisniewski (-)
│     │     ├──── Michael A. Wisniewski (1965-)
│     │     └──── Virginia Ann Wisniewski (1967-)
│     ├──── Barbara Jo Allen (1948-1950)
│     ├──── Johnny Egan Allen (1950-)
│     │     sp: Patricia Ann Potter (-)
│     │     └──── Paula Misty Allen (1970-)
│     └──── Peggy Lee Allen (1952-)
│           sp: Tony Lee Potter (-)
│           ├──── Sunny Kay Potter (1969-)
│           └──── Tony Lee, Jr. Potter (1978-)
└──── Robert Boldwood Allen (1931-)
      sp: Ella Sue Sizemore (1931-)
      ├──── Robert Boldwood, Jr. Allen (1956-)
      │     sp: Julie Ann Jordan (1958-)
      └──── Karen Leigh Allen (1958-)
```

Standing, 1. Paul Allen, 2. Virdie Ann Allen, 3. Weldon Allen, 4. John Allen, 5. Archie Lee Allen. *Seated*, 6. Virdie Allen, 7. Archie Allen, 8. Bobby Allen.

1. Virdie Mills Allen, 2. Weldon Allen, 3. Archer Allen, 4. Robert Allen (uncle), 5. James Ratliff (brother).

1. James R. Ratliff, 2. Bobby Allen, 3. Weldon Allen, 4. Paul Allen, and 5. Virdie Ann Allen Dunford.

Archie Lee Allen, 1921-1939, died of cancer. Started in the leg from a football injury. Had scholarships and planned to go to college.

Weldon Allen (son) and Alvirdie Allen (mother).

Sgt. Archer Tarpley Allen--picture taken 1907 or 1909, Nicaraguan Insurrection.

Robert (Bobby) Allen.

Alvirdie Elizabeth Mills

Alvirdie Elizabeth Mills, (b) 2-12-1885, (d) 2-19-1965 (possible heart condition and age complications-Robert Allen) Edward Ratliff, (b) ___, (d) ___; 1. James Jackson Ratliff (b) 10-12-1911, (d) ___; 2. Wauthor Jerome Ratliff, (b) ___-___-1913, (d) 8-14-1913; second husband, Archer Tapley Allen, (b) 08-30-1888, (d) 06-09-1964, (m) 03-01-1914; 1. Weldon Tarpleigh Allen, (b) 01-18-1915, (d) ___, 2. John Keaton Eagon Allen, (b) 06-05-1917, (d) 04-25-1943; 3. Virdie Ann Allen, (b) 11-11-1919, (d) ___; 4. Archie Lee Allen, (b) 12-31-1921, (d) 10-17-1939; 5. Paul Woodrow Wilson Allen, (b) 6-25-1924; (d) ___; 6. Robert Bolwood Allen, (b) 1-26-1931, (d) ___.

I asked Robert (Bobby) Allen a few years ago to write a history of his family and am very grateful that he did in 1991, or I would not have much of the following:

"Oct. 11th, 1991

"Dear Gloria,

"Am very sorry that I have not answered your letter sooner. I have been very busy visiting West Virginia, Ella Sue's sister in Atlanta, the Veterans Hospital in Richmond, Virginia and my son's home in Lakeland, Florida. Also, have had several friends from West Virginia to visit us over the summer and fall.

"Gloria, Dad was born in Swansonville, Virginia in 1888. Dad worked in and around the mills in southern Virginia and in North Carolina. Dad's education was through the sixth grade. I don't think in the area that he lived, a high education was offered for the common folk. As I understand it, Dad, being the baby in the family was spoiled and it seemingly led to bouts of mischief throughout his teen years. Dad was an astute horse trader and always had a handsome charger and a very grand buggy.

"Dad's mischief was one of the reasons he became a marine. One day, while working in the mill some co-workers dared him to throw some machinery out of the building. He did this. Also, the foreman was Dad's brother-in-law and his name coincidentally was Ben Mills. Realizing the consequence of this, Dad enlisted in the marines. My Aunt Sally, Dad's sister and all the family protested vigorously saying that they would take care of all the damage incurred.

"Dad joined the marines and subsequently was sent to

John Keaton Allen, 1917-1943, Opal Foley Allen shot down in Tunisia, North Africa-April 25, 1943.

Nicaragua where the marines put down an insurrection in 1907 or 1909 (?).

"Dad was decorated by Gen. Butler, the Commandant of the marines at that time. General Butler gained fame during this time and became noted politically after he left the Corps.

"One time, during a political barnstorming, General Butler was making a speech at Welch, West Virginia. Dad asked General Butler, Do you remember me? General Butler said "Absolutely, Corporal Allen." Dad became sort of a celebrity for a while.

"I believe this event happened during the 1930's. Dad was discharged from the marines in 1913, whereupon he came to West Virginia. He worked in the coal mines and he traded horses.

"Uncle George Mills became a friend of Dads and he introduced Mama to Dad. Mama had been widowed and left with two children, James and Jerome Ratliff. Jerome died as an infant due to some fever that was going around at that time.

"The union of Alverda Elizabeth Mills and Archer Tapley Allen, begat Weldon Tarpleigh, John Keaton Eagon, Verdie Ann, Archie Lee, Paul Woodrow Wilson and Robert Bolwood.

"James Jackson Ratliff retired as Lt. Colonel, U.S. Army serving over 31 years. He enlisted in the army in 1930, before I was born. (*I remember James spending the night at our house when we lived in Spanishburg before leaving the next day for Princeton to enlist-GCM*).

"The first time that I saw James, I was 5 years old. He went through the enlisted ranks from Private to Sgt. Major. He became a 2nd Lt. in 1942. After retirement, he settled in the Shenandoah Valley of Virginia at Strasburg, working in service stations, remodeling and construction. He married after retiring from the service and had a large family. (*Mom saw him, met his wife and two children at the time at a family funeral. She was very proud of him as I think while growing up, he spent some time with Mom and Dad. She was happy that he was happy with his family-GCM*).

"Weldon Tarpleigh Allen worked a short time in the coal mines after graduating from McComas High School in Mercer County, W.Va. In 1937, Weldon enlisted in the U.S. Army. He was assigned to the Signal Corp and graduated from the army school at Fort Monmouth, New Jersey. He attained the rank of Master Sgt, then Warrant Officer Grade 4. He resigned his commission as a Warrant Officer and took a Captaincy in the Reserves. Upon retirement, he obtained a degree as an Electronics Engineer. He also retired from the F.A.A. He resides in Richmond, Virginia.

"John Keaton Eagon worked as a chemist after graduating from McComas High School in Mercer County, West Virginia. He worked for the American Coal Company at Pinnacle, McComas, West Virginia.

"John enlisted in the marines in 1936. After boot camp at Parris Island he went to San Diego for advanced training. He spent the rest of his time in China, coming home in 1940. He enrolled in the Park Air College to become a pilot. He washed out because he took the Major's personal plane and flew under a bridge in St. Louis, Mo. *(Jimmie wanted to fly under the St. Louis Arch)*, but did not want to lose his license *(must have inherited some of the mischief from his father-GCM)*.

"He came home on the Thursday before Pearl Harbor and enlisted in the Air Force the day after Pearl Harbor.

"John's training was in Texas. He was shot down in Tunisia, North Africa, April 25th, 1943 on Easter Sunday. He was buried in the National Cemetery in Arlington, Virginia. *(He was married to Opal Foley, but I do not have the date-GCM)*

"Virdie Ann married Ernest Jackson Dunford out of which produced nine great children. All of them are living. Ernest passed away a few years ago. Virdie resides in Jacksonville, Florida.

"Archie Lee, Valedictorian, made all A's except one B in all his school years. (Also, I might add, John was also Valedictorian of his class and was a 1st. Lt. when he was killed). Had Archie not died, he would have had a choice to go to the Naval Academy or to West Point as he was appointed by Congressman Kee, who was the representative of southern West Virginia. All of my brothers were athletes. Some have said the injury that Archie suffered in a football game might have caused the cancer. The injury was to his leg, which was amputated, but too late to save him. A tragedy. Archie is buried beside Mama and Daddy in the Keaton Mills Cemetery at Egeria.

"Paul Woodrow Wilson was asthmatic as a child, coal miner, army veteran. He was on Iwo Jima when they hoisted Old Glory. This has become a great memorial which all can see in Washington, D.C.

"Paul is a master carpenter. He helped build many of the renown gambling casinos in Los Vegas, Nevada. He did a lot of the intricate finish work. He resides outside of Baltimore, MD. Paul has become disabled due to emphysema.

"Robert Bolwood, last child. Coal miner at the American Coal Company, Pinnacle, W.Va. Graduated McComas High School, Staff Sgt. U.S.A.F. during Korean War. Graduated Concord College, Marshall College and American University. Teacher and coach over 25 years. Retired due to massive heart attack. Resides presently Fernandina Beach, Florida.

"I can remember when Mom and I spent the day at Aunt Virdies at Crumpler. She had two or more large cast iron skillets on the coal burning stove filled with veal. She had breaded the veal and browned it, then just kept adding water as needed and let it simmer all day. Boy, was that good! All the cooking and visiting was done in the large kitchen. Later, in the evening the boys came home and went upstairs to the loft, where all slept. I thought that they were killing one another, but Aunt Virdie did not pay them any attention. It seems they were having a pillow fight and when they got tired or one got hurt, they quit. Beulah says that she was always 'scared to death' of them, that they played too hard. I don't know because I never stayed around the boys. Their only sister, Virdie Ann did survive, so perhaps they were not too rough.

"Bobby told me a few years ago that his father always worked and provided well for the large family. They always had pounds of fresh fish every Friday, brought in on the train, packed in ice. It would take pounds to feed all those big boys. He said that his dad had the Company store order him the best Buster Brown suit available, or at least, I think he said Buster Brown, for his graduation.

"I can imagine that there was never a dull moment around that household."

3. Descendants of Lydia Anner Mills
12 Aug 1996

Lydia Anner Mills (1887-1972)
sp: Lundy Rose (-)
```
├── Ray Vernon Rose (1909-)
│   sp: Leta Massie (1911-)
│   ├── Jortta Ray Rose (1931-)
│   │   sp: Robert Moye (-)
│   │   ├── Bobbie Diane Moye (-)
│   │   └── James Robert Moye (-)
│   ├── Benny Vernon Rose (1933-)
│   │   sp: Phyllis Waddell (-)
│   │   └── Teresa Ann Rose (-)
│   │   sp: Barbara Peiccies (-)
│   │   ├── Christina Marie Rose (-)
│   │   ├── Carol Ann Rose (-)
│   │   └── John William Rose (-)
│   ├── Lillian Irene Rose (1935-)
│   │   sp: Raymond McGuire (-)
│   │   ├── Sandra Gruhen McGuire
│   │   └── Donna Larae McGuire
│   ├── Newton Ashworth Rose (1937-)
│   │   sp: (-)
│   │   └── Scottie Dean Rose (-)
│   ├── Kareen Carol Rose (1939-)
│   │   sp: Henry Miller (-)
│   └── Minnie Anna Rose (1941-)
│       sp: James Walker (-)
│       ├── James Dean Walker (-)
│       ├── Tammy Reni Walker (-)
│       ├── Kimberley Rose Walker (-)
│       └── Edward Ray Walker (-)
└── Roy Vorden Rose (1911-)
    sp: Beulah C. Keys (-)
    ├── Roy Lendall Rose (1931-)
    │   sp: Jane A. Johnson (-)
    │   └── Christopher Rose (1959-)
    ├── Delores B. Rose (1933-)
    │   sp: Alton A. Shroda (-)
    │   ├── Larry B. Shroda (1956-)
```

└──── Laura A. Shroda (1961-)
└──── Lorena A. Rose (1935-)
sp: Harry H. Meadows (-)
├──── Linda Sue Meadows (1955-)
├──── Dwayne S. Meadows (1956-)
├──── Rhonda L. Meadows (1958-)
└──── Kenneth W. Meadows (1961-)

Lydia Anner Mills, (b) March 1, 1887, (d) March 9, 1972, (diabetes and congestive heart failure). Lundy A. Rose, (b) December 1, 1885, (d) August 16, 1965, (cancer); married Lundy A. Rose, October 22, 1908. They were married by Preacher Stephen L. Wood at her parent's home at Egeria, and were the parents of two boys: 1. Ray Vernon Rose, (b) August 22, 1909, (d) April 24, 1985, and 2. Roy Vorden Rose, (b) February 8, 1911.

They raised Bernadine Cole, daughter of Autie and Dolphus Cole. Aunt Autie died December 23, 1921. Bernadine was only 2 1/2 months old at the time of her mother's death.

Aunt Lydia was a retired postmaster and was a member of the Primitive Baptist Church for almost sixty years. Uncle Lundy was a retired miner and merchant. They are both buried in Roselawn Memorial Gardens Cemetery at Princeton, West Virginia. Uncle Lundy kept bees and had numerous hives located on a knoll beside the road. We tried to avoid that area but could not entirely because we had to use the road. I was, and am, very allergic to bee stings and had some bad times with stings. Aunt Lydia kept a square footed cut crystal bowl filled with honey on the dining room table at all times. The square of comb and honey cut from the hive just fit the bowl. We kids thought that having honey on the table was a special treat.

Aunt Lydia had a crystal bell that she rang when a meal was ready. Mr. and Mrs. Rose (Uncle Lundy's mother and father) lived in two large rooms on one end of the house. They had a sitting room and a bedroom. Uncle Lundy had put running water and installed a large sink where they could wash, but they still had to come out of their private place and walk down the path to the "outside" house. When they came in to eat, they just opened the door and walked through the living room into the dining room. They were so regal, sitting in the high-backed dining chairs.

In the evenings we might all sit on the front porch in swings and rocking chairs. They had a big swing on their end of the porch. After Mr. and Mrs. Rose's deaths, they moved out of the big house and built another one close to the road which also housed a grocery store and the post office. My nephew, Jeffrey Walker told me that he used to love it when Kerby would take them to visit Aunt Lydia because she always gave them candy. I remember Aunt Lydia as being a tall woman with not one pound to spare. In fact, she could be described as being gaunt. She was a strong woman in raising her family, taking care of her in-laws and for many years nursing Uncle Lundy before his death. When I spent my vacation at Granny McComas', I frequently spent the weekends with Bernadine. When I was very young and Daddy was still alive, we visited with them often. Aunt Lydia was in my house only once. She was visiting Aunt Dessie at MacArthur and Mom drove them over. I cooked a meal and we sat around the table and enjoyed a good visit. This was after Uncle Lundy had gone on and not many years before she died. I did not get to attend her funeral and unfortunately have not been to the cemetery. Of all the thirteen children of Martha and Keaton Mills, three are not buried in the Keaton Mills Cemetery. They are Aunt Lydia, Uncle Georgie and Aunt Stella.

Lydia Anner Mills Rose-March 1, 1887-March 9, 1972 (picture taken 1956).

Lydia Anner Mills Rose, Lundy Rose (picture taken in 1965).

Bernadine Cole Dillon --October 6, 1921 (raised by Lydia and Lundy), Elmer Cole--January 16, 1898-September 3, 1969, Lydia Anner Mills Rose (picture 1971).

4. Descendants of Ivory Mae Mills
21 Aug 1996

Ivory Mae Mills, (b) November 22, 1888, (d) June 15, 1890.

Ivory Mae Mills was the fourth child of Martha Ann Charity and Johnson Keaton Mills. Upon her death at the age of two, Grandpa Mills started the Keaton Mills Cemetery located on his farm in Egeria, West Virginia, at the foot of the Bluff Mountain. We have no pictures of her.

5. Descendants of Dora Hessie Mills
21 Aug 1996

Dora Hessie Mills (1890-1936)
sp: Fred Sneed (1893-1928)
├─── Infant # 1 Sneed (-)
├─── Infant # 2 Sneed (-)
├─── Infant # 3 Sneed (-)
├─── Infant # 4 Sneed (-)
└─── Eulalia Fern Sneed (1917-1938)
    sp: Henderson Earl Caudill (1911-)
    ├─── Evalyne Raye Caudill (1934-)
    │   sp: Jarrell Pierce St Clair (1954-)
    │   ├─── Jarrell David St Clair (-)
    │   ├─── Darrell Ray St Clair (1957-)
    │   └─── Harrell Dewayne St Clair (-)
    ├─── Donna Marie Caudill (1938-)
    │   sp: Fred Hatcher (-)
    │   ├─── Randell Dean Hatcher (1958-)
    │   ├─── Carol Damon Hatcher (1960-)
    │   ├─── Scott Daniel Hatcher (1963-)
    │   └─── Dillard Earl Hatcher (1966-)
    ├─── Randolph Washburn Caudill (1937-1942)
    ├─── Douglas Dale Caudill (1941-)
    │   sp: Barbara Foster (-)
    │   ├─── 1st Child Caudill (-)
    │   ├─── 2nd Child Caudill (-)
    │   ├─── 3rd Child Caudill (-)
    │   ├─── 4th Child Caudill (-)
    │   ├─── 5th Child Caudill (-)
    │   ├─── 6th Child Caudill (-)
    │   └─── 7th Child Caudill (-)
    ├─── Della Destine Caudill (1942-)
    │   sp: Charles Eugene Datson (-)
    │   ├─── Joseph Richard Datson (-)
    │   ├─── Nancy Eulalia Datson (-)
    │   ├─── Frances Margaret Datson (-)
    │   └─── Diane Gayle Datson (-)
    ├─── Wanda Kaye Caudill (1947-)
    │   sp: Douglas Norman Green (-)
    │   ├─── Tammy Kaye Green (1967-)

├──── Trisha Karen Green (1969-)
└──── Michael Earl Green (1970-)
├─── Alice Faye Caudill (1949-)
sp: James Leslie Byrge (-)
├──── James Douglas Byrge (-)
└──── Leslie Faye Byrge (-)
└─── Lorieda Gayle Caudill (1950-)
sp: (-)
└──── Stacy Ann Caudill (1970-)

Dora Hessie Mills Sneed, April 8, 1890-March 8, 1936. Eulalia (Totsie), daughter on lap.

Fred Sneed January 14, 1893-March 3, 1928.

Eulalia Fern Sneed Caudill, 1917-1938.

Evalyne Raye Sneed, 1934, first granddaughter.

Douglas Dale Caudill, 1941, grandson.

Dora Hessie Mills Sneed Rakes, (b) 04-08-1890, (d) 03-08-1936, Fred Sneed, (b) 01-14-1893, (d) 03-03-1928. Four babies died as infants.

1. Eulalia Fern Sneed, (b) 05-07-1917, (d) 04-03-1977. Hessie later married Luther Rakes, divorced, no children of this marriage.

Eulalia Sneed married Henderson Earl Caudill, December 3, 1938. They were the parents of eight children, 1. Evalyne Raye, (b) February 16, 1934, 2. Randolph B. (b) January 29, 1937, (d) February 24, 1942, 3. Donna Marie, (b) July 27, 1938, 4. Douglas Dale, (b) January 29, 1941, 5. Della, (b) December 25, 1942, 6. Wanda Kaye, (b) October 20, 1947, 7. Alyce Faye, (b) March 15, 1949, 8. Lorieda Gayle, (b) November 21, 1950.

Aunt Dessie said that Aunt Hessie and Uncle Fred were married in 1912 at Uncle George Walker's house at Josephine, West Virginia. A baby was born in 1913, 1914, 1915 and 1916 all died at birth. Only one cried. They named him James Keaton. All babies are buried in the Keaton Mills Cemetery, also Tot and her infant, Randolph. Uncle Fred and Aunt Hessie are buried side by side and all the babies in a row. Tot and her infant are nearby. Aunt Hessie was crippled and one hip was lower than the other. She always wore high heels to compensate. I think that her condition had something to do with losing the babies, however when she was pregnant with Tot, a new company doctor attended and probably newer and better treatment enabled this one baby to survive. She really produced a lot of children and grandchildren. Since she died in 1938, Evalyne was the only one she was privileged to know.

Aunt Hessie let us play with her tiny little shoes (4B) and we loved it. I remember one pair that she gave us, made of a bright blue leather and high heels. My foot was almost too big to get into them completely then, however that did not keep me from strutting around with my feet half in. My little sister, Beulah wears a 4B and her collection of many colored tiny pumps reminds me of Aunt Hessie.

I remember when Aunt Hessie and Uncle Fred came to our house in Spanishburg, where he died about a week later. We had been having heavy rains and the bottom was flooded. Uncle Fred drove the carriage and seemed "ok," but the next day he was confined to bed. We were all sent across the bridge to Grandma Mills' house and really could not understand what was going on. The doctor came and went and Mom and Aunt Hessie nursed Uncle Fred, but he died of pneumonia. A passage in Glennis Walker's book explains what happened. It seems that while working at the Pickshin Coal Company Tipple a lump of coal rolled off a railroad car striking Uncle Fred on the back. Grover Wallace, another employee seeing the lump rolling, called to him, but due to the noise from the tipple running, Uncle Fred was unable to hear the warning. His lungs and kidneys were injured from the blow to his back.

Apparently at the time of the accident, Uncle Fred did not know that he was badly injured. When he arrived at our house, due to the heavy rains, he had to carry Aunt Hessie and Totsy through the water. Getting wet and chilled probably caused him to contact pneumonia, thereby causing complications from his former injuries. We children could not understand how he could arrive, apparently healthy and be dead a week later.

Aunt Hessie lived at Egeria, Walkertown and Rhodell. She married Luther Rakes. They usually spent every weekend at our house on the "flat" rock at Egeria. They bought some land adjoining us and had the lumber company from Mullens build a house. They used a room of the house for a grocery store. When they went to buy supplies, they always bought pound boxes of stick candy, peppermint and white vanilla. I did not see any reason to buy the peppermint! I loved the vanilla.

Tot was growing up to be a beautiful young lady. She had blue eyes, fair complexion and dark hair. I can remember some of the neighborhood boys stopping by on the pretense of buying something just to get to talk with her and see if they could find out how her box would be decorated for the box supper at the schoolhouse so they could bid on it.

When they lived in a company house at Besoco, I remember going back with them and they turned on the electric light at the door and convinced me that it was magic. One bare bulb hung in the center of each room.

I remember going with them to Pickshin where Uncle Luther was applying for a job and sitting in the car parked near the company store and watching the bucket of slate go up the wire rope to the top, dump and come back down. Aunt Hessie told me that Uncle Luther had ridden up the slate dump in that bucket, when all the time he was in the company office seeking a job.

I was scared to even look at that bucket going up the high slate dump and the thought of riding in it petrified me. (Many years later my husband rode a bulldozer that was getting away from him from the top all way down to the bottom, he said that was the only safe way and besides he was paying for that dozer and was not going to lose it).

6. Descendants of George Winfrey Mills
21 Aug 1996

George Winfrey Mills (1892-1948)
sp: Angie Akers (1893-1975)
  ├── Amaco Mills (1917-)
  │ sp: George Wilson Stovers (-1954)
  └── Vernie Mills (1920-)

George Mills, Angie Akers (before married).

George Winfrey Mills, Angie Akers Mills.

Amacoe Mills Stowers and Vernie Mills, (daughters).

George Winfrey Mills, (b) June 5, 1892, (d) November 27, 1948. George Winfrey "Georgie" Mills, born June 5, 1892, and died November 27, 1948. He married Angie Akers, born May 7, 1893, daughter of William Bailey and Mary Jane Akers. They were married by Minister W.A. Bailey at Arista, Mercer County, West Virginia, January 3, 1917. They lived most of their married life in Mercer County, West Virginia, near Princeton. Georgie was in the lumber business for a number of years, then was in the coal mining business for twenty-nine years and served as deputy sheriff for a number of years in Mercer County. Angie died December 12, 1975. Both are buried in Monte Vista Cemetery, Bluefield, Mercer County, West Virginia. They had two daughters:

(1) Amacoe Mills, born November 7, 1917. Married George Wilson Stowers, August 1941, lived in Washington, DC and upon his discharge from the navy continued to live there. He died in February 1954. At that time Amacoe returned to Princeton to live with her mother and sister. She worked for Crozier Coal & Land--Page Coal & Coke Companies in the accounting office, located in Bluefield, West Virginia. In 1965, she went to work for the Mercer County Commission in the Tax Assessor's Office. She retired December 1988 and lives in Princeton with her sister.
(2) Vernie Mills, born May 6, 1920, owned and operated a beauty shop in Anawalt, McDowell County, West Virginia, then moved to Princeton and continued to operate a shop until 1959. In 1966, she went to work for the West Virginia Department of Highways in the Construction Office--District Ten in Princeton, West Virginia, as secretary to the Construction Engineer. She retired October 1988 and lives in Princeton with her sister.

I remember Uncle Georgia as always being there when we had a death in the family. Alastia (raised by Grandma) told me that he and his family were very faithful in visiting Grandma and checking to see if she was alright. My only memory of being at their house was when they lived at Matoaka. They lived in a lovely brick house on top of the hill. I could not understand why they were not using their indoor bathroom with the big tub until it was explained to me that they had a cistern and the only water supply was rain water and when there was a dry spell no baths in the tub.

Oh, yes, I do remember visiting them at their Spanishburg home with Aunt Dessie and Uncle Elmer. They lived there when he suffered the stroke and later died in the Princeton Hospital. Mom was called and was there with them a week. They kept a vigil at the hospital, but I don't believe that he ever came out of the coma to speak with them.

I thank Amacoe and Vernie for compiling and sending me the above account. (Sure would make it easier for me if I could get this from all the families-wishful thinking).

Since Matoaka was mentioned, I will tell you how it got the name. Matoaka is located on Widemouth Creek in Rock District, named by Captain D.H. Barger in 1903. Matoaka is the real name of *Pocahontas*, the Indian maiden. My mother had kept a clipping from a Princeton newspaper regarding Uncle Georgie's funeral. It is very yellowed, so it will not copy.

By: *Register Staff Writer*

Princeton--Funeral services were conducted Monday morning for George Winfrey Mills, of Shawnee Lake, who died Saturday night at the Memorial Hospital following a brief illness.

Mills was born in Raleigh County, June 5, 1892, and had lived near Princeton for the last twenty-nine years, where he was engaged in the coal business. He was a member of the Primitive Baptist Church.

Survivors are the widow, Mrs. Angie Mills; two daughters Mrs. Amacoe Stowers of Washington, D.C.; and Miss Vernie Mills of Anewalt; two brothers, Oley Mills of Egeria, Nathan Mills of Beeson, Mrs. Vertie Allen of McComas, Mrs. Lydia Rose of Beeson and Mrs. Dessie Cole of Crab Orchard.

The services were held in the home with burial following in Monte Vista Cemetery.

7. Descendants of Oley Johnson Mills
23 Aug. 1996

Oley Johnson Mills (1894-1952)
sp: Ella Graham (1897-1919)
├──Delmer Garlan Mills (1915-1997)
│   sp: Eulali Peyton (-)
│   ├── Lawrence Garlan Mills (1936-)
│   │   sp: Geraldine Tyree (-)
│   │   └── Daniel Mills (1968-)
│   ├──Glenn Mills (1938-)
│   │   sp: Martie Cox (-)
│   │   ├──Crystal Mills (1964-)
│   │   └──Alecia Mills (1966-)
│   └──Garlen Mills (1944-)
│   sp: Anita Conners (-)
│   └──Tracey Mills (1971-)
├──Arbrie Emmil Mills (1917-1942)
│   sp: Virginia Mooney (-)
│   ├── Elmer Kelley Mills (1941-)
│   │   sp: Margaret Cole (-)
│   │   ├──Loretta Kelly Mills (1961-)
│   │   ├──Arbie Scott Mills (1963-)
│   │   ├──Michael Edward Mills (1964-1964)
│   │   ├──Brian Luther Mills (1969-)
│   │   └──Janet Marie Mills (1974-)
│   └── Emil Loretta Mills (1943-)
│   sp: Dennis Meadows (-)
│   ├── Dennis Keith Meadows (-)
│   └── Wendy Dawn Meadows (-)
└──Lila Alastia Mills (1919- April 12, 1992)
    sp: Ule Tilly (1900-1960)
    sp: E.L. Hatcher (1901-1979)
    └──Joel Tilly (1935-)
        sp: Nancy Martin (1939-)
sp: Victoria Meadows (1896-1939)
├──Nina Athelene Mills (1921-1971)
│   sp: Andrew Graham (1896-1977)
│   ├── Wilma Jean (Nina's Daughter) Mills (1942-)
│   ├── sp: James W. Johnson (1937-)

- James W., Jr. Johnson (1964-)
- Liesl Dawn Johnson (1966-)
- James Bayre Graham (1954-)
  - sp: Unknown Unknown (-)
- Cathenia Ellen Graham (1955-)
- Patsy Sue Graham (1957-)
- Wesley Andrew Graham (1961-)
  - sp: Not Known Not Known (-)
    - Unknown Graham (-)
- Glendla Fern Mills (1923-)
  - sp: Karl Mason Walker (1923-1975)
    - Oley Dale Walker (1947-)
      - sp: Charlene May Thornton (1949-)
        - Tammy Yvonne Walker (1969-)
        - Jeffrey Dale Walker (1971-)
    - Linda Kay Walker (1949-)
      - sp: Earl Eugene Smith (1946-)
        - Crystal Michelle Smith (1980-)
        - Keith Alan Smith (1983-)
        - April Dawn Smith (1986-)
        - Earl Eugene, Jr. Smith (1966-)
        - Michael Oliver (Twin) Smith (1968-)
        - Richard Dwayne (Twin) Smith (1968-)
    - Jessie German Walker (1951-)
      - sp: Diana Leigh Thomas (1954-)
        - Karl Christian Walker (1976-)
        - Partick Shawn Walker (1979-)
        - Shannon Leigh Walker (1982-)
    - Connie Gay Walker (1952-1952)
    - Donna Rae Walker (1954-)
    - Drema May Walker (1955-)
      - sp: Daniel Ray McGrady (1950-)
        - Eric Michael McGrady (1985-)
    - Debra Fay Walker (1958-)
- Dora Mae Mills (1924-)
  - sp: John Wesley Richardson (1921-1987)
    - Wesley Dale Richardson (1949-)
    - Gerry Mae Richardson (1951-)
      - sp: William Phillip Kohler III (1952-)
        - William Phillip Kohler IV (1980-)
        - Emily Dale Kohler (1981-)

- Illene Mills (1926-)
- Oley Dale Mills (1928-1929)
- Ernest Dexter Mills (1929-1977)
  sp: Icie Emogene Walker (1931-)
  - Gary Wayne Mills (1950-)
    sp: Joyce (-)
    sp: Iris Regina Allen (1953-)
    - Robert Wayne Mills (1973-)
    - Christopher Michael Mills (1974-)
    - Eric Dale Mills (1977-)
  - Barbara Gale Mills (1951-1951)
  - Larry Dwayne Mills (1952-)
    sp: Donna Kay Dickens (1956-)
    - Scotty Allen Mills (1973-)
    - Mellisa Michelle Mills (1977-)
    sp: Donna Renée Mills (1960-)
    - Renée Mills (1990-1990)
    - Stephanie Elaine Mills (1993-)
    - Daniel Ernest Mills (1996-)
  - Jimmy Dean Mills (1956-)
    sp: Pauline Marie Taylor (-)
    - Douglas Keith Mills (1974-)
    - Lorie April Mills (1978-)
    - Kimberly Sue Mills (1983-)
    sp: Helen J. Pruitt (-)
  - Karen Sue Mills (1954-)
  - Kevin Lynn Mills (1970-)
    - Rebekah Lynn Mills (5-24-1997-)
    - Samantha Jean Mills (5-24-1997-)
    sp: Sheri Lee Peters (-)
- Lila Elizabeth Mills (1932-)
  sp: Joseph Hersel Crookshank (1924-)
  - Vicki Darlene Crookshank (1955-)
  - Sandra Jane Crookshank (1958-)
    sp: Delbert Calvin Eagle (1954-)
    - Delbert Calvin, Jr. Eagle (1979-)
    - Tabitha Ladawn Eagle (1981-)
  - Elizabeth Ann Crookshank (1963-)

Oley Johnson Mills, August 26, 1895-November 1, 1952.

Delmer Mills and Ernest Mills (half brothers).

Jeffrey Walker (Fern's grandson), Fern Mills Walker, Lila Mills Crookshanks, Dora Mae Mills Richardson, Ilene Mills Boyd.

Lila Alastia Mills Tilley (1919-1992), half sister to the above.

Eileen Mills.

Dora Mae Mills.

Oley Johnson Mills, (b) August 26, 1894, (d) November 1, 1952.

First married Ella Graham (March 10, 1914), (b) September 22, 1897, (d) March 7, 1919; 1. Delmer Garlen Mills, (b) January 25, 1915, 2. Arbrie Emils Mills, (b) March 26, 1917, (d) September 17, 1942, 3. Lila Alastia Mills, (b) February 24, 1919, (d) April 19, 1991.

Second marriage Victoria Ellen Meadows, (b) June 24, 1896, (d) August 8, 1939.

Married November 17, 1920; 1. Nina Athlene Mills (b) 11-28-1921, (d) 10-2-1971, 2. Glenola Fern Mills, (b) 3-4-1923, 3. Dora Mae Mills, (b) 07-27-1924, 4. Eileen Destine Mills, (b) 7-13-1926, 5. Oley Dale Mills, (b) 2-4-1928, (d) 7-12-1929, 6. Ernest Dexter Mills, (b) 12-17-1929, 7. Lila Elizabeth Mills, (b) 07-07-1932.

You may notice that Uncle Oley had two daughters named Lila. This is how it came about. When Lila was born, Sarah "Aunt Sally" Wood Walker was the midwife present. She named the baby Lila Elizabeth, being unaware of another Lila from her father, Oley's previous marriage. Lila from the first marriage always went by the name Alastia while Grandma Mills was raising her and I never heard her called Lila until long after she was grown and married. In her later years, she was known as Lila. I think that she did not like the name Alastia because she was called "Lastie".

I know how she felt. I was always call "Glora". I have a little Mexican "grandchild" in Florida who pronounces my name Gloriah and makes it sound like music. I love it.

Oley Johnson Mills died in a Princeton Hospital of an apparent heart attack. Ella Graham died probably of what was known then as "child bed fever" when her baby Alastia was either four or eleven days old. Victoria Ellen Meadows Mills died at the home of Dessie and Elmer Cole at Besoco of a stroke.

Uncle Oley lived, I believe all his life in the Egeria area. He was a farmer and a coal miner. During his employment at the Mead Coal Company, he accidentally came into contact with some very high voltage electrical cables, which came very near being fatal and he really never completely recovered from this.

After their big house burned, they moved to a small house around the curve from where the other had been. I remember the big, two-story house that had been in Aunt Victoria's family for many years. It was built in the old southern style with gingerbread trim. It was all wood and old and dry and I think it went up in flames quickly.

I have a note in my records that Uncle Oley played the five-string banjo. I do not know who told me this but would say that it is true because most country boys played some musical instrument.

Since they lived in Mercer County, Fern told me that they all walked the proverbial five miles to the Barn school.

I wondered how they managed when the house burned. Dora Mae told me July 30, 1995, at the cemetery reunion that she went to stay with Grandma and Alastia and all the others stayed with Uncle Nathan. They quickly built the house since two big families in one was rather crowded and moved into the house before it was finished and never finished it!

At the time of his death, he was walking from Egeria to Odd (about seven miles) to catch his ride to work. In the evening, he was dropped off at Odd and walked home.

His total of ten children all grew up to adulthood, except one, Oley Dale Mills who was born in 1928 and died in 1929. His oldest child, Delmer who was raised by Grandma Mills, worked on the farm and later in the coal mines. He married Eulalia Mae Peyton and they lived at Josephine for some time, before moving to Pennsylvania where they raised their family. As of this writing in 1995, he is eighty years old. After moving to Pennsylvania he did factory work until retirement.

The second son, Arbrie Emil Mills, who was raised by Aunt Dessie and Uncler Elmer Cole was killed in the Leconey Smokeless Coal Company Mine at Besoco on Stonecoal Gulf in Raleigh County, West Virginia, September 17, 1942. He was standing in water and came in contact with an electrical line. He is buried in the Keaton Mills Cemetery at Egeria, West Virginia. He and his wife, Virginia Mooney Mills had a son, Elmer Kelley and a daughter, Emil Loretta was born after his death.

The third, Lila Alastia was raised by Grandma Mills. Her mother died when she was eleven days old.

The first of Uncle Oley's second family with Aunt Victoria Meadows was Nina. Nina married Andrew Graham and they lived in the vicinity of the Hiram Meadows place on the Barn-Egeria road, in Mercer County, West Virginia. They were the parents of four children. Wesley Andrew Graham born June 12, 1951. He was married and divorced with one child. (I think that he died in 1993). James Bayne Graham was born January 7, 1954 and is married. Cathenia Ellen Graham was born December 26, 1955, and Patsy Sue Graham was born November 23, 1957. The above information was given to me by Nina's firstborn, Wilma Jean Mills Johnson. She was born November 24, 1942, and married James W. Johnson, December 21, 1962. He was born June 20, 1937. Wilma has worked for the Chesapeake and Potomac Telephone Company of Virginia with twenty-one years service. I am copying from a letter she sent me in 1986. Her service would now be thirty (unless she has retired). Her husband works for the Eastman Kodak Company. They have two children who were students at Virginia Tech in Blacksburg, Virginia, in 1986. James W. Johnson, Jr, born November 17, 1964 and Liesl Dawn Johnson born November 4, 1966. I just found a letter dated December 8, 1994, from Wilma giving me an update on her family and some information on her half brothers and sisters, which I will share.

"Sorry I am so slow in answering your letter, but we have been very busy this fall. We spent a week at Nags Head beach with our children and new grandson. Also, our daughter-in-law gave birth to a beautiful little girl on November 23, April Carolina. I am working on a new job (still Bell Atlantic) and am trying to learn the ropes of a new organization. I will be responsible for the Virginia and West Virginia Property Tax Report, as well as payment of the Virginia property tax bills. Now to your questons: Wesley Andrew Graham died in Philadelphia on July 25, 1993. I am not sure of the cause. I understand James Bayne lives at Odd and maybe Cathenia Ellen and Patsy Sue live in Kentucky. Also, I think that Wesley had two boys and was married twice. Patsy has a daughter. J.B. has children but I do not know what they are or how many. Now for my family: James Wister Johnson (Jamie) born on November 17, 1964, married Debbie Fay Hall on September 25, 1993. They are expecting their first child any day. Jamie graduated from Virginia Tech at Blacksburg (1987) with a degree in computer science. He completed his masters degree at North Carolina State in Raleigh. He is contemplating going for a Masters of Business Administration. He is a member of the technical staff at AT&T in Greensboro, North Carolina. Debbie is also employed at AT&T as a project management specialist. She received a degree in Business Administration from Highpoint College. Debbie was born April 7, 1960.

Leisl Dawn Johnson born November 4, 1966, married Corey Blake McLeMore May 19, 1990. She graduated from Virginia Tech. in Blacksburg (1989) with a degree in accounting. She completed and passed her Certification PA exam on her first try in 1991. She is now employed by the accounting firm of Foti, Flyn and Lowen in Roanoke, Virginia. Blake graduated from Virginia Tech. in 1987 and is employed by Lane Furniture Company in Rocky Mount. He was born on November 1, 1964. They have one son, Taylor Burton McLeMore, born on May 5, 1994.

I am sending you the only picture of my grandmother that I am aware of in existence. I found a small picture in my mother's pictures and had a negative produced. My aunts told me it is Ernest that is with her. They said it was made at the Lilly reunion not long before she died.

Fern was the second of this family. She attended the Barn school. She came to Beckley and was employed at the Pinecrest Hospital. She retired in 1983. She was given a plaque and was honored with a retirement party following twenty-one years of service. She married Karl Mason Walker and they were the parents of seven children. Mason served in the army during World War II. He was employed in the construction of the West Virginia Turnpike during the early 1950s and later drove a school bus in Mercer and Raleigh counties. Mason died in 1975 and is buried in the Keaton Mills Cemetery at Egeria. Their first child was Oley Dale, born July 6, 1947. He has served as one of our trustees for the cemetery for many years and we depend upon him to ask the blessing at our annual reunion at the cemetery. He has a beautiful voice that carries well and can get "quiet" from the crowd in a minute. He married Charlene May Thornton. They live at Glen Morgan. Second--Linda Kay Walker, born November 20, 1949. She married Earl Smith; Third--Jessie German Walker, born April 13, 1951. He married Diane Leigh Thomas. Jessie served as a sergeant in the U.S. Air Force. Their children are Karl, Shawn and Shannon; Fourth--Connie Gay Walker born July 2, 1952. She died July 2, 1952; Fifth--Donna Ray Walker, born March 24, 1954; Sixth--Drema Mae Walker born June 24, 1955. She married Daniel McGrady; Seventh--

Debra Fay Walker born August 17, 1958.

Dora Mae Mills was the third. She was born July 27, 1924. She married John Wesley Richardson, April 13, 1948. He died August 15, 1987. She lives at Rupert, West Virginia. They were the parents of two children. Wesley Dale Richardson born July 20, 1949. He is a doctor. Gerry Mae Richardson born October 13, 1951. She married William Phillip Kohler III, June 18, 1977. She is a teacher. They have two children, William Phillip Kohler IV born March 19, 1951, and Emily Dale Kohler born August 2, 1981.

Dora Mae also worked at Pinecrest. In fact that is where she met her husband, John. John was the one who suggested that we start a regular fund to maintain the cemetery. He loved coming to the Memorial Day reunion.

The fourth child was Eileen Destine. She was born July 13, 1926. She also worked at Pinecrest Hospital. She married Herbert Boyd, who was killed January 16, 1969, in a coal mining accident at Eastern Gas and Fuel Company at Keystone, West Virginia. They were the parents of three children, twin boys, Ronald Dean who lives in North Carolina; Donald Gene Boyd, lives in Florida, and Herbert Boyd who married Libby Burgess. Eileen lives in Beckley. The fifth child, Oley Dale born February 4, 1928, died July 12, 1929.

The sixth child was Ernest Dexter. He was born December 17, 1929, at Barn, West Virginia, and died January 24, 1977. He married Icie Emogene Walker April 7, 1949. She was born August 11, 1931, the daughter of Oda Oliver and Phoebe Marie Sizemore Walker. They lived on the Fitzpatrick Road in Raleigh County, West Virginia for fifteen years. He worked in the maintenance department of the Raleigh County schools for several years.

Ernest served as caretaker of the Keaton Mills Cemetery for a number of years. He did this without pay, or very little. In later years, we set up a fund and started paying a small amount yearly.

Ernest was last employed by Itmann Consolidated Coal Company as a continuous miner operator. On the day of his death, he arrived for work at the usual time as he had for the last ten years. He was fatally stricken with an apparent heart attack. He is buried in the Keaton Mills Cemetery. The cemetery he lovingly took care of for so many years. He always said that he would do the work whether he was paid or not. Since his death, his son Larry has continued his fathers' work. Emogene now lives at MacArthur, West Virginia.

The seventh child was Lila Elizabeth. She was born July 7, 1932. She married Jack Crookshank and they live in Rainelle, West Virginia. She has worked for many years in a sewing factory. Her mother, Aunt Victoria was a very good seamstress. It seems her daughter inherited her talent. Her three children are Victoria, Sandra and Elizabeth.

Lila Elizabeth Mills, (b) 7-7-1932, Joseph Hershel Crookshanks, (b) 4-24-1924, married 7-3-51; 1. Vickie Darlene Crookshanks, 6-25-1955, 2. Sandra Jane Crookshanks, 2-15-1958, 3. Elizabeth Ann Crookshanks 9-23-1963. Vickie and Elizabeth attended Concord College at Athens, West Virginia.

Sandra married Delbert Calvin Eagle. He was born 9-28-1954, married 3-4-1979; 1. Delbert Calvin Eagle, Jr., 10-15-1979, 2. Tabitha LaDawn Eagle, 2-14-1981.

8. Descendants of Della Dessie Mills
21 Aug 1996

Della Dessie Mills (1896-1980)
sp: Ernest Elmer Cole (1898-1969)
├── Lemma Lavada Cole (1918-1923)
└── Beulah Lorada Cole (1919-1923)

Elmer Cole and Dessie Mills Cole.

Della Dessie Mills, (b) March 16, 1898, (d) March 4, 1980 (stroke), Elmer E. Cole, (b) January 16, 1898, (d) September 3, 1969; (stroke), 1. Lemma Lovada, (b) January 4, 1918, (d) February 27, 1923, 2. Beulah Lorado, (b) June 30, 1919, (d) February 26, 1923.

Raised Arbrie Mills, son of Ella Graham Mills and Oley Johnson Mills; 1. Arbrie Emil Mills, (b) March 26, 1917, (d) September 17, 1942, (killed in the coal mines at Besoco, West Virginia).

In 1923, there was an epidemic of German Measels followed by membranes croup for babies and small children, which killed most of them. Beulah died at the age of four February 26, and her brother Lemma followed the next day at the age of five. They were recovering from the measels and the doctor assured Aunt Dessie and Uncle Elmer that they would be "ok." The croup choked them to death. This epidemic wiped out most of the babies and small children of Walkertown and Besoco. Aunt Dessie remembered at the age of eighty-three, in 1979 that the only youngster surviving were Holly Walker and another child, Hiram Meadows of Odd. The were taken to the hospital where a tracheaectomy was done and their lives were saved. Lemma and Beulah were born at Lego, West Virginia, and died at what is now Josephine.

During their married life they lived in various coal camps and on farms. At one time, they ran the company boardinghouse. They would have to set thirty to forty mine buckets on a long table and pack lunches for the boarders after they had cooked and served their evening meal. The buckets were three sectioned. The larger bottom part was filled with water; the middle section fitted inside a ring. This held sandwiches and the top section was shallow to hold pie or cake. Aunt Dessie and Uncle Elmer got to bed long after the miners were asleep and had to rise early in the morning to prepare their breakfasts. There was a 4 am shift, so the miners went to bed at the first hint of darkness.

They lived at Josephine, West Virginia, for many years before moving to MacArthur, West Virginia, where the last years of their lives were spent. Uncle Elmer was employed with the Leconny Smokeless Coal Company at Besoco for forty years.

I knew Aunt Dessie the best of all my aunts because she

lived the longest and we saw more of her. Beulah and I were able to help care for her in her last days. Totsie's girls were very helpful. One of them told me that when they lived at Rhodell and would see Uncle Elmer's green car coming up the hill on a Sunday, that they were very happy. Emogene, Ernest's widow lived near and for years took Aunt Dessie to get her groceries and other errands when she was able to get out and during the last when she could not get out of the house, Emogene checked on her every day, taking her to the doctors and to the hospital. In 1977, she slipped and broke her hip. After she got out of the hospital we took turns spending the night until Aunt Versie could come over and spend a few weeks. Later, we obtained a woman to stay with her, but she died before Aunt Dessie.

Aunt Dessie suffered a stroke and was paralyzed when they lived at Besoco and she was relatively young then. She had to be rolled over in a sheet. Mom went to take care of her and stayed a few weeks. Daddy was no cook in any way and we had to manage with what Lorena and I could cook. We were not old enough to have learned how to be a "good" cook so we were very happy when Mom came home. We spent a lot of time without her as she was called upon to take care of sick people all the time.

After that Aunt Dessie had a hired girl who lived with them as a family for many years. She recovered and had the full use of her arms and legs and did not seem to be affected at all, but it took a couple of years.

She liked house flowers and had the long porch on the front of the house filled with plants. She had some big depression glass bowls filled with flowers and when a storm came up, we scurried to bring them in before the wind blew them off the porch. They had chickens in a fenced-in area behind the house. I remember once when Dola Auer came to visit and within an hour, Aunt Dessie had a chicken killed, scalded and washed with salt, fried to a golden brown, a big bowl of mashed potatoes and other vegetables and hot biscuits. She had a big dining room table and even when we sat down without "company" being present, it was always filled.

Aunt Dessie taught me the proper way to clean a refrigerator. It was a slow process because she wanted it done right. Washed with soap and water, then baking soda and rinsed well and really dried with a soft cloth. I still do mine that way (once or twice a year). With our present-day self-defrosting we do not need to clean as often. When refrigerators first came out, women were proud of them and really followed the book instructions as to how to take care of them.

I just remembered the name of the flowers that Aunt Dessie grew the most. It was geraniums. This was the coal miners wife's house flower and every woman tried to see who could have the healthiest and prettiest. The leaves are waxy.

I have a piece of paper where Aunt Dessie wrote "Elmer worked his last day at Besoco May 14, 1959. Sent Miner's pension papers in March 24th, 1959. Was ok'd when quit work". I have a copy of Uncle Elmer's obituary:

Elmer E. Cole

Funeral services for Elmer Ernest Cole, 71, of MacArthur will be conducted Saturday at 2 p.m. in the Bethel Free Will Baptist Church at MacArthur with the Rev. F.C. Calhoun officiating. Burial will follow in the J.K. Mills Cemetery in Egeria.

Cole died in a local hospital Wednesday at 7:30 p.m. following a short illness.

Born Jan. 16, 1898 in Coal City, he was the son of the late James and Virginia Farley Cole.

A retired miner having worked at Besoco for 40 years he was a member of the UMWA and was a deacon of the Bethel Free Will Baptist Church.

He was preceded in death by a son, Arbrie Mills, a daughter, Beulah Lorado Cole and a son Lemma Lavada Cole.

Survivors include his wife, Mrs. Dessie Mills Cole; a sister, Mrs. Velma Crysel, Josephine; two grandchildren and five great-great-grandchildren.

The body is at the Williams Funeral Home at MacArthur where friends may call after 5 p.m. Friday, and will be taken to the church one hour prior to services.

Pallbearers will be S.C. Brooks, C.D. McKinsey, Earl Ratliff, Vincent Daniels, Homer Green and W.B. Aldridge, all deacons of the church."

Aunt Dessie's funeral was held at the same church and the Reverend. F.C. Calhoun also officiated. Both are buried in the Keaton Mills Cemetery at Egeria, West Virginia. They are buried beside their two children, Lemma and Beulah. Arbrie, who they raised as a son is buried nearby.

Elmer Cole and Dessie Cole at the cemetery 1967.

Lemma Cole and Beulah Cole, children–both died in 1923.

Dessie Cole, Elmer Cole, Arbrie Mills (raised as a son), died in 1942.

9. Descendants of John Corbit Mills
9 Jul 1997

John Corbit Mills (1898-1937)
sp: Thelma Eulaila McComas (1903-1970)
    Lorena Shelma Mills (1922-1964)
    sp: Kerby Laymon Walker (1917-1977)
        ├─── Arthur Kirk Walker (1939-)
        sp: Rose Elizabeth Beale (1940-)
           ├─── Denise Elaine Walker (1960-)
           sp: Timothy Patrick Thomas (1959-)
               ├─── Benjamine Patrick Thomas (1993-)
               ├─── Rachel Alexandria Thomas (1995-)
               └─── Hannah Marie Thomas (1998-)
           ├─── Arthur Kirk, Jr. Walker (1962-)
           └─── Rhonda Elizabeth (Betsy) Walker (1972-)
        ├─── Wathor Jeffrey Walker (1941-)
        sp: Dale Vandall (1945-)
           ├─── Wathor Jeffrey, Jr. Walker (1964-)
           ├─── Wendi Dawn Walker (1967-)
           sp: (-)
               ├─── Weston Hayes Walker (1990-)
               └─── Forrest Scott Walker (1993-)
           ├─── Heidi Lynn (Adopted) Walker (1969-)
           sp: Troy Colonnese (1966-)
               ├─── Holden Von Colonnese (1993-)
               └─── Paul Elliot Colonnese (1996-)
           └─── Troy Alan Walker (1972-)
              sp: Brandy Danylle Tadlock (1973-)
                  ├─── Paige Danylle Walker (1995-)
                  └─── Garrett Walker (1997-)
        └─── Linda Carol Walker (1943-)
        sp: Richard E. Jarrett (1943-)
           ├─── Richard E., Jr. Jarrett (1967-)
           sp: Michelle Leigh Rader (-)
           Divorced
               └─── Nicholas O'Brian Jarrett (1991-)

```
            └──── Jason Anderson Jarrett (1970-1997)
         └──── Kerby Randal Walker (1945-1986)
         sp: Carolyn Anne Lilly (1947-)
               ├──── Hondo Lane Walker (1968-)
               │   sp: Corrine (-)
               │      ├──── Boy One Walker (-)
               │      └──── Boy Two Walker (-)
               ├──── Michele Leigh Walker (1970-)
               │   sp: Greg Morgan (-)
               │      ├──── Boy Morgan (-)
               │      └──── Girl Morgan (-)
               └──── Julie Arlene Walker (1975-)
   ├──── Gloria Cathryn Mills (1923-)
   │    sp: James Vincent, Jr. Mallamas (1924-1997)
   ├──── Corbit Keaton Camden Mills (1924-1974)
   │    sp: Mary Ann Gregg (1930-)
   │          ├──── Donald Corbit Mills (1951-)
   │          │    sp: Shirley Susan Wheeler (-) (divorced)
   │          │       └──── Donald Corbit, Jr. Mills (1974-)
   │          ├──── Gary Sidney Mills (1955-1995)
   │          │    sp: Thelma Ann King (-)
   │          └──── Deborah Ann Mills (1959-)
   │               sp: Franklin Perry Carson, Jr. (1955-)
   │                  ├──── Matthew Perry Carson (1981-)
   │                  └──── Jeremy DeWayne Carson (1986)
   ├──── Allene Lavada Mills (1926-)
   │    sp: Richard Albert Cummings (1919-)
   │          ├──── Kevin Wayne (Twin) Cummings (1955-)
   │          │    sp: Mary Louis Davis (1955-)
   │          │    Divorced
   │          │       └──── Eric Wayne Cummings (1976-)
   │          └──── Karen Wynne Cummings (1955-)
   │               sp: James Michael Shepard (1952-)
   │                  └──── Michael Shane Shepard (1979-)
   └──── Beulah Lorado Mills (1927-)
        sp. Samuel Raymond Snuffer (1925-1996)
        │    Divorced 12/11/63
        Married Howard Cecil Austin 1972
        │       Divorced 8/17/73
        │
```

Married Ernest Clyde Shuemake 10/5/91
Divorced 7/1/94
- Stephen Wayne Snuffer (1949)
  sp. Sharon Louise Wiley (1948)
  Divorced
- Stephen Wayne Snuffer
  sp. Linda Dirrim
    (Married 1997)
- Stephanie Lynn Snuffer (1968-)
  sp. Arlan Eugene Geneseo (1965-)
  - Justin Michael Geneseo (1989-)
  - Joseph Andrew Geneseo (1995-)
- Richard Stephen Snuffer (1972-)
  sp. Cindy Akers (-)
  - Jessica Ann Snuffer (1991-)
- Brian Matthew Snuffer (1972-)
  sp. Jennifer Lee Wenhold (-)
    Divorced
- Brian Matthew Snuffer
  sp. Melanie Dawn Stump (1997)

Johnny Corbit Mills and Thelma McComas Mills.

Sisters Mayna McComas Walker and Thelma McComas Mills, Guy Walker and Johnny Corbit Mills.

Lorena Mills Walker, daughter of Thelma and Johnnie Mills.

Arthur Kirk Walker and Wathor Jeffrey Walker, sons of Lorena Shelma Mills Walker and Kerby Laman Walker.

Linda Carol Walker. Parents: Lorena Shelma Mills Walker and Kerby Layman Walker.

Gloria Mills-1941.

Time marches on--

Gloria Mills Mallamas-1959 (Western Union office).

Gloria Mills Mallamas-1966.

Allene Mills-1942.

Allen Mills Cummings, twins, Karen and Kevin.

Later--Karen Wynne Cummings and Kevin Wayne Cummings.

Corbit Keaton Camden Mills, (named after grandfather, Keaton Mills and grandfather, Dennis Camden McComas). Father John Corbit and both grandfathers, Keaton Mills and Dennis Camden McComas.

Beulah Mills Shuemake-60th Something Birthday.

Steve Snuffer (son).

Beulah Mills Snuffer Shuemake.

John Corbit Keaton Mills, (b) March 17, 1898, (d) November 6, 1937, Thelma Eulalie McComas, (b) April 25, 1903, (d) July 12, 1970; married April 12, 1918. John Mills died at the age of thirty-nine of a self-inflicted gunshot wound at home at Egeria, West Virginia. Thelma Eulalie McComas died at the age of sixty-seven of acute cardiac arrest--acute myocardial infarction in the Beckley Hospital, Beckley, West Virginia. They were the parents of the five following children: 1. Lorena Shelma, (b) January 22, 1922, (d) January 3, 1964 of lung cancer, 2. Gloria Cathryn, (b) July 7, 1923, (d), 3. Corbit Keaton, (b) November 1, 1924, (d) June 24, 1974 of cirrhosis, 4. Allene Lavada, (b) April 6, 1926, (d), 5. Beulah Lorada, (b) June 23, 1927, (d)– .

Mom and Dad had a double wedding ceremony with her sister, Mayna and Guy Walker at their home in Pinoak. After their wedding, both couples left by horseback on their honeymoon. Mom wore a brown tailored suit with a long jacket and skirt and at one time we had a picture of her sitting on the horse. She looked lovely with her long black hair up on the sides and up in back. They used what they called "rats" which were egg-shaped and made of bone or a hard celluloid material. These were covered with hair and puffed out on the sides. She looked much older than her fifteen years.

They journeyed to Egeria where they lived in the family home for a year. Dad worked in the fields and Mom helped with the household duties. The women cooked, canned, dried fruits and vegetables. They did the washing at the foot of Flat Top Mountain where the water ran clean and clear. They would build fires and boil the clothes in a big tub. The white shirts that the men wore to church on Sundays and to funerals had to be starched stiff by boiling flour and water into a thin, smooth paste. The ironing was done by putting flat irons on the stove to get hot, using one until it got cool and then grabbing another. Some of the irons had a covering with a wood handle which latched onto the iron. When they got old, they would slip out and some just had to be held with a quilted hot pad.

They moved to a log cabin at the foot of Walker Mountain on the road to Odd. This log cabin where Lorena and I were born was located at Barn, West Virginia, in Jumping Branch District, said to be named after an early settler's unusually large barn. They gathered up Daddy's horses, a cow, some pigs, chickens, potatoes and canned goods and moved into the cabin. Mom said that Grandpa Mills was very generous with giving them a share of everything they had worked for. Mom said the years she lived in the log cabin just keeping her own little house were the happiest years of her life. About three years later, Lorena arrived so they were not alone. Lorena was born there and by chance I just made it.

They planned to move to Besoco and were all packed to move. Even the kitchen stove had been taken down. Mom kept telling them that she would not make it. They had to unpack beds, the stove and enough to get by a few more days after I arrived.

I don't know how long they lived at Besoco. Corbit was born there in 1924. Their next move was to Lego because Allene was born there. It seems that they were moving at the wrong time again. They were moving next door to Aunt Crancy and Uncle Tressie McComas, but did not get unpacked, so Allene was born at their house. Aunt Crancy got the honor of naming Allene. While living in the Besoco area, they were partners in a grocery store with Aunt Dessie and Uncle Elmer Cole.

Later, they moved to Spanishburg on the Bluestone River in Rock District, named for Spanish Brown, an early settler. The Spanishburg house is the first that I can remember. It had a tin roof. The rain would put you to sleep. It was a two-story house, but you could still hear the rain falling on the roof.

The house was located across a creek in sight of Grandma Mills' house. There was a footlog with a wire railing going across the creek. It stretched from one bank to the other. The banks were almost straight down and rather deep. When Allene was just a toddler, somehow she managed to get to the creek. When we found her, she was hanging by a piece of her clothing to a short, scrub brush on the bank.

I was not old enough to go to school. I do remember being allowed to go with Lorena one day. The small yellow school bus stopped on the narrow road coming from Lusk Hollow. Lorena had to walk down from the house and cross a footlog. Sometimes, the water was too high and over the footlog and she would have to miss school that day.

We had been playing while waiting for the school bus and I had playfully put on two straw hats, which I forgot to remove and was very embarrassed when we got on the bus. The older girls on the bus all wanted to hold me and made me feel very welcome.

Miss Bottom was the school teacher. She was from Princeton and I guess drove the curvy road back and forth each day unless she boarded at Spanishburg. She gave me paper and crayons to occupy my time. At lunch, I played with the others on the school yard and really had a good day. I loved the play-yard time. The school is located on a level spot and is known as "The Bottom". At present, there is a large new school with several buildings located on this spot.

I will always remember Miss Bottom because she was so pretty. She was rather short and a little on the heavy side. She had a peaches and cream complexion and a lovely, kind face.

We had a fire in the Spanishburg house, but did very little damage as it was discovered just after it started. Mom was making rag dolls for us and sent me upstairs to get some rags from her trunk when I smelled smoke and noticed flames. The chimney ran up through the attic and out the roof, all exposed with no fireproofing insulation around it and had just gotten too hot. We started a water brigade with buckets of water and soon had the fire out.

I remember an incident regarding glass canning jars and the grape arbor. (Do you remember having to wash the dirty jars because your hand was small enough to go inside?)

The grape arbor had four posts and the heavy vines across the top was almost like a roof. Mom stored the empty jars in one corner under the arbor awaiting the new canning season. For some reason, some of us started throwing rocks at the pile of jars. I don't know how many jars we broke, but when Mom found out about it, she told each of us to go and get a switch. Of course we brought back tiny branches. She promptly sent us back for bigger ones. She lined us up and switched us on the legs. Needless to say we never did anything of that nature again!

Today, March 23, 1995, while writing this, I heard news on television that a teenage son had skipped school. When the mother was informed, she switched him on the legs and arms. He promptly called 911. Policemen arrived on the scene and she was handcuffed and taken to jail and held without bond. A different time.

Beulah was born while we lived at Spanishburg. She was born in the Princeton hospital. She was the smallest, weighing in at about four pounds. When she was put on the bed, she was placed on the pillow and covered with the big blanket. This was a blanket about the size used now for a crib. I remember hiding under the blanket one evening so that I would not have to go out in the cold, damp evening across the creek to bring the cows home. I don't know how many years we lived at Spanishburg. Our next move was to Morgans Ridge. Morgans Ridge was just what it sounds like. A bare, windswept ridge that I believe was cold even in the summers. We had the nicest house that we ever lived in. Was one of the old colonial type with a covered porch all across the front. When the sun was out, we children would sit or play on the porch because for a short time, it would be warm. I remember sitting on the porch with my thread and needle, trying to sew, but my thread would always pull out of the needle. I had seen women thread the needle and tie a knot in the end and their thread never came out of the needle, so I tried that, tying a knot in each end of the thread. Of course, I could not sew that way. I did not understand that they had doubled their thread and made one knot. It was many years before I understood that.

Daddy worked in the nearby mines, farmed and raised and traded horses. He was in good health then and I believe that era was our most comfortable.

It was winter when they took Lorena and I to Princeton to the hospital to have our adenoids and tonsils removed and it was a horrible cold time. We had to have a dose of castor oil and turpentine the night before. Lorena took hers without protest. Even though Aunt Mae McComas gave me a nickel to take mine, I still put up a fight. They put the turpentine on a spoonful of sugar. To this day, I cannot stand the smell. We were given ether and I thought that I was smothering when I was getting awake and it took Mom and a nurse most of the night to hold me in bed. On the trip home, the car could not make it beyond the main road since we had a heavy snowfall. They had to wrap us up and take us across that bare ridge on horseback. I cannot remember ever being so miserable, unless it was the time we walked across that narrow ridge, returning from the school

Christmas party, carrying our little baskets of candy and froze our fingers.

I remember the pie bake sale, or box supper held at the school. Each girl prepared a decorated box with pie, cake, sandwiches and other goodies to be auctioned off. No names were put on the boxes so the boy friends had to bribe sisters to tell or take their chance on getting the one they wanted. The young man buying the box got the honor of eating with the girl and sometimes got to "walk" her home. I was too young for this sort of thing but to console me, Mom bought enough bananas and one of each thing that she put in Lorena's box for me. I put it up on the shelf in our bedroom and made periodic trips to my hidden treasure.

The Christmas play at the school was wonderful. All children, regardless of age got a part. We practiced weeks before Christmas. Mothers brought white sheets to hang on a wire across the front of the room to serve as the curtain for the play. The teacher made the little paper baskets which she filled with candy for each of us. Mine had a couple of coconut Bon bon's on the top and I guess that was why I protected the basket and carried it in my hand until one hand got too cold, then transferred it to the other hand, while putting that hand into my pocket to warm it up. I still got all my fingers frostbitten. We were walking with a friend who lived on the main road and we stopped at her house. Her two older sisters, who had long been out of school took the baskets out of our frozen fingers, rubbed them and put cold water on them so that they would not warm up too fast. They had a big fire going in the fireplace, so we finally got warm but our fingers were very painful. I cannot remember a mother being there. I think that the little girl had been a "late" child and her mother had died. The two sisters took good care of her and seemed to act as her mother. I do remember having a playhouse in a little building near her home. She had dolls, tea sets and lots of nice things to play with.

Many years later at Egeria, I helped teacher Corda Walker fill the same type of baskets with candy she had ordered in bulk. She had ordered the baskets already made. I also remember Bonnie Harvey bringing her own decorations for the school Christmas tree. She had red and green roping and lots of silver and glitter. We no longer made the colored construction paper chains and strung popcorn.

Christmas at Morgans Ridge was big red apples, packed in individual pressed paper cartons and each wrapped in purple tissue paper, oranges and big sticks of peppermint candy. Daddy bought groceries at the general store on the ridge which he passed on his way from work. The apples and oranges were ordered special for Christmas. We did not have turkey. We had roast chicken, or chicken and dumplings and ham, (usually our own cured). I don't remember us ever having a Christmas tree so we really appreciated the big tree at school each Christmas.

I remember going with Mom to the coal camp. We would pack the horse with eggs, milk and vegetables and walk beside it over the hill to the coal camp. We went through the woods on a path. When we arrived at the bottom, we crossed a slate dump that was burning in some areas. The slate had been separated from the coal and compacted to fill in low lands. The pressure would start fires and a smoky mist was constantly rising from crevices like a volcano. Rotten eggs! This fire later got out of control and they had to move several houses.

We would go from house to house selling our produce, especially visiting the lady who ran the boardinghouse. We would then take our "script" and visit the company store to purchase the staples we needed. There were big doughnuts and other bakery goods under a glass counter. Mom always got some for us to eat then and take back to the others. Going back, we had to go up the hill. When we got home and unloaded the tired horse and turned him out to pasture, I am sure he was a happy horse. Mom would be tired, but she would unpack, put things away and start the evening meal to have it ready when Daddy got in from work.

From Morgans Ridge, we moved back in the Egeria area. The house was beside the road on what was called "the flat rock". There was nothing flat about it. A hill of solid rock and at the top where the house was, there was some level land. Although the road to Egeria has still not been paved all the way, they did black top that rock to make it smooth. We had about thirty acres and leased other land from the coal company. We did a lot of land clearing there. There was a sawmill located by the creek over a hill in the back and Daddy bought a "house plan". This was enough lumber, cut into the right lengths to build a four-room house with a loft. That lumber stayed stacked in the front yard until we moved to the last place which was on Sand Branch. It stayed stacked there until after Daddy's death when Mom had Grandpa McComas and a Mr. Thompson come over from Pinoak and build us a new house. The neighbors came in and in one day tore the old house down. We had tables under the trees and cooked a big meal for the workers. We lived in a building about the size of a two-car garage. It was a "granary" with a loft. We put a bed up for Grandpa and Mr. Thompson and all the rest of us put our mattresses on hay in the loft. We had the cookstove, table, cabinets etc. in one corner. It wasn't bad. The house was built of cinderblock which Mom's brother, Uncle Tressie McComas made; four big rooms with bedrooms upstairs. We grew up there. We could go through the field and get to the Egeria school in a few minutes. At the other house, we had to walk the proverbial five miles to the Barn school and the first year at Sand Branch, we still had to attend the Barn school because we lived in Mercer County and the Egeria school was in Raleigh. Finally, the counties made an agreement so that we could attend the Egeria school.

    I don't know how Beulah's little legs held up all those years. Mom always told us not to run off and leave her, but of course we did. (For anyone reading this book who does not know-- Beulah is under 5 feet tall and wears a 4-B shoe). I have always called her my little sister because she is little. Tough though - she made it!

    After we moved to Beckley, sister Lorena and family lived there until she became ill with lung cancer. They sold and moved near Beckley to be near doctors and hospitals.

    Both Lorena and I graduated from Egeria High School. Allene and Beulah graduated from Woodrow Wilson in Beckley. Corbit went into the army before graduating. When he returned from the army, he worked for years in a local gasoline station. Filling stations then were "full service" places and he won several awards from the Esso Company for doing a good job. Can you remember when you pulled into a station having your windshield washed, oil checked, tank filled etc. and get a smiling face to boot?

    When the economy went bad and people were being cut off by the hundreds, he and some cousins headed for Chicago. He worked for Republic Steel for years.

    From Glennis Walker's Book:

"Corbit Keaton Camden Mills - born Nov. 1, 1924 at Besoco, West Virginia and died June 24, 1949. Corbit was a veteran of World War II, serving in the field artillery of the 3rd, US Army under Lt. General George S. Patton in France and Germany. Following the end of the war Corbit was employed for fifteen years with the Republic Steel Company of Chicago, Illinois. He is buried in the Keaton Mills cemetery at Egeria".

Mr. Hornbeck, our school principal said that Corbit could go down to the corner and come back and tell you a story of all the things he saw and everything that happened. Unfortunately, he is not around for me to record his "tales".

While fighting in World War II, he captured four prisoners in the woods. He took them and marched them back to headquarters. Those soldiers did not have a chance against a West Virginia boy who had lived in the woods and gotten his first "sweet sixteen" rifle at the age of ten or so. His captain wanted to take the German Lugar that he had taken from one of the prisoners, but he refused to give it up and got away with it. When he came home from the war, he brought it with him.

Lorena married Kerby Laymon Walker at the age of sixteen. Kerby was a farmer and coal miner. They were the parents of three boys and one girl. Arthur Kirk, the oldest, lives at Elkview, West Virginia. He served in the air force. He was stationed in Canada for a time and their firstborn girl, Denise, was born there which Betty said caused some inconvenience when she first enrolled her in school. Arthur has worked for many years for the Appalachian Power Company and I think is about ready to retire. His wife, Betty works for a group of doctors. They have a son and two daughters, all redheads.

Lorena and Kerby lived at Egeria until in the fifties when she became ill with lung cancer. They moved to the Beckley area. Both are buried in the Keaton Mills cemetery.

Their second son, Wathor Jeffrey served in the navy during the Korean War. He went to Tucson, Arizona, and was a policeman for a few years, then started his own car parts shop. He now has grandchildren around to entertain him. He likes to go into Mexico, where he has a cabin to fish.

Their third child, Linda Carol, married Richard Jarrett and while he was in the air force lived in various states. They lived in the D.C. area for many years and now live in Georgia. He works for AT&T and she works her crafts. She spins, weaves, dyes, does caning and basketry. She used to keep exotic rabbits and make thread from the hair. She has a big loom and weaves yards and yards of material. She sent me a "rainbow" blanket of wool and silk for my birthday (July 7, 1995). I admire people with such talent because I could never even learn to crochet.

Their fourth child, Kerby Randal, known to us as Randy served in the navy and was at sea when Lorena died. When she found that she had lung cancer, her hope was to live to see Linda Carol married and Randy grown. She got her wish.

Allene worked in the Beckley C&P telephone office as a personnel representative. She married Richard Cummings, an officer at the local recruiting station. They later moved to New York, where she worked for the C&P telephone company. When her husband was called back from the reserves, they decided to make a career in the air force. After ten years of marriage, they became the parents of twins, a boy and a girl. They had to make the trip to England on a ship when the babies were just a few months old. Allene says this was one of the worst experiences of her life. One had to stay with the children while the other went to eat and they were all sick. They lived in California when the twins were born. They returned to California, then transferred to Illinois. They later retired to Winter Park, Florida.

Richard served with the US 14th Air Force in China with the Flying Tigers in World War II, and was commissioned lieutenant in 1943. Allene worked and taught ceramics on the naval base in Orlando. She made many beautiful figurines, plates, bowls, vases, etc., which are scattered all over the world. I would only have to describe my color scheme and she would make me something to go with my house. She became a qualifed judge and now judges shows. She used her own kiln after her retirement. Unfortunately, she has had to curtail her activities since she suffered a stroke and lost partial use of her right arm and hand.

Beulah married Samuel Snuffer and they are the parents of one son. She worked for C&P Telephone Company in Beckley until he was transferred to Rainelle by his company. They later returned to Beckley. They were divorced and she later married Howard Austin. They were divorced and her last marriage was to Ernest Shuemake, now divorced.

Beulah retired from the Beckley Veterans Hospital, where she was a supervisory telephone operator and now lives in the family home in Beckley. She keeps busy with her grandchildren and four great-grandchildren and her church work.

I attended Beckley College one year, then I worked at the local Western Union office as a teleprinter operator for thirty years. I retired early as they closed all the local offices over the country. After retiring, I worked with my husband in the construction business and spent some time in Greensburg, Pennsylvania and later in Virginia, where we strip mined coal, but never really moved from the house we built in 1949 in Beckley. I now live in Florida in the winter and in Beckley in the summer.

I do some writing, collect old books, new books, cookbooks, dolls, ceramic elves, and just any old thing. I spend a lot of time on genealogy research and find that the more I search the more I need to. This could be never ending, so I decided this year to bring to a close and publish the book with what I have.

I married James Vincent Mallamas, Jr. He served in the marine corps in the First Marine Raider Battalion, Company B. He was with Edson's Raiders in World II in the South Pacific Arena. His service number was 304743. There were not many marines in the early forties. At the time of this writing we still attended Edson's Raider reunions held every February in Quantico, Virginia. Nineteen hundred and ninety-seven was the fiftieth reunion and there are still several old Raiders around. They are a family. A book on Edson's Raiders was published in 1995.

Jimmie designed and built several homes in Beckley and Flat Top Lake. Later, he started into heavy construction– roads, dams and storage warehouses. He bought a plane and while working for an engineering company in Richmond and for ourselves, we were fortunate in being able to fly all over the country. At the age of forty-seven, he suffered a massive heart attack. He was told by his doctors that he would never work again, not even drive a car. He did a tremendous amount of work after recuperating. He developed lands and strip mined coal between heart surgeries. Presently, at the age of seventy-one he is "retired" and just does the repairs around the house and has a one man plane almost completed. (From Glennis Walker's book.)

"John Corbit Keaton Mills - born March 17, 1898, and died November 6, 1937, of an alleged self-inflicted gunshot wound at his Egeria home. It appears according to records at

Raleigh County Courthouse he was first named Leslie Sullivan Mills, evidently the name was never changed on the records. Known as Johnny, he married Thelma Eulalia McComas, April 12, 1918. She was born April 25, 1903, and died July 12, 1970. Johnny was a farmer and coal miner. He and Thelma are buried in the Keaton Mills Cemetery."

    It was not "alleged". We were there. We saw it. Daddy had been unable to work for some time and was very depressed at not being able to support the family. He had been too ill to be up and about and been confined to bed about two weeks. He hemorrhaged at night and his pillowcase would be soaked with blood. He took most of his meals in bed, but that night when supper was ready, Mom went in and asked him if he wanted to get up and eat with us. He said that he thought that he could and came into the kitchen and sat at the table. We had all been served and had taken a few bites when he got up from the table and stepped a few steps into the room adjoining the kitchen and picked up his gun (rifle or shotgun-I do not know which) that was leaning against the wall where he always kept it. He placed it to his forehead and pulled the trigger. This knocked him straight back with his head near the kitchen door. Blood was spurting from the hole in the middle of his forehead and I remember trying to get Allene and Beulah out, telling them not to look as I thought the image would remain with them. Mom was screaming and running to yell for the neighbors, but there was nothing to be done. I think that he was dead right after hitting the floor.

    I remember lots of relatives and friends and sitting with cousin Vertie Ann Allen on some boards in an unfinished building where beams of sunlight came through the cracks and warmed us.

    I do not remember much about the funeral or burial. I do know that the Elders came to the house and the services were held there.

    At that time we did not need people telling us that those who took their own life had no place in heaven. I believe that God has a special place of peace in heaven for these troubled souls.

    I buried this entire horrible memory way back in the back of my mind, as I am sure all the others did. Over the years, sometimes it would emerge. Now, the edge has worn off and I can remember so clearly and am able to write about it.

Weeks preceding Daddy's death, Mr. Butler, a well-known Bible scholar throughout the community spent days with him reading and discussing the Bible. In fact, Mr. Butler sometimes spent the night since he was elderly and a little "wobbly" on his legs and it was hard for him to walk the short distance to his house. I remember getting a bowl of cold water for him every morning. He told us if we always washed our eyes out with cold water in the morning that we would always have good eyesight. Must have worked for him. He was up in years and still could read the Bible and he never wore glasses.

The evening of Daddy's death, Tildon Walker, also a Bible scholar was on his way to spend the evening and "talk the Bible". Daddy had sent word for Tildon to come over.

Mr. Butler (I never knew his first name--he was a man you called "Mr.") was the Egeria postmaster for many years. One room of the house was used for the post office. Later, his daughter, Anna Belle took over. Anna Belle was a school teacher for a short time, until she had to enter Pinecrest Tuberculosis Sanitarium. After the disease was arrested, she stayed home and took care of the post office and her parents. Her sister, Ada, taught at the Egeria school and other schools in the county for many years.

Anna Belle used to give us a prize for memorizing Bible verses. I always started with "Jesus wept". She sold candy, aspirin and other small things in the store she ran in conjunction with the post office, so she usually gave us a candy bar.

The Butlers were our closest neighbors. Mrs. Butler was of the Dunkard faith. There were no others in the neighborhood. Once a year, a few came from other places and they held services. All religious meetings were held in the school gymnasium. It was the same size as the four-room school building. It had fold-down wooden slat chairs. Mrs. Butler wore a black bonnett and had a special one for church, also a small white, stiffly-starched bonnet and I think that the women took the big black bonnets off, uncovering the small white one when in church. They wore long black gathered skirt dresses with long sleeves. We thought that they were strange since we did not know anything about their beliefs. I think Mr. Butler was a Baptist, but he may have been a Dunkard also.

After the funeral and burial was over and all the relatives had departed for their homes, we were a lonely and sad family. The next day Mrs. Crouse came over and helped Mom do the washing. They filled big tubs with water from the well which was on the little porch and very handy and placed on the outside fire to heat. Three stacks of flat rocks had been placed so they would not fall over and also be level. It was easy to place the tub on top, fill it with water and leave the room to build the fire underneath. They scrubbed on the washboard, rinsed and wrung out by hand.

We were lucky in having the well right at the door and the water was pure mountain water. Cousin Bobby Allen said that he used to look forward to their visits just to get to drink the good water, but I think they enjoyed being with us also because Uncle Archie filled the car with all the family and spent many weekends with us. During squirrel hunting season, we could always expect our hunting relatives and friends and looked forward to it.

I am sure Mrs. Crouse went home with blisters on her hands from all the scrubbing, wringing, and twisting, but that was the way it was then. When a disaster struck and a neighbor needed physical and moral support, they got it.

I remember making "cocoa" that evening, using an old blue and white enamel coffee pot. I just mixed the milk, sugar, and cocoa and put the pot on the hot coals where they had heated the wash water. We did not call it "hot chocolate" just plain cocoa.

Today, I attended the Foley reunion at Camp Creek State Park and I learned Mr. Butler's name. It seems the generation after me called him Jim Butler, putting both names together as one.

Jack Foley told me of an incident involving my brother, Corbit and himself. They would cross over the corner of Mr. Butler's property to take a "near-cut". He warned them not to do this. They ignored him until one day, they heard a bullet whiz by. They stayed off his property after that.

One day they were hiding in the woods watching Mr. and Mrs. Butler rob the beehive. Mr. Butler had a face mask and hood pulled over his head and Mrs. Butler was standing on a wooden crate, puffing the smoke maker. Suddenly she was stung by a bee and one of the slats in the crate gave way at the same time, causing her to fall backward. Mr. Butler noticed the absence of smoke which he needed because the bees were all around him, looked back and asked, "Rowena, where are you?" The boys were afraid to go on his property to help so they ran to get Mom and Daddy, who later took Mrs. Butler to have her broken leg set.

Someone showed me a group picture and asked me if I knew the man standing to the left. I sure did. It was Mr. Butler. He looked like a prophet with his long white beard.

After reading Rachel's account of Mr. Butler shooting and killing their best horse because he got out and strayed on his property, I am sure glad those boys decided to avoid his property. James Butler, (b) 1867, (d) 1947. Rowena Butler, (b) 1869, (d) 1957. Both are buried in the Agee Cemetery at Egeria.

10. Descendants of Autie Ester Anthrim Mills
21 Aug 1996

Autie Ester Anthrim Mills (1900-1921)
sp: Dolphus Cole (-)
├─── Trama (Twin) Cole (1920-)
│   sp: Edna Mae Harold (-)
│   ├──── Connie Lynn Cole (1946-)
│   │   sp: Robert Stephen Hager (-)
│   │   └──── Robert Stephen, Jr. Hager (1966-)
│   │   Stephen Cole (1950-)
│   └──── sp: Amerio Bennett (-)
├─── Trema (twin) Cole (1920-)
└─── Bernadine Cole (1921-)
     sp: Elmo Dillon (1917-)
     ├──── Autie Elane Dillon (1941-)
     │   sp: Ben Farley (-)
     │   └──── Galen Matthew Farley (1973-)
     ├──── Lemuel Rhea Dillon (1944-)
     │   sp: Judy Carol Hylton (-)
     │   ├──── Michelle Lynn Dillon (1968-)
     │   └──── Curtis Rhea Dillon (1970-)
     └──── Delmer Clifton Dillon (1951-)

Autie Easter Anthrim Mills Cole, April 25, 1900 - December 23, 1921, Dolphus Cole.

Autie Easter Anthrim Mills, (b) April 25,1900, (d) December 23, 1921; Dolphus Cole (b) (-) (d) (-) married July 2, 1919; 1. Trema Cole, (b) June 10, 1920, (died as a small child); 2. Trama Cole, (b) June 10, 1920, (d) January 1964; 3. Bernadine Cole, (b) October 6, 1921 (d)(-).

Autie was the tenth child of Johnson Keaton and Martha Ann Charity Walker Mills. She is buried in the Keaton Mills Cemetery, Egeria, West Virginia. Trema and Trama, twins were born at Pinoak, West Virginia. Trema died as a small child and Trama was killed in an accident at Winona Coal Mine in Mercer County, West Virginia. Trama married Edna Harold. They lived at Rich Creek, West Virginia. He is buried in the Bowling Cemetery at Spanishburg, West Virginia. Bernadine was just two and a half months old at her mother's death. She was raised by Aunt Lydia Mills Rose. Bernadine married Elmo Dillon in 1940. They lived at Lashmeet until his death and she still lives there. They were the parents of three children: 1. Autie Elaine Dillon, born in 1941. She married Ben Farley; 2. Lemuel Rhea Dillon, born in 1944. He married Judy Carol Hylton. They live at Rock, West Virginia. Children are Michele, born 1968 and Curtis Ray, born 1970; 3. Delmer Clifton Dillon, born 1951. He lives at Lashmeet, West Virginia.

Since Aunt Autie died before I was born, I know nothing about her and have been unable to even get the dates of Uncle Dolphus' birth or death. I think that he was killed in an automobile accident. I do not know where he was buried.

11. Descendants of Nathan Crandall Mills
9 Jul 1997

Nathan Crandall Mills (1902-1967)
sp: Versie Lusk (1907-)
┣━━ Oma Wanda Mills (1926-)
┃   sp: Charles Clinton Akers (1924-)
┃   ┣━━ Wanda Mae Akers (1946-)
┃   ┃   sp: Tola Houston Walker (1950-)
┃   ┃   ┣━━ Denise Lynn Walker (1971-)
┃   ┃   ┣━━ Kevin Garfield Walker (1973-)
┃   ┃   ┗━━ Rebecca Ann Walker (1977-)
┃   ┣━━ Brenda Lee Akers (1948-)
┃   ┃   sp: Clifford Edward Hall (1946-)
┃   ┃   ┗━━ Clinton Ray Hall (1970-)
┃   ┣━━ Connie Gail Akers (1950-)
┃   ┃   sp: Randall P. Cook (1940-)
┃   ┃   ┣━━ Randall P., Jr. Cook (1972-)
┃   ┃   ┣━━ Angela Renee Cook (1974-)
┃   ┃   ┗━━ Crystal Gail Cook (1978-)
┃   ┣━━ Clinton Crandall Akers (1952-)
┃   ┃   sp: Vicky Darlene Joy (1955-)
┃   ┃   ┗━━ Clinton C. II Akers (1975-)
┃   ┣━━ Debra Kay Akers (1954-)
┃   ┃   sp: John Wayne Barbour (1949-)
┃   ┃   ┣━━ Bobby Wayne Barbour (1975-)
┃   ┃   ┗━━ Rachel Ann Barbour (1979-)
┃   ┗━━ Harold Wayne Akers (1958-)
┣━━ Basil William (twin) Mills (1928-1995)
┃   sp: Betty Sue Akers (1929-)
┃   ┣━━ Robert Basil Mills (1949-1949)
┃   ┣━━ Sandra Dian Mills (1950-)
┃   ┃   sp: Jerry P. Burkett (1949-)
┃   ┃   ┗━━ Curtis William Burkett (1978-)
┃   ┣━━ Donna Mae Mills (1952-)
┃   ┃   sp: Laurel A. Farmer (1950-)
┃   ┃   ┣━━ Donna Jean Farmer (1971-)
┃   ┃   ┣━━ Laura Anita Farmer (1972-)
┃   ┃   ┗━━ Jason William Farmer (1978-)
┃   ┣━━ Gary Nathaniel Mills (1953-)
┃   ┃   sp: Bonnie Good (-)

```
                    ┌──── Vickie Lynn Mills (1973-)
                    ├──── Drema Kay Mills (1974-)
                    └──── Gary Wayne Mills (1975-)
            sp: Brenda Gail Grimett (1950-)
     ┌──── Elisa Ann Mills (1954-)
            sp: Steve Seabastean (-)
                    ┌──── Petreca Marie Seabastean (1974-)
                    └──── Medhell Lee Seabastean (1977-)
     ├──── Larry Ray Mills (1956-)
     └──── Darlene Sue Mills (1957-)
            sp: Claude N.B. Farmer (1957-)
                    └──── Anthony Nathaniel Farmer (1978-)
──── Dasil Keaton (twin) Mills (1928-)
     sp: Myrtle Marie Hatcher (1935-)
            ┌──── Carolyn Elaine Mills (1952-)
            ├──── Keaton Dasil Mills (1954-)
            ├──── Arlene Elizabeth Mills (1958-)
            └──── Nathan Mills (-)
──── Loma Marie Mills (1929-)
     sp: Francis Xavier Combs (1926-)
            ┌──── Delila Marie Combs (1946-)
                   sp: Joey Zebroskey, Jr. (1947-)
                          ┌──── Deidra Sherie Zebroskey (1966-)
                                 sp: Carl Pennington (1966-)
                                        └──── Joseph Pennington (1993-)
                          └──── Regina Joe Zebroskey (1971-)
                                 sp: Eric Thomas (1972-)
                   sp: Richard Troy Davidson (1942-)
                          └──── Felecia Ann Davidson (1963-1997)
                                 sp: Roger Dale Marcum (1962-)
                                        └──── Roger Dale Marcum, Jr. (1983-)
            ├──── Patricia Ann Combs (1948-)
                   sp: Kenneth Bruce McGlothlin (1948-1979)
                          ┌──── Prema Ann McGlothlin (1975-)
                                 sp: Brandon Rich (1973-)
                                        └──── Kennith Brennen Rich (1973-)
                          └──── Direet Carmey Shrewsbury (1984-)
                   sp: Ernest Shrewsbury (1950-)
                          └──── Dereck Carmie Shrewsbury (1984-)
            ├──── Frankie Dale Combs (1951-1998)
```

```
           sp: Linda Louise Corey (1949-)
           ├── Stephanie Lynn Combs (1968-)
           │   sp: Delmer Doss (1963-)
           │   ├── Jeffrey Doss (1988-)
           │   └── Tiffany Doss (1991-)
           ├── Frankie Dale, Jr. Combs (1971-1996)
           └── April Snow Combs (1978-)
               └── Brooke Combs (1996-)
         ├── Evelyn Louise Combs (1953-)
         │   sp: Everett Silas Phillips (1950-)
         │   ├── Heather Lavonda Phillips (1972-)
         │   │   sp: Mike Newhouse (-)
         │   ├── Zachary Phillips (1977-)
         │   └── Brandon Kenneth Phillips (1979-)
         └── Francis Shawn Combs (1969-)
└── Elouise Lana Ann Mills (1932-)
    sp: Willie Blackburn, Jr. Reed (1923-)
    ├── Carol Jean Reed (1948-)
    │   sp: Gary Elden Dixon (1944-)
    │   ├── Monica Jean Dixon (1971-)
    │   │   sp: Darrell Wayne Wells (1963-)
    │   │   └── Chandler Elizabeth Pauline
    │   │               Wells (1996-)
    │   ├── Deonna Terese Dixon (1973-)
    │   │   sp: Jeffrey Earl Cook (1966-)
    │   │   ├── Taylor Garrett Cook (1944-)
    │   │   └── Jeffrey Tanner Cook (1997-)
    │   └── Amanda LeAnn Dixon (1980-)
    ├── Charles William Reed (1951-)
    │   sp: Barbara Joyce Shannon (1954-)
    │   ├── Charles William Reed, Jr. (1972-)
    │   │   sp: Nelda Ann Scroggs (1972-)
    │   │   ├── Jonathan David Reed (1991-)
    │   │   ├── Jacob Lee Reed (1991-)
    │   │   ├── Jessica Nicole Reed (1944-)
    │   │   └── Joshua William Reed (1995-)
    │   ├── Michael David Reed (1973-)
    │   └── Brian Lynn Reed (1974-1974)
    └── Archie Lynn Reed (1952-)
        sp: June Kay Smizer (1953-)
```

```
            ├───── Justin Lamar Reed (1978-)
        ├───── Jeremy Lynn Reed (1980-)
        └───── Travis Lee Reed (1982-)
    ├───── Charolette Yvonne Reed (1954-)
    │   sp: Lonnie Edwards Mullins (1950-)
    │       ├───── Autumn Michelle Mullins (1976-)
    │       │   sp: Anthony Edwin Todd (1970-)
    │       │       └───── Taylor Danyelle Todd (1997-)
    │       └───── Phillip Blackburn Mullins (1979-)
    ├───── Marsha Elaine Reed (1965-)
    └───── Janneta Angeline Reed (1971-)
        sp: Richard Eugene Massie (1969-)
            ├───── Alexandria Lee Ann Massie (1944-)
            └───── Dylan Chase Massie (1998-)
```

Versie Lusk Mills, April 19, 1907, and Nathan Crandall Mills, June 25, 1902 - July 5, 1967.

Francis (Penny) Combs and Loma Mills Combs.

Basil Mills (1928-1995) (twin) and Betty Mills.

Dasil Mills (twin) and Myrtle Mills.

Nathan Crandall Mills, (b) 06-25-1902, (d) 07-05-1967; Versie Lusk Mills, (b) 04-19-1907, (d) (-) ; 1. Oma Wanda Mills, (b) 11-18-1926, (d) (-) ; 2. Basil William Mills, (b) 1-25-1928, (d) 6-5-1995; 3. Dasil Keaton Mills, (b) 1-25-1928, (d) (-) ; 4. Loma Marie Mills, (b) 5-11-1929, (d) (-) ; 5. Elouise Lana Ann, (b) 2-28-1932, (d)(-).

Uncle Nathan was a coal miner and a farmer and lived on the last "homeplace" of Grandma Mills at Beeson at the time of his death of a stroke. He was sitting at the table and slumped over. He died in the Princeton hospital about a week later, almost like Uncle Georgia.

He was a strong, big man and he and Aunt Versie did their share of cutting trees, grabbing stumps and clearing new ground. I used to wonder why they did so much hard work building a cabin, clearing new ground and just when they got it into shape, they would move on and start the whole process over. They owned several different farms during their married life.

Their marriage is a very interesting story. Aunt Versie's father did not look with favor on any suitors for her. Their courtship consisted of two personal meetings and exchanging letters, which were usually "slipped" to her by friends.

On the morning they planned to elope, she prepared the morning breakfast and got the men off to the fields. She was dressed as usual with her apron on. One of her brothers became suspicious and came back to the house just after she had left and was hurrying up a path to the top of a hill, were Mom and Daddy were waiting on the road in their open top "tin lizzie" to take them to the justice, he got off a shot and some bullets went through the car. They made their getaway without injury and were married that evening.

The legal age for a marriage license without parental consent was twenty-one. Uncle Nathan had Aunt Versie to write twenty-one on a piece of paper and put it in her shoe so that when she was asked her age, she could truthfully answer that she was "over" twenty-one.

Uncle Nathan seemed to remember that his bride was hard to come by and treasured her over many years. They worked side by side, clearing new ground, building houses and growing vegetables to can, corn to be ground for the winter cornmeal and also to feed the animals and he was the only one that I knew who grew tobacco. He would dry the leaves, then dampen and roll them into cigars. He also made twists to be used for chewing.

They lived at Lester, Pickshin, Odd, Egeria, Spanishburg and Beeson. I remember getting to spend some time during summer school vacation when they lived at Pickshin. The company houses there were all on the hillsides, propped up on stilts against the back of the hill. This made a very high "basement" area where we kids could play. With all the open space under the wood floors, I don't know how they kept warm in the winter. The kitchen coal burning cook stove always had a fire going and had either fireplaces or a burnside stove in the other room.

In the summer the ice man would come by with big blocks of ice. The colored woman next door would get a block and wrap it in white cotton cloths and then paper to help keep it for a while. She did not have one of the oak ice chests which people look for now as antiques. She would chip off pieces of ice and give to us kids.

When the blackberries were ripe on the other side of the hill, we had to get out early in the morning before other people got all of them. By the next morning, more would be ripe. Aunt Versie canned them for winter use.

Blackberry Time

Pa took vacation from his job at the mill
    to go blackberry pickin' up on the hill,
on the hill where berries hung rip on the cane,
    sweetened by sun and soft summer rain.
With his shirt buttoned tight at collar and wrist,
    A homemade bucket gripped in each first.
pants tucked in boots gainst chigger and snake,
    Pa'd be pickin' fore I was awake.

Long about noon, he'd come down the hill
    and I'd trot beside him, eating my fill
of berries still warm with the heat of July,
    and plenty left over for jelly and pie.

Then, trailed by a hound and purple-mouthed me,
    He'd head for the house and a glass of iced tea.
He'd swat Ma's behind, and she'd give him a shove.
    I don't recall Pa ever talking 'bout love,
but he took vacation down at the mill
    to bring us berries from up on the hill.

P.J. Evans, Vienna, West Virginia

    Oma was born at Pickshin, Raleigh County, West Virginia. Basil and Dasil (twins) were born at Pickshin, Raleigh County, West Virginia. Loma was born at Beeson, Mercer County, West Virginia. Lana was born at Odd, Raleigh County, West Virginia.
    Oma married Charles Clinton Akers, October 2, 1945. He was born August 30, 1924. She was born November 21, 1940. Basil married Betty Sue Akers, February 27, 1948. She was born November 21, 1930. Dasil married Myrtle Marie Hatcher, May 5, 1951. She was born March 8, 1935. Loma married Francis Combs, May 29, 1945. He was born February 15, 1926. Lana married Willie Blackburn Reed (Junior). He was born September 6, 1923.
    Most all had large families so there are many grandchildren around. In 1995, Aunt Versie was the only living aunt

that I had on the Mills side and I have two on the McComas side—Aunt Jewell, widow of Mom's youngest brother, Glacie, and Aunt Mae, widow of Uncle Reathie. She is about ninety-five and still "spry" as they say. Jimmie and I get to stop by in Virginia to visit her sometimes when we attend the Edson Raider reunion at Quantico, Virginia. She lives along nearby. Some of her children are in the area. Uncle Nathan is buried in the family cemetery at Egeria, West Virginia.

12. Descendants of Kelly Alderman Mills
9 Jul 1997

Kelly Alderman Mills, (1904-1931)
(b) February 16, 1904, (d) November 26, 1931.

Kelly Alderman Mills was killed by a gunshot wound to the temple by a .38 Caliber pistol in the hands of Leslie Meadows. Glennis Walker wrote about this in his book. He said "allegedly" Leslie Meadows shot Uncle Kelly. I think there is enough documentation to substantiate that this really happened. Leslie was never indicted or had to serve any time for this murder, however there are records in the Mercer County Courthouse at Princeton, West Virginia, regarding the sheriff's investigation etc.

It was a Sunday. Cousin Delmer Mills (Oley Mills' son) and Uncle Kelly were returning from Beeson, where they had been to spend the weekend with Grandma Mills, when their car broke down. Leslie offered to take them to Odd to get a part for the car. Uncle Nathan was with them. Uncle Nathan lived at Odd, just over from the post office and Wallace General Store, so he got out and went home.

Delmer, Uncle Kelly and Leslie came back to Leslie's house and stopped. Leslie went into the house and got a quart of home brew. He came back and got into the car and gave the home brew to Uncle Kelly. He took the lid off and was talking so Delmer got out of the back seat of car and walked around the curve to his Dad's and went to bed.

They were not mad or quarreling when he left. Someone told Delmer later that he was only gone about five minutes when it happened. Uncle Kelly had the can lid in his hand when he died.

Leslie would not allow anyone to come into the yard. He said he would shoot the head off anyone who tried to come in. Effie Roles, who lived up the road came over and he did relent and allow her to come in. Charlotte, his sister-in-law from across the road was there. She was married to Frank Meadows, who was Leslie's cousin.

I talked with Delmer at his sister Alastia's house in Beaver, September 11, 1983, and made some notes then I recently wrote him and asked some more questions. He cleared up some points.

Uncle Oley lived just around a curve, not a half mile away, but it was some time before someone came to notify them.

I had always thought that it was the next day before they could get the sheriff there and did not move the body until then, however, Delmer says it was that night. Someone probably went to Ghent and called Princeton from there, because there were no telephones in Egeria, or someone may have driven over to Princeton.

It was some time around midnight when Uncle Oley came to our house to tell us. We all got up and built a fire in the fireplaces. Daddy went with Uncle Oley and we were on pins and needles, afraid that they would get shot.

We sat through that long night, waiting for the daylight. Somehow, we thought that everything would be alright once it was daylight. It was erie.

I remember absolutely nothing about Uncle Kelly's funeral. I asked Delmer and he said they took his body to Uncle Oley's where the services were held and burial later in our family cemetery. Cousin Ilene said that she thought that someone made his coffin. I know that Brammer Store stocked padding, lining, and hardware for making coffins. The hardware came in either black or brass.

Ilene also said that after that, Grandma Mills could not stand to come back to their house and never visited them again. She had lost Uncle Laurence, her youngest just two years before in a mining accident. Uncle Kelly was her last son at home, so I guess she had all that she could take.

Delmer said that it was not dark when he got out of the car and started walking to Uncle Oleys. If it was only a few minutes after he left, what could have been said or done to cause this drastic action? Did Leslie have the gun on him, or did he get it from the house when he went for the home brew?

Leslie never denied shooting Uncle Kelly. He claimed self defense. He said that Uncle Kelly was coming at him with an axe. An axe was found beside the body. How did he wield the axe and still have the lid to the jar of home brew in his hand?

Leslie was never indicted or tried for the crime. Two attempts were made. During the second attempt, a key witness, Frank Meadows who suffered from heart trouble died just before the prosecuting attorney and stenographer arrived at his home to take his testimony. It was thought that he would testify that the axe Uncle Kelly was supposed to have attacked Leslie with was taken from his house after the fact and placed at the murder scene. We will never know.

Anyway, Leslie served no time for the murder, however, I feel that he did not get off "scott free". I have heard people talk about him seeing ghosts. Someone said that he once stopped his car in the middle of the road. The person riding with him wanted to know why he had stopped in the middle of the road. He was supposed to have answered, "How can I move? Kelly is standing in the road".

Cousin Ilene Mills told me on October 6, 1994, that she talked with Charlotte Meadows Lewis (Leslie's wife's sister and Frank Meadow's wife at the time of the killing) while attending Charlotte's son Ralph's funeral and that Charlotte said that Uncle Kelly was walking down beside the house when he was shot and that he staggered and grabbed at the side of the house and that the bloody handprint was still on the house. She also said that Leslie was not well at that time and that he had not slept a good nights sleep since the incident.

Aunt Dessie Cole told me on November 18, 1979, that Dr. McComas was brought from Flat Top to examine the body and he said that Uncle Kelly "had been kicked forty some kicks". I wondered why they went for Dr. McComas after Uncle Kelly was dead, but guess he had to sign the death certificate.

From all that I can find out, Uncle Kelly was a mild mannered man and not one to pick a fight.

Leslie Meadows died in 1994, leaving children, grandchildren and great-grandchildren. Uncle Kelly's life was cut short at the age of twenty-seven and left none of these. He is buried in the Keaton Mills Cemetery, Egeria, West Virginia.

13. Descendants of Laurence Evestus Mills
21 Aug 1996

Laurence Evestus Mills (1905-1929)

Laurence Evestus Mills, (b) October 18, 1905, (d) October 25, 1929. Killed in coal mining accident.

Laurence Evestus Mills, (b) October 18, 1905, (d) October 25, 1929.

Uncle Laurence was killed in a mining accident in Springton Coal Mine in Mercer County, West Virginia, at the young age of twenty-four.

He still lived with Grandma Mills and told her when leaving for work that morning that he would be home late as he was going to Matoaka after work to buy a car. He had saved for the car and left home carrying six hundred dollars in cash. (This sounds logical to me, since I have some old car advertisments of that time and the price of the cars was that amount). People did very little credit buying then and of course not for something so foolish as a car.

After the accident, his body was removed from the mines and taken to the undertakers. They said no money was found in his clothing. Uncle Georgie Mills was a deputy sheriff of Mercer County at that time and made a full investigation but was unable to turn up the missing six hundred dollars. Could the accident have been a contrived one?

Of course the missing money does not necessarily mean that this is true. It could be that some greedy person from the many who had access in retrieving his body from the mine and transporting to the undertakers could have taken the money. Also, he may have made his plans known to his co-workers and someone may have "done him in". We will never know.

Uncle Laurence was buried in the Keaton Mills Cemetery. I know that he liked cars because the only memory that I have of him concerns his car.

At the time of the following incident when Uncle Laurence transported me to Granny McComas', I was not old enough for school. I was six years old when he was killed. He was tall, dark, and handsome, as the saying goes and loved to dress well and drive his car. To my memory and pictures he and Uncle Oley shared a strong resemblance. They had oval faces more like Grandpa Mills, while my father, Uncle Nathan and Uncle Georgia had the more square face of Grandma Mills. All were handsome, well-built men. I barely remember Uncle Kelly, but believe he was of a smaller build like Daddy. I have no pictures of him.

Grandma Mills lived in the curve on the main road at

Spanishburg and we lived in the tin roof house across the creek, just beyond the walled-in "sulphur" water springs, where people came from Princeton and all around to fill their jars with the stinky sulphur water that was thought to be healing and healthy.

There was a round, pagoda-like structure made of cement with steps leading down where the spring was enclosed in the center. The top was vented with a pipe rising from the center about five feet tall. It looked like a huge umbrella. Someone had pitched a car tire around the pipe. I have planned to go over there to see if the tire is still there, or if it has deteriorated away.

It was a Sunday. Uncle Laurence was to take me to Pinoak to spend some time with Granny McComas. I think he had a Ford car with no top, or the top was down and it was black. (You know, Henry Ford said, "You can have your Ford in any color you want, as long as it is black"). Black was all that he made. I had been put in the car and was waiting when somehow, someway another car hit us from the rear or side–I don't know. There was no room for passing on this road, the view was good so another car could surely see us. Very few cars were driving the roads then, so thinking back, I am inclined to believe that one of his buddies was playing a trick, bumping to see how much damage could be done. They were always bragging about whose car was the best and toughest built.

I was all shook up and got a few scratches and bruises. After Grandma Mills checked me and found nothing serious, we went on our way to Pinoak. After Uncle Laurence dropped me off at Granny's, we sat on her porch so we could watch him drive down the road. Granny's house was located on a high peak of a hill and one could sit on the porch which ran the entire length of the house and watch traffic wind its way around the curves and down to the bottom where the road was level, then out of sight. There was a hanging swing located at each end of the porch, however they were a little high for a little one, so Granny brought a little chair out for me.

When the car went out of sight, I realized that I was not at home and a sudden wave of homesickness overcame me. I started whimpering and Granny thought that my cuts were hurting, so she went in and got her "good-for-everything" Sayman's salve and rubbed the boo-boo's gently and I was "ok." I had a good visit of a couple of weeks. I got to stay in the "girls" room and have a room all to myself.

When I watched Uncle Laurence's car go out of sight, that could very well have been the last time that I ever saw him.

James Vincent Mallamas, Jr., June 27, 1924-February 13, 1997.

Tribute To My Late Husband
Best Husband Contest

January 23rd, 1989

I believe that my husband, Jimmie is the best husband in Central Florida, the United States of America and the world because:

1. In the almost forty-one years that we have been married, he has never left the toilet seat up.
2. He is very romantic, tender, kind and good and treats me like an adored woman.
3. When he awakens in the morning he says, "Good morning sweetheart." He always tells me that he loves me before going to sleep or leaving for work.
4. He can fix anything, including hurt feelings, plumbing, electrical etc.
5. He has a wonderful sense of humor and makes people feel better by just walking into a room. He can tell tales of his former lives, such as when he fought with Napoleon, etc.
6. He is handsome and at the age of sixty-five, still has mostly black hair. He has a lovely crooked (wolf) grin.
7. He was a marine for seven years and still has the values and stick-to-it-iveness instilled when he was a young man.
8. He has taught me how to show love. I was a quiet shy, old-maid-type when he met me in 1944. He brought me out of it.
9. He accepted my family as his own. He loved my mother and said that we were cheated when she died at the age of sixty-seven. My nieces and nephews are as close to him as his blood relatives. My cousins by the dozens love him.
10. The only four-letter word that he uses in my presence is LOVE. He never uses the dirty bathroom word that seems to be accepted socially now.
11. He is a real man.
12. I can step out of his beat-up (he says "customized") 76 pick-

up truck, dressed in jeans and dirty and he will say, "Hello lovely lady." With age and wrinkles, this is appreciated and keeps romance in our marriage.

13. His indomitable spirit.

He suffered a major heart attack at the age of forty-seven. He turned a power shovel over on himself and was pinned for hours under steel bars in a very small space, consequently one month later, he threw a blood clot from the bruises. I was allowed to see him for five minutes only on the hour and his doctors did not give much hope for his survival.

He survived to work and have open heart surgery two years later. In 1986, he had heart surgery two more times. On May 6, they performed two bypasses and all seemed to be going well, however by ten the next morning, they were rushing him to surgery again as the old twelve-year bypass had collapsed. In the crowded elevator taking him to emergency surgery (ten people and the hospital bed with all the tubes and appliances dangling), I remarked to him that they must think that he had been a general instead of a sergeant since he was getting the V.I.P. treatment. Almost out of it, he said, groggily, "Yes, and I was a damn good one, too." This was his spirit as they wheeled him into the operating room to have his chest sawed open two days in a row. I sensed that his cardiologist had given up, but his surgeon did not and he came through. He had to spend a month in the hospital. His fighting spirit brought him through and he was back working the second week out.

Some of our friends thought that I brought him through. I was there for him, but he did it. He is some kind of a man!

He entered the marine corps before completing high school. After the combat was over, he attended California Junior College and took the test and received his diploma. After getting out, he took the college entrance test and was accepted by West Virginia Tech, a very well rated engineering college.

He is a practicing Architect and a Florida General Contractor. He has built bridges, roads, warehouses, houses, dams, strip mined coal, deep mined coal, lost a finger and part of a thumb in logging, designed and built buildings and thinks that he could help solve the housing for the homeless with his special designed, small, lightweight concrete houses. I do not exaggerate when I say that he can fix anything. Some things he cannot do physically now, however he sure can show someone the proper way to do it. Some men would have given up after the first heart attack and lived as an invalid, but not Jimmie.

He tried to be a pilot in the marines, however his lack of a high school education kept him out of the program. After getting out and starting his own business, he took a few lessons and bought his own plane and flew extensively for eight years. He still has his pilots license but cannot get the medical.
14. Although we were not able to have children, he has helped support and educate nieces and nephews.
15. He makes everything that we do an adventure.
16. He has not gotten tired of me.

This is not a lot of mush. It is all true. I could say more good things about my husband, but this is too long now and you may not read all of it.

If James Vincent Mallamas, Jr. is not chosen as one of the best husbands in the "Oprah Winfrey Best Husband Contest," it is not because he isn't.

Sincerely,
Mrs. James V. Mallamas, Jr.

The foregoing was written for the *Orlando Sentinel* for the contest being run in many newspapers. In made the *Sentinel* but did not get through Oprah's people.

Jimmie died February 13, 1997. April 18, we would have been married forty-nine years. He is now resting beside his father in the family cemetery. Footstones reading:

James V. Mallamas, Sr. (Feb. 14, 1893-July 23, 1970) West Virginia, Sgt. Co. B. 59th Inf. 4th Div. World War I. U.S. Army.

James V. Mallamas, Jr. (June 27, 1924-Feb. 13, 1997) West Virginia, Sgt. Co. B. 1st. Marine Raiders 1st. Marine Div. World War II.

This letter from Barbara Ruble, a daughter of one of our Raiders. The Rubles had a "bunch" of girls and brought them all to the Raider reunion held in Quantico, Virginia, every February. We watched them grow up.

July 18, 1997

Dear Gloria,

I was extremely sorry to hear that Jim passed away.

My mother told me. I will always remember your husband as a devoted, caring and compassionate person. His kind spirit and warm nature must have touched everyone he came into contact with. Out of all my Father's Marine Corps friends, your husband made the biggest impression on me because I could sense that he was in touch with his emotions and feelings, even as a big, tough Marine. I always envied you too, as his wife, thinking how lucky you were to be by his side, sharing life with such a wonderful man. You were always such a lady and it was such a pleasure to talk to you.

I hope that you are doing well and feeling good. Please accept my sincere condolences. Take care of yourself.

Sincerely,
Barbara

While cleaning my desk I found the following in a "cubby hole." Jimmie had lettered it neatly (he never wrote in longhand). He could letter as fast as I can write.

The next war to end all wars should be fought by all Industrialists, Commissars, Capitalists, Union leaders, Government leaders, Judges, Diplomats, Dictators, Presidium members, Congressmen and Senators.

When these idiots have eliminated themselves to the last man, he should be hanged and Soldiers that have seen the hell of war be given the opportunity to create an everlasting peace upon the earth. History has taught us that diplomats create wars and soldiers bring peace. I am surprised that he did not mention BUREAUCRATS. Guess that government leaders takes care of that - *Gloria.*

Sgt. James V. Mallamas, Jr. (1943)

Modern Mountain Man: A Tribute

By Olive Fielding Marrical

Randy Walker

When a researcher for the National Park Service asked Kerby Walker to assist in a cultural study of the majestic New River Gorge in southern West Virginia, the amateur archaeologist reacted with disbelief.

"You mean you're going to pay me?" he asked incredulously. Later he explained, "I couldn't believe someone would pay me to do something I liked so much."

That "something" was an ambitious exploration of the rugged river corridor comprising one of the National Park Service's least known acquisitions. A fifty-mile, spectacularly scenic stretch of this northward-flowing stream, oldest river on the North American continent and one of the oldest in the world, had been designated by Congress in 1978 as the New River Gorge National River.

Federal protection of this unique waterway was long overdue. It rises as a trout stream in the mountains of North Carolina and flows serenely through Virginia, sinking deeper to become a major river for its last ninety miles through West Virginia. Rivaling Egypt's Nile as perhaps the world's most ancient river, the New River reaches its nadir in the park area, entrenched at an awesome depth in this circuitous cleavage of the West Virginia hills. Bare peaks rise above the forested hills, and breathtaking vistas of the cavernous view below vie with more famous American scenic landmarks in beauty and grandeur. The area is the wildest most spectacular spot in West Virginia, and one of the nation's brightest natural jewels.

It is the heart of the Great Southern Appalachian Forest, North America's most biologically diverse forest and a botanist's dream. Its divergence of species is rivaled only by the forests of central China and surpassed only by equatorial rain forests. Among unique qualities are Appalachian Cove forests, found in sheltered valleys and exceptionally rich in plant and animal variety. Wildlife abounds--deer, black bears, wild turkeys, beavers, raccoons, chipmunks, woodchucks, foxes, skunks, a wide variety of birds, among others. North America's oldest fishing hole, the river is renowned for its outstanding smallmouth bass and channel catfish. Understandably, the area was a favorite hunting ground for America's early Indian inhabitants.

The New River in the park area is a powerful, high-volume river. Its rocky bottom, sudden drops and winding bends create rapids with strong currents which have made it popular as a whitewater boating stream. Roaring creeks noisily crashing down over huge boulders to the river's edge add to the scenic splendor, and abandoned mines and ghost towns enhance the air of mystery and intrigue.

The origin of Sandstone Falls, which span the entire width of the river nine miles north of Hinton, is said to date back 330 million years. It achieved distinction is 1884 when a block of sandstone from the area was shipped to Washington, DC, to be placed in the Washington Monument.

In an area along the river with an extensive series of

flat rocks, river action has created fascinating round, natural cisterns, abraded by rocks and debris caught inside during floods, causing them to deepen. Fish trapped inside when flood waters recede, lacking nutrients, are smaller than those moving freely in the river. The pools burst into color in the fall when Utrivularia gibba, a carnivorous plant with yellow blossoms on slender stems, appear.

Among these rocks is a man-made work of art, two exquisite bas reliefs carved by one of a group of Italian stone masons who tented on the rocks while building a stone railroad bridge years ago. His handiwork produced a sailor in a sou'wester holding the wheel of a ship, near his family's heraldic device, its motto carved on a ribbon.

When the New River Gorge was designated as a National River, the Park Service was charged by Congress with "conserving and interpreting outstanding natural, scenic and historic values and objects" in the 62,000-acre, untamed wilderness through Summers, Raleigh and Fayette counties. Its research team was committed to "charting the history of human impact upon this magnificent region," wrote Paul D. Marshall of Charleston, West Virginia, in his preface to the three-volume report of the comprehensive study his firm conducted for the National Park Service.

Assigned to direct the archaeological portion was David N. Fuerst, a Cleveland, Ohio, native who earned his master's degree in anthropology/archaeology at Southern Illinois University. Seeking people knowledgeable about the New River area, Fuerst found that the person most often recommended was Kerby Randall Walker, who lived in a rural area near Beckley, Raleigh County. A modern mountain man, the tall, raw-boned machinist by trade not only loved the out-of-doors, but had become a student of the land. He learned all he could about Indians who had roamed the hills, as well as plant and animal life, rocks and minerals, and history of the area. He joined the survey team timidly, yet eagerly, along with William Stone, whom Fuerst recruited in Lookout, Fayette County.

The choice, according to Fuerst, was ordained. "I believe God has a plan for everybody," he declared. "The three of us working together was like an interchange. My academic background was inspired by their knowledge of the woods. Bill Stone was enthusiastic. Kerby was inspirational.

"Once in awhile during your lifetime," Fuerst continued, "you'll meet someone who's pure---just plain good, and it's going to rub off. That was Kerby. He had a wealth of knowledge, but was a very simple, humble man. And he was able to laugh at himself. He was slow about accepting me, but finally I knew he trusted me when he sat down and gave me some of his moonshine. I knew we had become friends for life."

For four months in the fall and winter of 1980-1981, the three men trudged through the rugged mountains, eight to ten hours a day, six days a week. They traversed some fifty miles on either side of the river, from Fayetteville to Hinton.

A natural corridor linking the Ohio Valley to Piedmont, Virginia, the New River area historically was part of a great system of Indian trails. In the park vicinity, the trails crisscrossed, forming a network of paths, many of which are still visible in the woods as deeply worn tracks.

Fuerst realized that most of the Indian sites already known were in rock shelters. "But at a point in the woods near Fayetteville, where two streams came together near a trail I knew was an Indian path, there was a rise in the center with pine trees growing out. While I wondered about the possibilities, Kerby immediately recognized it as a valid site. Upon searching, we soon found a beautiful point about 4,000 years old."

The incident changed Fuerst's direction. "By the end of the day, I began thinking of going beyond the known spots I had intended to use. Kerby inspired me to find new Indian sites."

During their continuing trek through the densely-wooded, rock-strewn terrain, Kerby and Bill kept reminding Fuerst about snakes. The Timber Rattlesnake and Copperhead are the only poisonous snakes in the Gorge, frequenting wooded hillsides and rock outcroppings. Both reptiles are very well camouflaged. Only one of the many non-poisonous snakes has a reputation for being aggressive, the Northern Water Snake. It can bite repeatedly, injecting saliva containing an anti-coagulent which may cause even a small bite to bleed profusely. "But we didn't see one snake the entire time," said Fuerst. "We did run into three small black bears once."

By the time they completed their exploration, the archaeological trio had charted and compiled inventory data on

248 previously undocumented Indian sites, as well as reaffirming 40 others already recorded. Fuerst credited Kerby with the success of their finds. But Kerby considered this a small number compared with many other areas he had come to know. He had told Marshall and Fuerst earlier that the New River Gorge was "poor country for Indian sites, because they found it difficult for travel." In fact, because of its treacherours rapids, Indians called it the "River of Death" as testament to the wild, untamed nature. The rapid current and need for frequent forage around falls rendered canoe travel impractical and dangerous in the deep, narrow gorge of the river now in the national park. Instead, Kerby pointed out, their trails bypassed New River by following overland routes east and west. "The Indians made the paths; the buffalo followed," he reported. Other parts of the state were much more fertile fields for uncovering signs of Indians, Kerby had found.

At first Marshall and Fuerst were skeptical of Kerby's uncanny sense regarding possible Indian camp location. "I can see the Indian sites in the woods," he told them. Asked how he was able to spot them, he responded simply, "You have to think like an Indian." He went on to explain that a potential site usually is a rock shelter facing south, so it is warm and dry, land that is comparatively level and near water.

Fuerst noted that, "Kerby didn't have a degree after his name but he had more knowledge than many professional archaeologists." His studies and experience notwithstanding, it was a remarkable instinct, a closeness to the land, that led this born woodsman to the sites, Fuerst believed.

While growing up on a small farm several miles from Beckley, one day Kerby found two old Indian arrowheads in the furrows of his father's newly-plowed field. Thereafter, he habitually followed in the wake of the plow, tirelessly searching for the hand chiseled, distinctively-pointed pieces of flint which brought reality to his imagined scenes of Indians cavorting in the field.

As he learned more of their habits, Kerby began to look for old Indian campsites in areas near the farm, and eventually expanded his explorations to other sections of West Virginia and, sometimes, to Virginia, Kentucky and North Carolina. But southern West Virginia became his field of expertise and, in some thirty years of ferreting out relics of the native American's past, he amassed over 1,000 arrowheads and other artifacts. Most of them he filed neatly, identifying the locale where they were found.

Some were red, others beige, black, white or gray. As he showed them, he talked of their age and the type of stone used, explaining, for instance, that one point found near his boyhood home "had to be brought there, because it's Kanawha flint, found only in Kanawha and western Fayette Counties." His most exciting find was an arrowhead estimated to be eight thousand years old.

However, he confessed later, "I'm ashamed of the way I was getting them. Now I've learned how to dig a site properly, to protect the artifacts so that they can be documented and preserved. I don't believe in potting (digging) or destroying sites. That's why I was so eager to help find sites in the park."

Once while exploring at Camp Creek in Mercer County, West Virginia, he had come across an Indian burial site which someone had uncovered. Sadly, Kerby related, they had left human remains exposed. Kerby carefully reburied them.

With a slow grin, Kerby revealed that he had made a few arrowheads himself. Undistinguishable from the genuine Indian variety, his were fashioned in the manner of native Americans, using a piece of leather to hold the flint, a rock to rough it out and the point of a deerhorn to finish it.

Kerby had virtually lived in the woods from the time he was able to walk. He searched for Indian trails, walked them for miles and became well versed in their locations and history. Indian trails were followed by Trans Allegheny pioneers across the mountains into what was then western Virginia, and other trails entered that state from Ohio.

Kerby's early life in the rural mountains meant helping to gather all sorts of greens which grow in the wild---poke, dandelion, lamb's ear and others. He especially liked ramps, those pungent plants which hill people treasure so much that spring feasts featuring them have become famous. And in the fall, when his father went hunting, Kerby went along, scouring the forest for "sang," the ginseng roots which they dried and sold.

"We got enough money to pay for the hunting license and shells for the gun," he said. "Once when my dad needed tires, we gathered enough 'sang' in one week to pay for new ones." Years later the ginseng and goldenseal he collected and sold "fed my family" when coal mine shutdowns caused layoffs at the machine shop where he worked.

At an early age Kerby began reseeding to ensure future supplies of the plants. "We looked for 'sang' in late August and early September, when it was making seeds. I always scattered the seeds around so there would be new plants. The herbs grow slowly and they had to be at least six years old to have roots big enough to be worth digging."

The age and shape of the root dictate its worth on the market. The closer a root's resemblance to the shape of a man, the greater its value. The lower stem of the plant has a notch for each year of growth, Kerby noted, and he had found some roots "over 60 years old---maybe even 100." The largest root Kerby unearthed weighed about three ounces before it was dried. Once when he went to pick wild blackberries, he found a patch of ginseng that netted him a pound, then worth about $40, in fifteen minutes. Dried ginseng was bringing about $180 a pound in 1985 and, in just one day, Kerby dug $105 worth of roots on Bolt Mountain, a few miles from his home. Most of the ginseng harvested in the Appalachians is shipped to the Orient, where it is a cure-all. "They consider it an aphrodisiac and believe it will make you live longer," said Kerby.

Many people swear by its medicinal powers. The Cherokees, Iroquois and other tribes in eastern United States were digging and using ginseng long before white men who came to the mountains discovered there was money in it. "Digging is fun---walking through the nettles," Kerby laughed.

Although harder to get, goldenseal brought less money, Kerby said. The Cherokees, who used it to heal many disorders, first introduced it to early American settlers. They were so impressed with the native American herb that they exported it back to Europe. The medical profession valued it so highly that it was listed as among the most important medications in European trade as late as 1939, and also esteemed by American medical researchers whose national pharmacy text listed several extract uses.

Kerby cultivated ginseng, goldenseal and ramps behind his home, Pine Villa, along with unique "sarvis" trees. This tree produced tiny, bright red berries about the size of a pea and an interesting bit of folklore as well. Kerby explained that, when early settlers died during the winter, they were buried but no service was held because the severe weather made travel difficult. "Sarvis" trees were the first to bloom in the early spring, and that prompted a memorial service for all those who had died during the winter. "Sarvis" was the pronunciation for "service," traced back to the British and Scottish settlers in West Virginia, such as saying "darby" for "derby."

The resourceful woodsman found another means of earning money when unemployed as a machinist. He fashioned custom knives, daggers and hatchets from hard T-1 steel, silver nickle and brass, with elkhorn and hickory handles. They included historic Bowie knives similar to those popular in the South during the mid-1800s and the deadly "frog stickers" favored as survival weapons by legendary knife fighters of the Mississippi steamboat era. The latter measured more than a foot long and were as keen as they were gleaming. Although they were popular, "I doubt that the daggers ever again will be in demand. They're just too heavy to carry," Kerby said, grinning. "Most hunters prefer small skinning knives."

As a nature lover, he was a friend to deer, wild turkeys, squirrels and other animals he encountered in the woods. "I killed a squirrel last year, and I really didn't mean to," he related. "I felt bad about that." And he created works of art from tree knots, burls and strange-shaped twigs and limbs. One he named "Dancing Hillbillies" was a clever use of twigs from a Mountain Laurel and a white Snowball bush, with heads of oak tree knots.

His penchant for collecting quartz crystals and rocks led to friendship with a man in North Carolina who operated a diamond mine. The owner charged a fee for people to dig at the mine, and, in exchange for quartz and other minerals, Kerby built up a "credit" for such digging. Late in June 1986, Kerby and his wife, Carolyn, journeyed to North Carolina for their first vacation in several years, leaving their three children in the care of grandparents. A week earlier David Fuerst, en route from Ohio to the University of North Carolina, had stopped at Kerby's home to introduce his bride to the Walkers. They had been married June 21.

On July 2, Kerby and Carolyn were at the diamond dig, along with the owner and a friend. The two men left, telling Kerby to collect money from anyone else who wanted to dig. Kerby went to a nearby stream to wash, then told Carolyn he felt like he was going to pass out. He leaned over, began gasping for air and collapsed. Almost simultaneously, the two men who had departed returned, Kerby's friend stating, "Something told me to come back." One man started CPR while the other hastened away to summon aid. Tragically, though at the age of 41, Kerby died of a heart attack. It was a devastating loss, yet somehow the setting seemed most appropriate for this remarkable, gentle giant of a man---beside a cool stream, in a beautiful, peaceful, wooded area, amidst the nature he so loved.

Randy was a machinist in the navy and continued that kind of work when he got out. He married Carolyn Ann Lilly and they were the parents of one son and two daughters. He made many beautiful knives. His hobby was looking for arrows and other Indian artifacts. He knew the woods and how to track where the Indian trails were. He died suddenly of a heart attack at the age of forty-one July 2, 1986, while digging for rubies in North Carolina the same age as his mother was at the time of her death. He was so interesting to talk to. One could sit for hours as he showed Indian artifacts and tell you just where he found them. He is buried in the family cemetery and we have a five hundred dollar memorial for the maintenance of the cemetery. (GCM)

James Peyton Mills

(We could not find that this Mills family was related to us, but somewhere back there, they probably are. Anyway, we lived the same way.)
by Virginia Graham

James Peyton Mills and Miriah Minter were married in Henry County Virginia, February 31, 1849, and remained there for several years, then decided to move to Stokes County, North Carolina, in hopes of finding things less crowded and perhaps better farming. When they arrived there, James Mills found a reasonably priced one hundred-acre farm. By this time they had three girls and seven boys.

All had to help with the chores. Miriah would bake a stack of pies about two feet tall on Sundays. It took a lot to feed so many. James Mills and the older boys would butcher several hogs at one time. The hogs had fattened on acorns in the woods. The family ate the vegetables and meat they had raised and often went fishing and hunting to help put food on the table.

The children had to make their own toys to play with. There was no money to spend on unnecessary things. The girls dolls were made out of corn husks or old socks that could not be mended any more. They enjoyed going to church and hearing the word of God and seeing their faraway neighbors.

James Mills family in Wayne, West Virginia, kept writing, telling him of how good farming and life was in Wayne County, so they decided to move to West Virginia. They sold some of the cattle and loaded their covered wagon with the necessary things and left behind what they could not take.

The mother and girls rode in the covered wagon and Mr. Mills and the boys, dogs and cattle walked. Some times they had a hard time getting across the streams and they had to drive the cattle across. A few times, they got to load the wagon on a flat boat with men on each side, paddling. The cattle had to swim. The Mills family came by way of the New River trail.

After they arrived in Wayne County, they located a farm and all were busy getting things in order. They had to get out of bed about four o'clock in the morning to get milking, churning, clothes washed on the washboard and all the chores done.

When it was mealtime, the Mills children came to the table quietly and stood behind their chairs until Mr. Mills said grace and then they each sat down and waited until their father filled each plate and it was passed around to each child. There were no loud noises or playing at the table.

There was lots of bean stringings and apple peelings. Neighbors would all go to help each family and when the job was done, they would have a party. The family loved it when it was time to make molasses. Friends would come to help and the smell of the cane juice cooking would really fill the air. The jars had been washed and dried ahead of time, so the youngsters would just play and gather firewood while the older people cooked the molasses.

This Mills family lived a long life and their great-great-grandchildren are scattered all over the United States. Many still in Cabell and Wayne counties.

James and Miriah Mills were laid to rest in Springhill Cemetery in Huntington, West Virginia.

He was born in 1824 and died in 1903 and Miriah was born in 1826 and died in 1920. They had a hard life, as most of our ancestors did. We are proud of the lives most of our families had and of their strength. I hope our future generations will be proud of our lives and our strength when they in later years are researching us.

Virginia Midkiff Graham
Huntington, WV 25701

The foregoing article was sent to me by Patricia Chambers Schaffer, Virginia Beach, Virginia. Her father was Joe Chamber, originally from Huntington, West Virginia.

Foley Family in Egeria

Handed to me July 29, 1995, by Rachel Foley Vogtsberger at the Foley reunion at Camp Creek State Park.-- *Gloria*

I had suggested to her at the 1993 reunion that she write about things that she remembered about growing up in Egeria and her family. She said that she tried to get Jack and Betty to write, but no luck, so she sat down and did this. Her memories certainly portray that time.

The Things I Remember About My Family
(By Rachel-1994)

I was born in 1921, in Modock, West Virginia. I was the eighth child. My dad decided he would buy a farm so his children could have fresh air and good fresh food. We moved to Egeria, West Virginia in 1923. I was three years old. I was too young to remember much about our move. Dad had grown boys to help on the farm. My sister Ruth had to go back to Matoaka to finish high school. Croby, my oldest brother, always helped on the farm. After Ruth finished high school, she went to Morris Harvey College in Montgomery, West Virginia. My brother Shad went there also. They both were school teachers. Hallie, Shad's wife, was a schoolteacher early in their married life.

Things began to get harder for my dad to make a living on the farm. He and my brothers went into the lumber business, cutting the big trees on our farm. I remember Shad had a truck to carry the lumber to Besoco to sell. They cut timber for ties and headers for the coal mines. On the fourth of July, Shad would use the truck to take his children and us children to Shawnee Lake for a picnic. I can remember we would always have watermelon, the only one that year. It was a great outing for our family. Shad and his wife, Hallie, lived in a house that he and our dad built on our farm. He and his family lived there many years helping my dad with the lumber and farming.

(This same house was where one on my nephews, Wathor Jeffrey Walker was born. After Shad and Hallie moved to Barn, Lorena and Kerby lived there. While their first son, Arthur Kirk had been an easy delivery with midwife, Mrs. Lilly present, Jeffrey's was a difficult one and Kerby had to go for the doctor.)

We had a good time with Shad and Hallie. They taught night school and would go places with us. On Friday night, we would meet at their house and play cards and pop popcorn. On Sunday afternoon, we would go to the schoolhouse and play softball. All the family would go, even Mom and Dad. The gym at the schoolhouse was used as a church. Mom and Dad would always have the preachers over for dinner on Sunday. It was usually chicken, we raised our own.

In the summertime, there would be a revival meeting. We would have two preachers. I can remember Johnny Foley and Preacher Doss being there. Opal Foley would come with her dad and sing in church. I always wanted to be like Opal and sing like she sang. Dolly, (Johnny's wife), one summer before she died, she was in our kitchen washing lettuce for a salad. We had to draw water out of the well and it was very cold, she said, "This water is freezing". I don't know why, but I will always remember her saying this. When she got pneumonia and died, I thought it was because she washed her hands in the cold water. The lettuce salad was made with green onion, bacon and lettuce. Bacon was fried and the hot grease was mixed with vinegar and poured over the lettuce mixture. This was called wilted lettuce. Johnny's boys stayed with us all summer many times. They liked the farm. Naomi and Francis would come also.

We had two beautiful horses to do the plowing. Their names were Fox and Nig. Our postmaster had a farm near us, his name was Jim Butler. One day, Nig got out of the fence and went into Mr. Butler's corn patch. Before we could get him out, Mr. Butler grabbed his shotgun and killed Nig. Nig was like one of our family. I don't think Croby ever forgave him. These were the horses we would ride out to Mr. Brammer's store at Barn, West Virginia, and buy our groceries. I can remember the candy jars he had where we could buy one cent pieces of candy. He also had dress goods for ten cents a yard. My Mother and Hallie sewed for me. One I remember was a colored stripe she made it into a shirt waist dress. They would make dresses from print cloth used for flour sacks. When my brother, James and I finished high school, we went to Stoco High School at Lego, West Virginia, to take a test. Our school was not a credited school. I wore that dress. Our mother had given us money for lunch, twenty-five cents each. James and I decided instead of buying a hot dog and coke for lunch, we would spend our money for an ice cream sandwich. That was something we never had very often.

Our schoolhouse and gym was used for all our entertainment and for church. Someone asked me what I remember most about my parents. It never took me long to answer. It was the love for family and God. I can remember my dad sitting on the front porch with his Bible reading after all the chores were done. We all loved to sing and had a choir of our own. During the summer, Dad would have a music instructor to come from Matoka or nearby to teach us the music from our church hymnal which was written in square strong notes. Henry had a strong base voice. I can still hear him sing "On the Jerico Road" in the base voice. We often went to other churches to sing. Dad and Mom were so proud of us.

The gym was used for basketball and Jack was the captain of the team and the boys would go to other schools to play the boys there. I think at one time they were champions. The girls had a good team. I always played center. I was the tallest. And of course the square dancing we had every Saturday night was a big event. On Halloween, the gym was decorated with corn shucks and pumpkins. The string band was boys from Egeria.

In 1930, things got hard for us on the farm. This was during the depression when Hoover was president. We would sell our farm produce for groceries. Potatoes were selling for one dollar per bushel. We could grow good potatoes getting one hundred bushels to an acre. We all had to help on the farm. The girls would help our mother gather vegetables and fruits to can. The older boys had gone into the military service, they would send money home to help out on a monthly basis. Five of the six sons served in the military. Shad was deferred because of his dependents–six. Our sister Ruth was a mountain of strength to us. She was teaching in Helen, West Virginia. She would come home every summer and help out. One summer she came home and saw that our mother was pregnant. Mother was trying to keep it a secret because Ruth thought that we had enough children, nine at this time. She asked mother if she was pregnant and mother answered her by saying "you left the yeast cakes you were taking for your acne and I took some that was left and got pregnant." Of course she and Ruth had a big laugh about this. The result was a beautiful baby boy named Johnny Jackson, born September 14, 1927. I was six years old and would sit by Mom's bed and rock Jack. Mom had her babies at home. Our dad died of a stroke when he was fifty-four years old. Jack was twelve years old at this time. We called Dad "Papa". I can remember Papa holding Jack on his lap and telling him bedtime stories on the front porch. Jack missed not having Papa when he was growing up but our Mom did all she could to be both Mom and Papa. And of course, our oldest brother, Croby, stayed home with Mom until he died.

Croby was engaged to a girl by the name of Roxie Hubbard. Roxie went away to school and found another boy and married him. Croby was hurt and never married at all.

My sister Ruth went with a boy from Egeria named Nathan Shrewsbury. For years we thought they would marry but they broke up when Ruth went away to teach. She later married Sonny Collier from Beckley, West Virginia and he lived four years and died with tuberculosis. She was a widow for several years. Then she met and married Rudolph Rogers from Point Pleasant, West Virginia. They both taught school in Point Pleasant before moving to Ft. Lauderdale, Florida. They both died there. They are buried at Point Pleasant.

My sister, Betty, and I were teenagers together. We would date the same boys. Betty was always fixing her hair different. I remember her ordering a blonde bleach to put on her hair. She was a beautiful blonde. None of the other girls had hair like that. I didn't think Mom or Papa wanted her to do that, but she did it anyway. One night Betty and I wanted to go to a dance at the schoolhouse. We asked Mom if we could go, she always said ask your Papa. We asked Papa and he said if your brothers go with you. We didn't want our brothers to go with us, but to go we persuaded them to go. After the dance, some of the boys would ask to walk us home. This particular night, we walked home with our date and our Papa and the schoolteacher who lived with us (Mom kept the schoolteacher for twenty dollars per month; room and board) were sitting on the porch. The boys were saying good night when a light was turned on us and it was the schoolteacher. He told my Papa that he should not allow the girls to be out with boys at night. Betty and I cried that he said that. We hated him (the schoolteacher) for that, because our Papa had trusted us to take care of ourselves.

Betty had heavy, thick hair and she wore it in a page boy, perfectly turned under. Even after playing basketball in the gym, she combed it back into place. Yes, she was a beautiful blonde page-boy girl.

The only time Papa had spanked Betty and me was when Mom told us to wash the dishes. We argued about who was going to wash or dry. We didn't want to do them in the first place. Papa had a razor strap hanging on the wall. He took that down and gave us both a swat with that razor strap and it felt like I was being killed. Betty never even cried.

Betty had a few accidents. She fell off of her bike and broke her arm. She fell out of the barn loft and broke her shoulder. The boys were throwing rocks across the chicken house and she was hit in the head. It caused a scar she still has. I can remember we kept our apples in the barn loft under hay to keep for winter. I can still smell those apples.

We had dairy cows and James did most of the milking before we went to school. One time, we were all gone and Croby was supposed to milk one of our good cows. He couldn't get her to stand still. When we got home, he had her inside the house in the pantry trying to milk her. Her name was Jersey.

Henry had a bad accident. The boys had stacked lumber up in the "v" shape on sawhorses. Mom had made taffy, Henry and James wanted to go inside to get some taffy. They tied the dog to a leg of the sawhorse and the dog pulled all of that lumber over on top of Henry and James. James escaped without injury, but Henry was smashed very badly. Croby had to go for the doctor who lived at Flat Top, West Virginia. By the time the doctor got there, Henry was smashed so badly, he looked bruised all over. There were no broken bones, and he recovered nicely.

(The doctor Croby had to go for at Flat Top was Dr. McComas, my cousin on Mom's side. One time, I had poison oak on my face so bad that when I opened my mouth to eat, the scabs cracked. Henry was driving the mail truck then, so Mom and I went with him in the morning. He dropped us off at Dr. McComas' house. His office was in the house. He opened a little door in an oak "washstand" and filled a small metal salve box with some pink salve. My face healed and left no scars." *GCM*

Buford went to business college in Beckley, West Virginia. Afterwards, he worked in Beckley for a year or so. One summer he decided to go to Florida and work. We had a relative there, Harry Foley (Uncle Lundy's son). Buford stayed with him for a while. He got homesick and came home. When he came back he brought some clothing for Jack. They were short pants and Jack was starting to school that year. Jack did not want to wear those short pants, and I don't think that he did. Jack never liked the first grade of school, so every day about noon, I would take him home. I was in the seventh or eighth grade.

Some of the fun times we had were pie and cake walks and box suppers. The girls would bake the cakes and pies and hope their boyfriends would bid on their pie. The box supper was a full meal put into a decorated box. We would spend hours decorating our box, again hoping our boyfriend would get our box. Another thing we would do was go chestnut and chinquapin picking. On Mothers Day, we would go walking through the woods and gather the flowers called trillium or ladyslippers for a bouquet for Mom. Maybe violets would be added. Our Mom loved flowers. When the huckleberries and blackberries were ready to pick, we would spend a whole day picking and filling big lard pails with berries. We would spend days cleaning the berries and canning for winter. Shad and Hallie would help us. Everything was done with the entire family. Shad's favorite was strawberry jam. Even though our mother had asthma, she was always helping. Many days it was hard for her to do the housework. But I can remember she would always get up and bake three or four big pans of biscuits and make gravy for breakfast.

In 1930, Henry and Buford joined the CCC Camps to get money to help the family out. My mother cried when they left. When President Roosevelt was elected, he gave these boys a break. He also helped the boys and girls who wanted to go to college with the NYA program. They could work and pay for their room and board. I took advantage of that and went to Concord College in Athens, West Virginia, getting my certificate to teach.

The first summer I went to Concord, I went with Ruth. Ruth was going to school every summer working on her masters. That fall I stayed on at Concord. I would get so homesick. Henry would come get me and bring me home in his Model A rumble seat Ford every Friday. He was carrying the mail then for twenty-five dollars a month. His route was from Egeria, to Barn, to Odd, to Ghent and return.

Shad and Hallie moved from Egeria to Barn, West Virginia on Hallie's mother's farm. Her mother, Mrs. Fink had died that year. I can remember the beautiful quilts that her mother made. I guess that I got interested in making quilts when I was a young girl. My mother, Hallie, Mary Harmon, and several other women would get together and quilt. Mom would take Betty and me with her. The men would go sometimes if there was something to be done on the farm. I can remember the good chocolate cake Mary Harmon made and served at the quilting bees.

There was a teacher and his wife, Mr. and Mrs. Stoveall who lived near us in Egeria. They had no children. One day, they came to my mother and asked her if she would give Rachel to them to raise since she had so many children. My mother, of course said that she could not give away any of her children. My mother and dad wanted all of their children to get an education. When the older ones finished school, they had to help the younger ones.

When Shad and Hallie moved to Barn, West Virginia, they had three children. They had three more born at Barn, West Virginia. We didn't see them as much after they left Egeria.

I finished two and a half years of school at Athens and got a job teaching at Terry, West Virginia. Ruth had been teaching there but wanted to leave and go to Florida. She talked to the superintendent of schools and told him she wanted her sister to have her job. That is the way I got my first job, and that is the way Ruth looked after the family when she could. This was the year I met Irvin Vogtsberger. We were both rooming with Mary and Lu, my cousins, in Beckley, West Virginia. I fell in love with him the first time I saw him. When I realized he was from Wisconsin, I thought it was so far away. I would have to leave my family, but we were married in March and we left West Virginia to go to Jacksonville, Florida. Later we moved to Minnesota. I have been here for forty years. Irvin died in 1993 with cancer.

Croby, Mom and Jack were left on the farm and Croby decided he would go to work in the mines. They moved to Rhodell, West Virginia, and Croby worked in the mines. Jack was still a young man. He graduated from high school at Stoco, and was drafted immediately into the army. He served with the occupational forces headquartered in Yokohama, Japan. He returned home to Rhodell and started working in the coal mines. This was not to his liking so he ended up in Fairfax, Virginia, where he and his wife (Joanne) raised their family.

Mom and Croby moved to Coal City, West Virginia. Croby worked in the coal mines. He had a heart attack in the mines and died at the age of fifty-six years. Mom stayed on at Coal City until she died at age seventy-seven in March 1964.

While at the Foley reunion July 29, 1995, Jack recalled when he and my brother Corbit used to ride their old "put together parts" bicycles over the Booge Harmon Mountain to Pinoak to Uncle Tressie McComas' where they sometimes stayed for weeks to work in his sawmill. They rode those bikes back down the mountain, both completely without brakes! They did survive.

Rachel mentions going huckleberry picking. I remember one time we all went up on the Bluff Mountain. James and the boys with long legs would run off and leave us girls. We crossed logs, sat on them to rest and continued on. I would pick clean--no leaves in my bucket so it took me longer to fill, but when completed it was just a purplish-blue top. Mom always made a cobbler first, then canned or made preserves of the rest. In the winter, she would open a quart of the huckleberries and serve hot cobbler with milk for supper. Nothing better and cultivated blueberries has almost nothing to do with the taste and flavor of huckleberries although they do look alike and are in the same family.

Sometimes we did go berry picking down past the schoolhouse where we ended up at a creek which had a large pool where we went swimming, or playing in the water. We had to let our clothes get dry before returning, but usually got caught. Moms can tell.

While attending the Barn school, I spent a night with

the teacher who boarded with Hallie Foley's mother (in the house where Shad and Hallie later moved into to take care of her mother) and boy, was her mother a great cook! She cooked up a big meal and then later after the dishes were washed, she made candy.

I slept in a small room off the living room and it had stacks of quilts. Beulah and I stopped to visit Hallie a few years before she died and she showed us numerous quilts. Hallie had them on the bed. She would peel one after another off the bed to show us.

At that time, a grandson was mowing and taking care of the farm, but not doing all the gardening and farming that Hallie and Shad used to do. When they first moved there, one of the first things they did was to erect large chicken houses and raise thousands of chickens. At that time, the feed companies sponsored chicken raising and contracted to buy all the eggs. Shad also worked in the mines. He could drive over the hill to Odd and go to Besoco. This is a road that turns up just before you get to the Odd Post Office and grocery store, if you are going from Ghent to Odd. It is rather steep and was at that time a dirt road (I think that it still is) and passable most of the winter.

After Hallie and Shad moved in with her mother, they had two more children, both boys, however the first one did not live. I think that he was born with a heart condition. The doctor told Hallie not to have any more children, that they would probably be born with the same heart condition, however the next boy was perfectly healthy.

I remember Mom going out to stay with them until the baby was born and Betty tells me (July 31, 1995) that she remembers Mom getting her ready for the funeral--that she wore little white shoes. Betty was six then and said the older people were crying and she did not know how she was supposed to act. She thought that she should be mourning, but did not understand just what it was all about.

When Hallie and Shad lived in the house on the farm, I remember standing at the stove and watching her make chocolate pies. She put the milk, eggs, sugar, cocoa, a little flour for thickening and some butter, then she would stir vigorously because lumps would form which she beat out. It would look like it might be getting too thick, if it did, she added a little more milk. They ended up being perfect and she always invited any kids hanging around to help eat them.

The house that Rachel mentions that was built on their property for Hallie and Shad to live in was a two-room house. Betty Foley Mills asked me a couple years ago, "How did we live in a two-room house?"

I answered, "Oh, but Betty–they were large rooms."

I remember babysitting the children while Hallie, Shad and Buford went to Beckley on business and to do Christmas shopping. Lorena went along to do our Christmas shopping. Hallie put a kettle of beans on the back of the stove and all day I added water as they cooked down. By nightfall when they got back the beans had cooked to a thick soup. I don't remember whether I made corn bread or Hallie made it after she got back, but they sat down at the table and ate bowls of that bean soup as if they had nothing to eat all day. People usually got a cup of coffee and a piece of G.C. Murphy's good pie at the counter when in Beckley at the 5 and 10 cent store.

Buford had promised me that morning before they left that he would bring me something--to take good care of the children. He forgot and I was so disappointed. I had looked forward to it all day. Lorena had a shopping bag full of gifts for us for Christmas, not the plastic bags of today but a real shopping bag with sturdy handles. The night was light and we walked home across the fields. We were not allowed to take a peek into the shopping bag.

Close to this house along the road, there was a shallow water hole that froze over in the winter. It was a wonderful place for ice skating, but I never had the nerve. The Mitchem boys, James, Jack, Corbit and most of the boys just sailed across. Rachel, Betty, some of the Thompson girls kept right up with the boys. This was skating with just the bottom of your shoes, no ice skates. The house is no longer there. It was either burned down or torn down, but has been gone many years.

Also, the house that Mr. Noel Christian, the teacher from Beckley lived in has long been gone. The chimney may still be there. I forgot to look when we passed last Sunday, July 30, 1995. He and his lovely wife moved to the community and became a part of it immediately. He worked hard at getting the peoples confidence and did so much to help the young people. He had croquet in the yard. He grew rows and rows of colorful gladiolus. He would have us over Saturday nights to play cards and he always made chocolate fudge. He really could make it.

One Saturday night when he was not at home, James Foley and some other boys went in and had their usual Saturday night card game. When Mr. Christian and his wife returned from Beckley, they never said a word, although they knew the boys had been there. Mrs. Christian sewed her own clothes and she made a red dress for me. I had sold cloverine salve to get four yards of material. She used one of her patterns and it was a neat dress.

Mrs. Christian was from Kentucky. They did not have children while they lived in Egeria, about four years, I think. She could have been lonely, but she filled her days with reading, sewing, cooking and general housekeeping. I suspect that she graded some papers for him, especially English Literature. He said that he had to learn with the students. I know that she graded the stories we wrote because I have one of mine with her comments on it. I would sit with her and talk for hours because I did not play cards. She won a contest for making the most words from a sentence. She used the dictionary and worked for weeks. She won a box of candy with twenty-four bars in it.

They took Allene for a weekend visit to her parents in Kentucky and Allene never forgot it. When Jimmie, Beulah, Allene and I were driving from Florida to Corbit's funeral, something reminded her of the trip and she told us every little detail.

After Mr. Christian got a teaching position in Beckley, they had two girls. She died before he did, but it was not until after the girls were grown.

Several years ago when James Foley arranged a reunion held on the farm, opposite the graveyard for anyone who had ever attended the Egeria school or had taught at the school, Mr. Christian was there. He also brought Mr. Peregoy, who said that he had not had the opportunity to make the trip to the Egeria School while he was the superintendant of the schools and he had always wanted to.

Betty Foley, Macil Walker, Lotie Walker and myself were the total graduating class of 1941. We were all at the reunion and in 1995, we were all still alive. Betty has promised me a picture of the four of us for years and now she says that if I do not get it this year, I have her permission to beat her.

One time when I was spending the night with Betty, we went down to the school and played volleyball until it was too dark to see. We strung a net, or rope (I don't remember if we really had a proper volleyball net) from the gym to the schoolhouse.

When we got back to the house, Mr. and Mrs. Foley were in bed. We were so hungry and there was a pot of green beans on the stove. We just all dived in and ate from the pot. I guess we got some corn bread to go with the beans.

After reading Rachel's account of Mr. Butler shooting and killing their best horse because he got out and strayed onto his property, I am sure glad those boys decided to avoid his property.

James Butler, (b) 1867, (d) 1947. Rowena Butler, (b) 1969, (d) 1957. Both are buried in the Agee Cemetery at Egeria.

Old Timey Sayings

Here is a list of "old timey" sayings that you might have heard your parents or grandparents use. Some may be trite, but hope these sayings, some humorous, some not, will continue to be a part of our conversations in years to come.

You can't hit the ball if you don't swing the bat.
You won't get criticized if you are doing nothing.
Don't hang up a calendar before sunup on New Years Day or you will have bad luck all year.
If a girl takes the last biscuit from the plate she will end up an old maid.
Don't plant beans before you hear the first whipporwill's cry.
It is bad luck to get out of the wrong side of the bed. (How do you know which side is right?)
It is bad luck to put your left shoe on first or to swing your left foot out of bed first.
If a girl places a piece of wedding cake under her pillow, she will dream about the man she will marry. (Bet the only result is a smashed piece of cake).
Your first dream while sleeping under a new quilt will always come true.
Two wrongs do not make a right.
If you spill salt, quickly throw some over you left shoulder or you will have bad luck.
If you make a wish on the first star that you see at night, it will come true. (How we kids loved and practiced that one).
Don't count your chickens before they are hatched.
A bird in hand is better than ten in the bush.
An apple a day will keep the doctor away. An onion a day will keep everybody away.
Behind every cloud there is a silver lining. (There are times you need this one).

Where there is smoke, there must be fire. (We all knew that one).
Beauty is only skin deep. (Heard this one from aunts, grandmas and adults).
Beauty is in the eyes of the beholder.
If you break a mirror, you will have seven years bad luck. (I sincerely believed this).
A faint heart never won fair lady.
A black cat crossing in front of you will bring bad luck. (Common saying).
If the month of March comes in like a lion, it will go out like a lamb. (We still believe this).
If a bat flies in your house, it is a sure sign of imminent death in the family. (This scared us).
Birds of a feather flock together (Aunt Dessie Cole used this a lot).
Children are to be seen and not heard. (Yes, we were made aware of this one–).
Little pictures have big ears. (Cousin Rema Walker used this one).
You will be judged by the company you keep.
Pretty is as pretty does. (Heard that one often).
Don't cut off your nose to spite your face. (Very common).
If you can eat a sour crabapple without making a face, you can marry the one you want. (Grandma Mills told us this one).
A penny earned is a penny saved. (A dollar wouldn't help much in these times).
You can take the girl out of the country, but you can't take the country out of the girl.
Skinny as a rail.
It's raining cats and dogs.
It's like looking for a needle in a haystack.
Poor as Job's turkey.
It takes one to know one.
A watched pot never boils.
Snug as a bug in a rug.
Knee high to a grasshopper.
Easy as rolling off a log.
Lay down with dogs; get up with fleas.
Drunk as a skunk.

A whistling girl and a crowing hen will never come to a good end.
Let sleeping dogs lie.
Look what the dogs dragged in.
If I had known you were a-coming, I'd baked a cake.
Clean as a hound's tooth.
He's a chip off the old block.
That's the way the cookie crumbles.
Don't bite off more than you can chew.
Crooked as a dog's hind leg.
Sleep tight and don't let the bed bugs bite. (I put my little foster children to bed with this).
Make hay while the sun shines.
Kissing wears out, cookin' don't.
High as a Georgia pine.
I'm the chief cook and bottle washer.
Fit to be tied.
He's loaded for bear.
Sober as a judge.
Two sheets in the wind.
Not worth a hill of beans.
Naked as a jay bird.
Too many cooks spoil the broth.
If the shoe fits, wear it.
Don't beat around the bush.
That takes the cake.
Cross that bridge when you get to it.
You don't judge a book by its cover.
Beggars can't be choosers.
When in Rome, do as the Romas do.
Pleased as punch.
Don't open up a can of worms.
So much water over the dam.
You were left holding the bag.
Wet as a whistle.
Don't cry over spilt milk.
You had better save that for a rainy day.
It is better to wear out than to rust out.
Lost time is never found.
Mad as a wet hen.
They will get their "come-uppance". (My mother)

Some Sensible Observations

The driver is safer when the roads are dry. The roads are safer when the driver is dry.
Alcohol makes a man colorful; it gives him a red nose, a white liver, a yellow streak, and a blue outlook.
Don't get in the habit of telling people where to get off unless you are a bus driver.
One father is worth more that a hundred schoolteachers.
There are two ways of being rich. One is to have all that you want. The other is to be satisfied with what you have.
An old man was asked what had most robbed him of joy in his life. His reply was, "Things that never happened".
Marriage used be a contract. Now, many regard it as a ninety-day option.
Make the most of life before most of life is gone.
Do what good you can today. You may not be here tomorrow.
Face powder can catch a man, but it takes baking power to hold him.
Don't wait for the hearse to take you to church.
Three hints for making a speech, be sincere, be brief, be seated.
If you can't make light of your troubles, keep them in the dark.
Carve your name on hearts, not on marble.
Smile a while and give your face a rest.
The kindness we show tomorrow cures no headaches today.
A temper is a valuable possession, don't lose it.
Better alone than in bad company. (Judged by company you keep–birds of a feather).
Stop worrying. Worry kills life.
Be patient with children. You are dealing with soul stuff.
Before you give anyone a piece of your mind, you ought to make sure you can get by with what you have left.
Worry is interest paid on trouble before it is due.
No one is a failure in this world who lightens a burden for someone else. It is not so much what we know as how well we use what we know.
Remember that AMERICAN ends with I can.
Buy not silk when you owe for milk.
A mountain has no need of words–it says so much without them–

thus should be our lives.
Never speak loudly to one another unless the house is on fire.
Full of bad habits just waiting to be picked up.
Life is a highway, but you have to build it as you go. (This is my own-*Gloria*)

Stories

Written at Fort Blackmore, Virginia, in 1979. We were strip mining coal and sometimes, I had time on my hands after I had cleaned up the small travel trailer that we lived in–so I scribbled.

Some family members have heard some of these stories. My personal recollections are from actual memory of stories heard and incidents that actually happened in my childhood. I look at the lifestyle of country living now and sixty years ago and know that the pace has quickened. If we had had electricity, indoor plumbing, refrigerators, televisions, washing machines and machinery to make farm work easier, we would not have been in such a hurry to migrate to the city.

I dreamed and traveled all over the world in different periods of time in books, studied hard and waited until I could graduate from high school and go to the city and get a job.

I was not alone. In the thirties, during the Depression most of my classmates were struggling along the same lines, waiting for a better life.

All the Mills children were born either in Wyoming County or Mercer County and mostly raised in the Egeria area. Grandpa Mills sold the homeplace, 106 acres in 1923. His land holdings had dwindled from 1 or 2 thousand acres to 106.

They bought a place at Spanishburg and resided there until his death in 1924. After his death, they lost the place due to a "lost" note that Grandma thought had been paid off, however the court held that it had not, and it had to be paid.

She then rented a small house on the upper bank of the road near the grocery store and road entrance from the bridge located in Spanishburg. I remember an incident there when visiting one Sunday. The boys were playing in a sawdust pile at a sawmill in the bottom on the other side of the road. They did not want us girls to follow, but that was just the place we wanted to be, so we tagged along behind. They held us and put sawdust in our eyes. We went screaming and rubbing our eyes across the road to Grandma's house to have the sawdust washed out.

They learned of a few acres of land at Beeson that was for sale and Grandma, Uncle Kelly and Uncle Laurence bought it. Grandma lived there until her death and later Uncle Nathan's family lived there. That is where he died. Since then, Basil, Oma, and Aunt Versie have lived there.

Uncle Laurence was killed in the Springton Mines in 1929, at the age of twenty-four. Uncle Kelly was shot and killed by Leslie Meadows at Egeria in 1931 at the age of twenty-seven.

Grandma, Delmer, and Alastia continued to make their home at the Beeson place. Grandma died in 1936. She died of a broken hip, cancer of the liver, complications from the broken hip and age. Surely, she must have been worn out. She raised ten children to maturity.

Aunt Dessie described to me the method Grandma used to keep sweet potatoes for winter. Sand was sifted and thoroughly dried. She placed a layer of the dry sand in her large wood chest. (This was a chest that over the years had been used for linens, clothes, and packing for moving). A layer of sweet potatoes and another of sand were placed until the chest was filled. Aunt Dessie said that the sweet potatoes kept until spring, if they lasted that long.

Pumpkins could be kept most of the winter and of course the dried variety kept indefinitely. So without refrigeration, our ancestors managed to get a fairly-balanced diet during the winter.

In the spring, all members of the family got their molasses and sulphur tonic.

Probably the reason the fresh spring greens tasted so good was because we had had very little leaf vegetables during the winter months. The winter food consisted of canned, dried, pickled, or preserved. The only leaf vegetable was cabbage. The cabbage heads were pulled, turned roots up and the heads buried in rows in the ground, deep enough to keep from freezing. During the winter the snow would be scraped off and the heads dug up. Toward spring some of the outside leaves might be rotten, but the center would still be good, white and sweet. The cabbage made delicious cole slaw, cooked plain, or added to vegetable soup. We would open a quart of home canned tomatoes, add potatoes, onions, cabbage, and canned beef and viola!, a big pot of good, hearty soup. (Beef fat and all --we cooked with a good bit more of fat in those days–the days before cholesterol.)

Grandma's Arthritic Medicine

*Told to me August 27, 1991,
by Cousin Alastia (Lila) Mills Tilley Hatcher*

One day Alastia and Grandma were in the berry patch. Stooping to pick the berries got the best of Grandma and she collapsed on the ground. She told Alastia to go and get her brother Delmer to bring the horse and sled. They were able to put her on the sled and transport her to the house. She had Delmer go out and dig up a poke-weed root, skin it and slice down the sides, then she poured enough liquid out of a quart of moonshine to cover the poke root. After this soaked for some time, she would take drinks at intervals and soon was able to get up and walk. She explained that the poke root itself is poisonous, but the whiskey changes the poison and extracts something from the root that would heal arthritis.

I do not know anything about it to recommend this cure, but Alastia said that it worked for Grandma.

Always in the fall they went on herb gathering expeditions. Grandma collected large amounts of a plant she called Pepperile. This grew profusely at Spanishburg but not at Nubbins Ridge, where they moved later. She used this plant to treat pneumonia. Alastia said that it made a good tasting tea and she and Delmer learned to like it.

Uncle Doug Peyton of Spanishburg said that Nubbins Ridge was so named because corn did not grow well on the ridge, producing only "nubbins" (very small ears).

Chester set off a large charge of dynamite while serenading the celebration of Alastia and Ule Tilley's wedding. The blast threw rocks and dirt all over Grandma's porch, but no one was hurt.

Alastia said that Grandma always kept her "Run Johnny, run bag" packed. This was her midwife bag. When she was called out in the middle of the night she took Alastia with her. They were always boiling water and Alastia until she was a teenager, thought they boiled the babies.

    Grandma collected lots of a special fern which she boiled into a dark black thick liquid. She made a salve of this which she rubbed on her goiter. I do not know just what base she used but suspect it was either sheep tallow or beef fat. It did seem to shrink the rather large goiter on her neck.

The "Association"

My stories would not be complete without telling you about the Primitive Baptist associations. Every year, a three-day meeting was held with lots of hymn singing and plenty of good old hard shell preaching. This meeting was looked forward to and planned a year in advance. I can remember my Granny McComas buying a five gallon enamel blue and grey coffee pot just to use when the association was held in Pinoak.

I can remember three carloads of us leaving Pinoak for Monroe County one year and having several breakdowns, flat tires, etc., before we got there. I slept with five other children in an upstairs bedroom. The house was filled and the women worked late into the night after the men had retired to sleep on hay in the loft of the barn. They had to cook and prepare for the morning breakfast and lunch the next day. I will never forget the smell of mutton boiling. They raised a lot of sheep in Monroe County so they made use of it. All they did was boil and boil and the grown ups actually ate it and seemed to relish it. I like a good leg of lamb, roasted properly but I cannot stand mutton. Maybe if I was starving.

I remember sitting under trees with other young people and listening to the singing and preaching coming out of the windows of the little church. On Saturday, the big day, they usually set up benches and preached to a large crowd outside. While the brimstone and fire was being preached in the church area, horse trading, moonshine drinking and knife swapping was going on in the woods a distance away.

The business was taken care of on Friday. Deacons and clerks sent from all districts gave their reports and new people were elected for the next year. Also the location of the next years meeting was picked.

Washing of feet in the church; if you have never witnessed this ceremony, you may wonder just what happens. After the service has ended and prayer has been said, the elders start first. A big bowl or other vessel and towels have been provided. A brother will kneel at the feet of a seated brother, remove his shoes and socks and proceed to wash and dry his feet. After all the elders in the pulpit have completed their ritual, it is passed on to the members of the choir and those in the front seats. They use several containers of water. The women wash other women's feet.

So that all the preachers who wanted to preach might do so, there were meetings held in homes. There was always a lot of discussion on the way home and afterward about elders and their preaching, ("The Lord sure blessed Brother Lilly today. He sure delivered a powerful sermon").

The young people socialized under the trees while the church service was going on. I would say that many a romance started at these meetings that later developed into marriages. I know that my uncle Reathice McComas and Aunt Mae Cooper and her sister, Willie Belle and her husband, Gilvin Walker, met this way.

Sunday was the big finale. A lot of spirited preaching, singing and praying. Then a big dinner on the ground. Goodbyes were said and everyone headed in different directions for home.

They enjoyed their religion and fellowship so much. The weekend could be compared to kids going to the circus so far as enjoyment goes.

I never heard of one-hour service. The circuit preacher just made it to each church once a month. If your area happened to be the fourth Sunday, the fourth Sunday was sacred. You got a good three to four-hour dose of religion. Granny did not allow us to get up and leave. You sat there on those hardwood benches (no cushions) until dismissed. At dismissal, everyone held their song books and walked around, singing and shaking hands with everyone.

This is still done today. I attended services at the Camp Creek Church at Flat Top a few years ago and nothing had changed. Well, some things. Services did not last as long and our "dinner on the ground" was served on a large table in a shelter. Modern times, modern ways, same old shared spirit.

When I got my two weeks vacation at Grannys when school was out, I knew that I would be expected to attend church with them and be quiet and patient all day. We would walk down the hill, across a level half mile, around a curve and there on the left up on a hill was the church.

Grandpa carried the big porcelain pitcher and bowl for the water to be placed on a table for the preachers. The bowl and pitcher were always taken back home for safe keeping.

When it had been raining, the road would be muddy as none of it was paved. Granny would scold me for getting mud on my white bobby socks. How did she expect a little girl to walk in the mud and not splash some on her legs? I wanted to take my clean socks with me and put them on after we got there, but she would not let me.

This Rich Creek Primitive Baptist Church still sits at the top of the hill beside the road. The building has been remodeled and improved. This church was organized in 1851. My mother, Thelma McComas Mills' funeral was held in this church, in 1970.

I did not know until I was grown that there were other words that went with "The Association". The church at Pinoak was a member of the Indian Creek District Primitive Baptist Association.

Trip to Burton's Store

    Once a month, Grandma, Alastia and I would trudge through the forest, following a narrow path to Burton's General Store. We passed two houses during the entire journey. The first was a small timbering one-room shanty, located about half a mile from Grandma's house. This was not occupied by a regular country settler. It had been placed there for workers when getting out the timber (usually this was mine props). After the timbering operation closed, migrant familes moved in and out. During this particular summer that I spent with Grandma, it was occupied by a family with several small children. The path took us right through their yard at the front door. Children seemed to be everywhere.

    A few miles down the path (long miles to my young legs), we passed the second residence. This one we did not come very close to and I was thankful for that. They had mean dogs that started barking when we came within sight and never stopped until we were long gone. Their house was a good, safe distance from our path and there was nothing but rocks behind the give-and-take fence. No grass, flowers, or trees. Perhaps it looked more bare and ugly than it really was because rumors were that the people living there were mean and had strange powers over people. It was told that they hid in the woods and robbed people. I do remember that one time, on our way back, someone tried to grab Grandma from the back. She hit back with her walking stick and they disappeared into the woods. We thought that we heard a few "rustles" in the bushes later. We practically ran all the way home. My stomach started "tying in knots" as we approached this house going and coming and I always breathed a sigh of relief when we were out of sight.

    The visit at Burton's store was always pleasant. They were raising a granddaughter and a foster daughter, my age, so I got with them while Grandma shopped. This was never done hurriedly. She bought salt, sugar, flour, cornmeal, baking soda, dried beans--the necessary staples and always her can of sardines and box of salt crackers. She ate the sardines on the way back. She teased us because we would have nothing to do with the dead fish with their insides still in them.

I can picture her now, breaking the key loose, inserting it and rolling the thin strip of metal back. She relished the sardines. My thoughts at that time were, "How do grown ups stand sardines and coffee?"

She always bought a nickel pack of Wrigleys Spearmint gum. That was the treat for Alastia and myself. I always wanted one of those big round suckers, displayed on a round cardboard, cherry red, purple grape, orange orange, yellow lemon, and lime green. The flavors were real. Grape was, and is, still my favorite. I never got up nerve to tell Grandma that I preferred a sucker to a stick of gum, but I must have had an ocassional penny for myself because I do remember those penny suckers and how good they tasted.

I would look at those suckers, tacked to the board, in all their magnificent colors and think that the nickel that paid for the gum would buy five, but I never said a word. (Children were to be seen and not heard). Of course, I enjoyed the gum, but those suckers were special!

Hair Rollers

We made our own hair rollers out of strips of tin cans, which we wrapped in several layers of paper from the Sears catalog. We used the glazed color pages as they were thicker. Alastia and I would get her brother Delmer to cut strips for us, then we would set about wrapping and rewrapping so that the sharp edges would not damage our hair. (They did).

We would wet strands of hair and wrap around the tin strip, then fold the ends to hold. Sometimes we would "put our hair up in rollers" and sleep in those uncomfortable things all week so that our hair would be curly on weekends. We all bragged that our hair was naturally curly. The truth came out when we were caught in a rainstorm when out for a Sunday stroll. All our hair came out straight and stringy except cousin Delmers, which had some natural curl.

Today I use the same concept in rolling my hair, however my rollers are made of soft pink foam rubber.

Molasses Making Time

This was the best time of the year--in the fall when the cane was ready. Lots of hard work and lots of fun. First, the leaves had to be stripped from the cane stalks. They had sharp points and could cut your arms and hands all over. We always wore long-sleeve shirts. After the stripping, the cane was cut with sharp knives like bayonets. The stalks were gathered about six to a pile as this was about the amount one person could carry.

It was carried and placed in piles near the juice mill. The mill and the copper bottom pan was usually "community" owned and made the rounds in the fall to all farmers who had raised cane. A long pole came out from the center of the mill where the horse would be hitched to and go round and round while someone was hunkered down in the center feeding the cane to the mill. A large washtub was placed under the drain to catch the juice.

Meanwhile the ditch was dug to place the pan on and the fire was built to start cooking the juice down. The pan was usually six to eight feet long. The bottom was thick copper with the sides and ends hammered over a very thick board. The ditch was dug just to fit the pan. Wet clay mud was plastered on all sides, which over the period of cooking had to be re-wet often.

Each time the washtub was filled, it was poured into the pan. The juice was very green and had to be "skimmed" all the time. A long wooden paddle was used to dip the frothy green stuff off and then scraped off with another paddle into a pre-dug hole beside the pan. After boiling half a day the skimmings started to become yellow and later golden. Then, we could cut pieces of cane and dip into the boiling mass and lick it off. Good!

When, finally it was determined by the chief molasses maker that the syrup was just right, four men would insert two poles into hangers that had been built into the pan and carefully lift off the fire and place in a level spot so that the hot molasses would not spill.

The molasses was then carefully strained through cheesecloth into jars. Sure was a sticky mess. This always happened after dark, so we had to work with lanterns. The next day, all jars had to be washed off before putting them away for the winter.

The young people played on the mountain of dry pulp. Teenagers played kissing games, sang songs, played French harps and generally had a good time. The nice thing about a "stir-off" was the the dating couples got to walk home together.

Molasses was really a staple in our diets in my generation, just fading out of the picture in the next generation. Sometimes, molasses was the only "sweetner" in the house. Very little refined sugar was bought.

Practically every farmer had a patch of cane and all helped one another when it came time to make the molasses. If a farmer did not have enough land to plant cane, he would arrange to trade work or other produce for his family's winter supply of molasses.

We had a lot of gatherings to make molasses taffy. It sure was fun pulling and stretching and getting the sticky stuff all over us.

Cousin Bob Allen used to help relatives during the molasses making time and at the end of the day, when all the hard work was done and the molasses had been poured into jars, they would tell him that he could pick out a jar to take home. He always picked the jar with the most foam on top because he liked it. They would laugh at him because later the foam (skimmings) would disappear and the jar would only be two-thirds full.

The picture below show the method used to extract the juice from the can. The tired old horse or mule had to go "round and round" all day. Guess he got dizzy. They did give them a rest and alternate. The person feeding the mill had to keep his head down and be very careful using his hands to feed the cane. There were accidents sometimes and a hand or part of an arm could be lost.

Stackpole Temple to Heaven

One summer when I was at Grandma Mills', a preacher had come into the area to build a church straight up to heaven. He picked the forks of the road where it went three ways and all traffic had to pass that way. This was a sandy bottom, level road where the branches from the trees met in the middle and shaded the road. It was almost like an umbrella over the road.

He kept on building and preaching every Sunday. He would put on his carpenter's nail apron, climb up to the last board that he had hammered in and proceed to nail another in a haphazard manner. He would be preaching all the time to the few who had gathered below. When he finished, he would come down and pass a hat for donations. I was always nervous and wanted to leave before he came down because I did not have a penny to put in the hat.

I don't know how long he stayed until he moved on but he never did get the building to reach heaven. It was good entertainment for all us kids and the dating couples who liked to walk up the road to see and listen to the "odd" preacher.

Respected Teacher

Clouney Harvey was my teacher from the fifth through the eighth grade. He was always old. He was tall and gaunt like Abraham Lincoln. He dressed in a blue serge suit that had been pressed so often that it shined and the creases were sharp enough to cut. He wore black, soft leather shoes which sometimes had patches sewn on top. He taught us that patches were honorable, dirt was not.

He did not allow children to make fun of others because they were not well dressed or had some physical flaw. He was very stern. His wood yardstick was sharply pointed due to poking the coal fire in the burnside stove. Any student busy throwing spitballs, passing notes, or being inattentive in any manner could expect that pointed end to sail through the air right at them.

He had a silver dollar that had been worn smooth in his pocket that he used to teach the sense of touch. He would have everyone in line close their eyes and pass the coin from hand to hand to see who would be first to determine what it was.

Except for written tests, each grade would line up against the wall beside his desk to recite. The other grades, seated were expected to continue with their study until it was their time to come forward.

Friday afternoon was "spelling bee" time. All students, regardless of grade were equally divided around the wall on two sides of the room. The Parental Teacher Association parents were sometimes present to observe since P.T.A. meetings were held in the afternoon before dark. When you missed a word, you sat down.

The correct speller got to "turn down" all those who had missed the word. Sometimes, you got to cross the room at the end of the line and turn down students on that side.

Some things you never forget. I remember that I once "turned down" several with the word "raisin". This was the only fun thing for the week and we really looked forward to Friday and the spelling bee.

Clouney Harvey and his wife raised two boys and ten girls. All became teachers at some time in their lives. One boy went west and became a literary critic. Dozens of grandchildren and great-grandchildren are still following the profession.

I had three of his daughters as teachers, Bonnie, Lillie and Pansy Woods, who celebrated her one hundredth birthday a few weeks ago. A few years ago, I stopped by her daughter's house, where she was recuperating from a hip injury. She told me that when her husband died, she had just given birth and that she took to her bed for eleven days. Recovering her strength and renewing her spirit, she got out of bed and started directing the farm. She said at the time, she thought, "How in the world am I going to feed six children," but said that never were they hungry and she added in an afterthought "unless they were waiting for it to get ready".

Clouney Harvey's students from that country school were prepared to face the world when they left. If not, it was not his fault.

No, we did not really like him. He was too tough. Looking back years later I realize that he was not in the business of teaching us to love him. He was in the education business, teaching, reading, writing, arithmetic and DISCIPLINE. He gave us a good, basic education in spite of ourselves and respect and love can blend.

July 1996

While researching in the Raleigh County Library, I came across the following: Clounie Lee Harvey, eighteen, born Mercer County, residing Mercer County and Leona A. Walker, fifteen, born Raleigh County. James W. Lilly married couple August 16, 1893, at the residence of C.C. Walker. (Their first daughter, Pansy Harvey Wood died August 5, 1996, at the age of 102.)

The Green Beads

Written for *The Briar Patch*

While reading the story, "How I Earned My First Dime", by Berna Crawford in the first edition of the *Briar Patch*, I was reminded of the green beads that I paid all of a dime for at the local G.C. Murphy 5 and 10 cents store. Was there ever such a time when you could buy something of value for one thin dime?

This was in the early 1930s. I don't think that Governor Kump's "temporary" (Never To Be Removed) sales tax had been passed. The best that I remember, if you had a dime to spend, you could spend it and not have to wait until you had a few pennies to go with it, or if it was in effect at that time, the first fifty cents was exempt. There was something about the store giving you a tax ticket if your purchase was over fifty-one cents, but under a dollar, so when you made an additional purchase up to a dollar you did not have to pay the tax again.

Mom had hired Norean, a girl a few years older than me to do the washing. There was lots of water to be carried and heated, a lot of rinsing, wringing and hanging to be done. I helped. When Mom paid Norean, she gave me a dime all my own to be spent the way I wanted. She also let both of us accompany her to Beckley on the shopping spree. She left us at the jewelry counter to make our selections. In those days they called beads and pearls "a strand". There was a marvelous selection of many strands hanging on wire hangers which required all to be removed to get to the one you wanted. I know that we drove the clerk crazy. We examined–we agonized–we looked. Only the BEST would do. It took us at least an hour to decide. Of course the clerk (yes, you had plenty then) had time to wait on several other customers during our trying time. Finally, I settled on a strand of dark green beads shaped and moulded like flowers with odd shaped long and round beads in between. They were ornate, lovely. One could spend hours looking at each bead to find the different shapes. Norean decided to make her purchase a strand of pink pearls. Oh, they were fine pearls. I remember when we were picking wild strawberries, we rested on the grass and carefully examined those pearls. Norean and another girl who was the proud owner of a strand of pearls were trying to decide who had the best. The pearls were either glass beads covered with a pearl-like exterior or some kind of hard wax dipped in a pearl mixture. The boys produced a knife and each girl took the tip and tried to scrape from inside the holes where they were strung. Norean's were some kind of hard wax. The pink coating was very thick as though the beads had been dipped several times, so hers were determined to be real cultured pearls. Norean has been gone now for several years and I wonder if the pink pearls lasted to the end.

I do not know what happened to the green beads, but I do know that they accompanied me on a journey in a little brown paper bag that my Daddy thought was our lunch.

Granny McComas sent word that she would like for me to come to Pinoak and spend the winter with her and go to school there. Well, that was a long ways, so Daddy decided to deliver me to Grandma Mills at Beeson and let them take me to Grannys later.

So we sent out early in the morning for a walk of some fifteen to twenty miles. Now, we did not follow the main road all the way. There were paths and shortcuts. On the other side of Bluff Mountain going downhill there was this ARTIE-FI-CIAL TURN (I never did find out why it was called this.) Perhaps because it was made by man. This went down around a curve and almost doubled back. If you were walking, you could just cut across and save some distance. The road was very rugged and just passable to vehicles at some times of the year. It was so easy to break an axle.

We had covered about half of our journey when we stopped at a clear stream. Daddy was carrying my suitcase with my clothes and I was hanging on to the brown bag for dear life. He said, "Let's rest a while and have our lunch that your mother fixed for us". Alas, all my bag contained was the green beads and a few other precious little girl things. I had left the bag of food on the table.

Daddy reasoned that we could just have a good refreshing drink of cold water and rest in the soft grass a while and guess we could make it on to Grandmas where we would be well fed. He must have understood the importance of the green beads to a little girl. He never scolded me at all.

The next day, the backs of my legs were so sore that I could hardly stand up. After resting a few days, my cousin Delmer delivered me on to Grannys at Pinoak. I suppose that I took my beads with me, but somehow I can never remember wearing them or what became of them. I wish I knew. I think that I could give an artist a description clear enough to duplicate.

I do know that owning those beads at that time in my life meant more to me than Jade or that other green stuff, (Emeralds) would at present.

That dime was hard earned and well spent.

Gloria Mills Mallamas
138 Sunrise Avenue
Beckley, West Virginia 25801

Pork and Bean Sandwiches

My nephew, Jeffrey Walker (son of my sister Lorena), visiting from Tucson, where he has lived for the past twenty-five years, related the following tale to me. Kerby and Fred Walker put all the boys in the car and started to Camp Creek to fish and swim. They stopped at the general store at Flat Top to buy picnic supplies as they planned to be gone all day. When both searched their pockets, they found that neither had brought their billfolds. They emptied their pockets of change and came up with enough to buy a big loaf of white bread and a large can of pork and beans.

They left the boys to swim and went fishing. When the children got hungry and were tired of playing in the water, they kept telling them that they were hungry. Kerby told them to play a little longer and let them fish. Finally, when he could put them off no longer, he took out his trusty pocket knife and cut the bean can open and made bean sandwiches for all. Jeffrey said they were so hungry that they relished the white bread and bean sandwiches. Best food they ever tasted!

Family Recipes

Dora Mae's Southern Corn Pone

4 cups corn meal　　1 Tbsp. salt
1/2 cup white sugar　4 cups boiling water

Place meal, sugar and salt in large bowl. Add boiling water and stir until smooth. Cover with cloth and let stand overnight.
In the morning, add:

1 cup flour　　　　　2 tsp. baking powder
1 cup buttermilk　　 1 tsp. baking soda, dissolved in a
2 eggs　　　　　　　little water

Melt 2 tablespoons butter in large iron skillet, then pour remaining butter into corn meal batter and mix well.
Place in preheated over at 460° for 15 minutes, then reduce heat to 350° and bake 45 minutes.
Remove from oven and turn out on wire rack to cool.

　　　This is an old-time recipe. You can eat it warm or cold and it is delicious sliced thin and buttered for oven toast.

My cousin Dora Mae Mills Richardson (Oley Mills' daughter) brings this to our annual family reunions at the cemetery and she bakes it in a Bundt cake pan and it looks just like a pound cake. We put the real food on one table and the desserts on another. Helpful hands keep transferring her corn pone to the dessert table. She always places a tub of butter beside the corn pone. One year, she could not make the reunion and she was told in the future if she found that she could not come, to bake the corn pone and send it!

It seems that Dora Mae and Emogene Mills (widow of Cousin Ernest Mills) had an agreement that Emogene was to bring the butter. One year, Emogene forgot and we just about banished her.

Emogene Mills' contribution to the annual cemetery picnic. They clamor for it!

Eclair Cake

1 large instant vanilla pudding	1 box graham crackers
1 large Cool Whip	3 cups milk

Mix pudding and milk, fold in Cool Whip. Butter 9x13" pan. Put layer of crackers in pan. Spread half of pudding mixture on crackers. Layer of crackers; then pudding. Top with crackers.

Chocolate Topping

1/4 cup milk	1 tsp. vanilla
1/4 stick of butter	1/3 cup cocoa
1 cup sugar	1/8 tsp. salt

Combine milk, sugar, cocoa, and salt. Boil 1 minute. Remove from heat. Add butter and vanilla. Cool and spread on top layer of crackers.

Cousin Emogene Mills always brings this dessert. She makes two and stores one in the cooler and brings it out when the first one disappears.

Hamburger Casserole
(is also on the menu)

1-1 1/2 lb. hamburger	1/2 lb. sausage
1 small onion, chopped	1/2 tp. minced garlic

2 cans beef gravy (or brown gravy)
1-1 1/2 cups biscuit mix or enough to put biscuits on top.

Brown hamburger and sausage and drain. Mix gravy as directed. Put meat mixture in greased 9x13" pan. Pour gravy over top. Make biscuit mix up stiff like drop biscuits. Drop very small biscuits all over top and bake. Bake at 425° until biscuits are brown. Serve while hot.

Emogene's Famous Pea Salad

1 can peas, drained
2 hard boiled eggs
onion (small-chopped)
1 medium cucumber
3 Tbsp. mayonnaise
Salt and pepper to taste

Drain peas, dice eggs, onion and cucumber. Mix all ingredients well. Let set several hours or overnight.

    The following are dishes that Margaret Mills (wife of Elmer Kelly Mills, grandson of Oley Mills) brings to our reunions-in the nineties.

Pumpkin Cake Roll

3 eggs
1 cup sugar
2/3 cup pumpkin
1 tsp. lemon juice
3/4 cup cake flour
1 tsp. baking powder
2 tsp. cinnamon
1 tsp. ginger
1/2 tsp. nutmeg
1/2 tsp. salt
1 cup chopped walnuts
powdered sugar

Beat eggs; add sugar to eggs. Stir pumpkin and lemon juice into mixture. Add all remaining ingredients except walnuts and powdered sugar. Spread mixture into greased and floured jellyroll pan (15x10x1'). Top with chopped walnuts. Bake at 375° for 15 minutes. Turn out on towel sprinkled with powdered sugar. Roll up and let cool. Unroll and spread with filling. Reroll and chill. Slice and serve. Freezes well.

Filling:

4 Tbsp. soft butter 2 (3oz.) cream cheese, beaten
1 cup powdered sugar 1/2 tsp. vanilla

Mix together and spread on cooled cake and reroll.

Peanut Butter Fingers

1/2 cup margarine
1/2 cup granulated sugar
1/2 cup brown sugar
1 unbeaten egg
1/3 cup peanut butter
1/2 tsp. vanilla
1/4 tsp. salt
1 cup sifted flour
1 cup quick oats
6 oz. pkg. semi-sweet chocolate pieces
1/2 tsp. baking soda

Cream butter and sugars together. Add egg, peanut butter and vanilla. Mix. Add salt, baking soda, flour and oats. Spread in

9x13" greased pan. Bake at 350°, 10-25 minutes. Remove from oven and sprinkle chocolate chips over immediately. Let stand 5 minutes, then spread melted chocolate evenly over top. Cool until chocolate hardens, then spread topping on top. Cut into oblong pieces.

Topping:
1 cup peanut butter, 2 cups confectionery sugar (sifted), 1/3 cup evaporated milk. (Mix small amounts at a time).

My little sister, Beulah insists that I mention her "specialty" which she spends so much time in preparing.
Here tis'
WATERMELON.
(Of course, I always take the molasses stack cake.)

Cousin, Fern Mills Walker's specialty is chicken and dumplings. She brings a large pot which is usually emptied. I am not giving the recipe because if you do not know how to make chicken and dumplings, you are not a relative and not a country girl and there is no use me wasting my time on you.

Grandma Mills' Molasses Stack Cake

Grandma used a small aluminum dish pan to mix her cake. She filled it about half full of flour, made a round cavern in the middle, poured some molasses in, added some buttermilk, two or three eggs, some soft lard, a little baking soda and started mixing. When she had worked enough flour into the liquid to make a stiff batter, she removed it to the rolling board.

She rolled the dough rather thin and then placed a plate on it and cut quickly around the edges. She would then flip it onto a big black baking pan like our cookie sheets, but with high sides (called bread pans) and pop it into the wood-burning cookstove. She could get two layers in each pan. When they were brown, she removed them and stacked them with applesauce or applebutter. The traditional way was with dried apples. She would soak the apples in water and cook until soft. This was really good and I think we could reproduce it with present-day dried apples, but they would be of a lighter color and probably not quite as flavorful. I have tried rolling the dough and cutting it with a plate, but I always tear it up when trying to get it on the pan.

Now, I will give you a simple recipe that you really can make and it tastes almost like the cakes made by our grandmothers, or at least people tell me that when I take them to our reunions.

(You will notice that Grandma did not include any spices. None in the batter-sometimes, cinnamon in the applesauce). If she was using dried apples, none was needed as there was plenty of flavor.

Molasses Stack Cake

1 cup butter or margarine   1 tsp. baking soda
1 cup sugar (leave out if you do not want that sweet)
1 cup molasses   1 tsp. salt (leave
3 eggs   out if on salt-free diet)
5 cups all-purpose flour   1 cup buttermilk
Apple sauce or applebutter

Cream together butter and sugar 'til light. Stir in molasses; add eggs, one at a time, beating after each. Stir together flour, soda, and salt; add to creamed mixture alternately with milk, beating after each addition. Cut wax paper rounds to fit 8-inch cake pans. Grease and flour. Pour 1 1/3 cup batter into each pan. (Refrigerate remaining batter). Bake at 350° until done, about 15 minutes. Remove from pans and cool on rack. Wash pans, grease and flour. Repeat with remaining batter. I usually only get 5 layers unless I make them very thin. I find that you can put the batter in the pans, sprinkle with flour and flour your hands and just pat it to the edges.

I use a quart of home-canned applesauce or applebutter when I have it. If not, add cinnamon and nutmeg and a little sugar to "store-boughten" applesauce and cook it down a little.

I really enjoyed slices of Grandma's cake and several glasses of cold, sweet milk out of the springhouse one Easter Sunday after walking hills and valleys all day and having nothing to eat until we came back in the evening. Cousin Delmer, his girlfriend, Cousin Alastia, several teenagers from the commu-

nity and I went to a farm located on a hill on the main road coming from Bluff Mountain to an Easter egg hunt. I can't remember the name of the people, but they were an aunt and uncle of Amacoe and Vernie Mills. It would be Akers if it was their mother's brother. They had two sons, who had hidden the eggs earlier, so naturally they found most of them. I either found one or someone gave me one. I was carrying a small compact that had had rouge in it. It had a mirror in the lid. My egg was not colored, so I got bits of the caked rouge out of the tiny compact and rubbed it on my egg. I carried the egg all day, but would not eat it, although I was very hungry. We went through paths and woods, never on the main roads. On our way, we went up a hill that was too steep for grazing cows–might have been good for goats. There was a rumor that someone had lost a fifty dollar bill on the hillside. If so, it was a windy hill and could have blown anywhere. We went all over that hill from top to bottom and side to side. Now, looking back, I believe the older kids just told us that so we would run our legs off. I was the youngest one along and my legs were getting mighty tired by the time we started home late in the evening.

    I don't know why I had worn a two-piece light green wool dress on a hot day. Guess it was because I thought it was pretty. Mom had bought the dress from Oda Walker's wife. She had had twins and had not gotten back to her previous weight, so had put some dresses in a trunk. I remember, she got them out, one by one for us to see and I just loved the light green one, so Mom got it for me. I had to be careful not to snag it on branches as we walked through paths in the woods.

    We were hot and tired and had blisters on our feet when we got back to Grandmas. She had made two of the stack cakes the night before and we did not wait for beans and cornbread to be heated up, we just dived into the cake and milk. I have never tasted anything better in all my life.

Grandma's Rhubarb Dumplings

Another favorite of mine was the rhubarb dumplings Grandma made in the spring for breakfast. She would go into the garden and cut a few stalks of the tender rhubarb (when it is young it has a lot of red), wash and cut them into small pieces and put them into a pot of water, with sugar added. Then she made regular dumplings as you would for chicken, dropped them into the boiling mixture and cooked until the dumplings were plump and done. Served with creamy country milk, we treasured this breakfast because we only got it a short time during the spring season.

Grandma's Wheat Cakes

Grandma made the wheat cakes in a crock. They were made with buckwheat flour, milk, eggs and a little shortening. She would put two long "fish fryers" (these were made of cast iron, oblong and with low sides) and pour two cakes in each. The two fryers covered the top of the stove. The wheat cakes were served with butter and molasses. I never tasted syrup as we have now. Sometimes a syrup was made by carmelizing sugar and then adding water and more sugar to make a light syrup.

She always left a cup or so of the batter in the crock for a starter the next day. I can remember her putting a plate to cover the crock and setting it aside.

They were never called pancakes or hotcakes, sometimes, flapjacks.

Most of the farmers grew a buckwheat patch and took the grain to the local miller to be ground into flour for the winter supply.

I remember her baking corn pone in a cast iron dutch oven with legs on the hot coals in the fireplace when she did not want to fire up the cook stove. This and some potatos baked in the coals, washed down with milk was sometimes our supper.

I remember in the spring going our into all the fields and picking narrow dock, lambsfeet and other wild greens, which we would have with onions, cornbread and beans for supper. It was good. She once had some renters with a big family in half of the house and sometimes they would beat us to the fields. Of course we did not need as much. The next day Mother Nature would have replenished the fields. Grandma would show us which greens to pick and at that time learned what was edible, but now I could not tell you.

Old Fashioned Stack Cake

1 cup firmly-packed brown sugar
1 cup shortening
1 cup molasses
1 cup buttermilk
2 eggs, beaten
7 cups apple butter
1 tsp. baking soda
1 tsp. ground ginger
dash of salt
5 1/2 cups all-purpose flour

Combine sugar, shortening and molasses; beat until smooth. Add buttermilk, eggs, ginger and salt; mix well. Add flour about one cup at a time, beating until just blended after each addition. (Do not overbeat). Divide dough into 10 portions on a greased cookie sheet and pat into a 10-inch circle. (Better to use cake pans–I line mine with wax paper, grease and flour, then when baked you can just dump the cake on a cooling rack and peel off the wax paper, put your cake pans in cold water, wash and do the same thing over until all the batter is used). I cut out wax paper ahead of time the size of my cake pans and store between two pieces of cardboard. Do this when you have nothing else to do and it will save time when assembling this cake. Bake at 350° for 5 to 8 minutes. Remove to a cooling rack. Stack the layers spreading about 2/3 cup apple butter between the layers. I cook apple sauce with extra sugar, cinnamon and nutmeg added until thick and a light shade of red when I do not have apple sauce that I have canned. This is much better than the apple butter from the grocery store. If you can get apple butter from craft shows that is stirred outside in a big copper pot, then do it. It is about like our homemade apple butter.

One Egg Cake

A good-and-easy butter cake

2 cups sifted cake flour
1 1/3 cups sugar
2 1/2 tsp. baking powder
1 tsp. salt
1/3 cup butter
1 tsp. vanilla
1 cup milk
1 large egg

Heat oven to 350°. Grease well and dust with flour 2 round layer pans, 8x1 1/2" or 1 square pan 9x9x1 3/4".
Sift dry ingredients into bowl. Cut in butter. Add 2/3 of milk. Add vanilla. Beat 2 minutes, medium speed. Add remaining milk

and egg. Beat 2 more minutes. Batter will be thin. Pour into prepared pans. Bake layers 25 to 30 minutes, square 30 to 35, until top springs back when lightly touched.

I make a frosting with a little butter, milk and confectioners sugar and a tablespoon of rum. This makes a light cake and excellent to use for an upside down pineapple, peach or other fruit cake. The texture of this cake makes it perfect for birthday or wedding cakes.

Since there are only 2 cups of flour, this makes two small layers. I sometimes bake in a large cake pan in just one layer, cool, then cut and put custard, or cream filling between and seven-minute icing on top. I also make Beulah's customary strawberry birthday cake this way.

Milky Way Cake

8 small Milky Way bars	1/2 tsp. salt
2 sticks margarine	1/2 tsp. soda
2 cups sugar	1 1/4 cups buttermilk
4 eggs	1 cup chopped pecans
2 1/2 cups all-purpose flour	1 tsp. vanilla

Chop candy bars; combine with one stick margarine in top of double boiler; heat over hot water until melted, then set aside. Cream sugar with remaining stick of margarine add eggs and beat until light and fluffy. Combine flour and salt. Stir soda into buttermilk; add alternately with flour, beating smooth after each addition. Stir in nuts, vanilla and melted candy-margarine mixture. Pour into lightly-greased tube pan or 3-eight" layer pans. In tube pan bake at 275° for 1 hour and 10 minutes. For layer pans bake 30 to 35 minutes at 350°.

Frosting:

2 1/2 cups sugar	1 cup evaporated milk
1 package (six ounces) semi-sweet chocolate chips	
1 cup marshmallow creme	1 stick margarine

Combine sugar and milk in saucepan; cook to softball stage. Add chocolate chips, marshmallow creme and margarine; stir until melted and thoroughly blended. Cool; spread on cake.

If you do not like fruitcake for Christmas, this one is a good substitute. The Mayonnaise cake, the fruit cocktail cake and this Milky Way Cake were very popular when the recipes first came out and I have had people ask me if I still have them, so I looked through piles of clippings and found them. I have never found them in a regular cookbook, although I have something over a hundred old and new cookbooks.

Indian Cake

4 cups apples	2 tsp. soda
2 cups sugar	1 tsp. salt
1 cup cooking oil	2 tsp. vanilla
2 eggs	3 cups flour
1 tsp. nutmeg	1 cup chopped nuts
1 tsp. cinnamon	

Pare and chop apples finely. Cover with sugar and let stand at least 1 hour. Add oil, eggs, nutmeg, cinnamon, soda, salt, vanilla, flour and nuts. Bake at 350° for 50 minutes.

Golden Spice Cake

2 2/4 cups sifted pastry flour	1/4 tsp. nutmeg
1 tsp. soda	1/2 cup butter
1/2 tsp. salt	1 cup sugar
1/2 tsp. cloves	1 egg, well beaten
1/2 tsp. cinnamon	1 Tbsp. molasses
1 cup buttermilk	

Sift flour once, measure, add baking soda, salt, and spices. Sift together again. Work butter with spoon until creamy. Add sugar gradually, beating until light and fluffy. Add egg and molasses. Blend well. Add flour, alternately with milk, a small amount at a time, beating until smooth after each addition. Turn into greased loaf pan (6x10x2") and bake in moderate oven (350°) 45 to 50 minutes. Frost with butter frosting.
(Or throw all ingredients into the mixer bowl and beat well, dry ingredients with butter first, then adding milk, molasses and egg).

West Virginia Jam Cake

2 cups sugar	1 tsp. soda
1 cup shortening	1 cup chopped nuts (black WV walnuts)

3 eggs	1 cup raisins
1 cup buttermilk	1 cup ground coconut
1 cup berry jam	large apple, grated
3 cups sifted flour	Chopped dates (optional)

Cream sugar and shortening; add eggs and beat well. Combine buttermilk and jam; add alternately with sifted flour and soda, beat well. Add nuts, fruits and coconut; stir until well distributed through batter. Bake in 3x9" layer pans for 30 to 40 minutes at 350°.

(If black walnuts are not available, use pecans or other nuts and add 1/2 teaspoon black walnut flavoring.)

Filling:

2 cups sugar	1 cup chopped nuts
2 Tbsp. flour	1 cup chopped raisins
1 1/2 cups sweet milk	1 cup grated coconut
1 cup butter, or margarine	1 cup grated apples

Mix sugar and flour together; add milk and butter and cook until thick, stirring occasionally. Remove from heat; add nuts, fruit and coconut. Spread between layers, on top and sides of cake. Decorate with maraschino cherries if desired.

This makes a magnificent cake–something to be proud to take to a reunion.

Carrot Walnut Raisin Cake

2 1/2 cups walnuts, divided	3 eggs
1 1/4 cups sifted all-purpose flour	1 cup granulated sugar
1 tsp. salt	1 cup vegetable oil
1 tsp. baking soda	3 cups grated carrots
1 tsp. baking powder	1 1/2 cups raisins

Drop walnuts into boiling water; boil 5 minutes. Drain well; spread in shallow pan. Toast at 350° for 15 to 20 minutes, until golden brown, stirring often. Set aside 1/2 cup of halves and large pieces for decoration. Chop remainder coarse. Resift flour with salt, baking soda and baking powder. Beat eggs; beat in sugar and oil. Add flour mixture; mix to smooth batter. Stir in carrots, raisins and chopped walnuts. Turn into greased 10" tube pan. Remove from pan and spread with cream cheese frosting. Decorate with walnut pieces.

Cream Cheese Frosting:
1 pkg. (3oz.) cream cheese, at room temperature
1/2 cup soft butter
3 cups sifted confectioners' sugar
1 tsp. vanilla, brand or lemon extract
Cream all together.

Carrot Cake with Cream Cheese Icing

Makes 10 servings.

2 cups all-purpose flour	1 cup granulated sugar
2 tsp. ground cinnamon	3 large eggs
1 tsp. baking powder	2/3 cup milk
1/4 tsp. salt	3 medium carrots, grated
2/3 cups softened butter	1/2 cup coarsely-chopped walnuts

Icing:
1/2 cup (1 stick) butter- softened
4 ounces cream cheese
1 tsp. vanilla extract
2 1/2 cups confectioners' sugar

Topping:
1/4 cup finely-chopped walnuts
2 Tbsp. light brown sugar

1. Preheat over to 350°. Grease a 9" round cake pan. Dust with flour; tap out excess.
2. Mix together flour, cinnamon, baking powder, and salt.
3. Beat together butter and sugar at medium speed until light and fluffy. Add eggs, one at a time, beating well after each addition. At low speed, alternately beat flour mixture and milk into butter mixture. Stir in carrots and nuts. Pour batter into prepared pan.
4. Bake cake until top springs back lightly touched and a toothpick inserted in center comes out clean, 40 minutes. Transfer pan to a wire rack to cool for 10 minutes. Turn cake out onto rack to cool completely.
5. Prepare icing, beat together butter and cream cheese at medium speed until completely smooth. Beat in vanilla. Beat in confectioners' sugar until well blended. To prepare topping, mix together nuts and brown sugar.

6. Place cake on a serving plate. Spread icing on top and sides. Sprinkle with nut mixture.
If desired, icing can be omitted. Instead, dust top of cake with confectioners' sugar.

Sour Cream Pound Cake

2 3/4 cups sugar	1/4 tsp. baking soda
1 cup butter or margarine	1 cup dairy sour cream
6 eggs	1/2 tsp. lemon extract
3 cups sifted all-purpose flour	1/2 tsp. orange extract
1/2 tsp. salt	1/2 tsp. vanilla

In mixer bowl, cream together sugar and butter or margarine until light and fluffy. Add eggs, one at a time, beating well after each addition. Sift together flour, salt, and soda. Add to creamed mixture alternately with sour cream, beating after each addition. Add extracts and vanilla; beat well. Pour batter into greased and floured 10" tube pan. Bake in 350° for 1 1/2 hours or until cake tests done. Cool 15 minutes. Remove from pan. When cool, frost or sprinkle with confectioners' sugar, if desired.

Applesauce Spice Cake

2 1/2 cups all-purpose flour	1/2 tsp. ground allspice
2 cups sugar	1 16-ounce can (1 1/2 cups)
1 1/2 tsp. salt	applesauce
1 1/2 tsp. baking soda	1/2 cup shortening
1/4 tsp. baking powder	1/2 cup water
3/4 tsp. ground cinnamon	2 eggs
1/2 tsp. ground cloves	1 cup raisins
1/2 cup chopped walnuts	

In mixer bowl, sift together flour, sugar, salt, soda, baking powder, cinnamon cloves, and allspice. Add applesauce, shortening, and water; beat 2 minutes. Add eggs; beat 2 minutes more. Stir in raisins and nuts. Pour batter into two greased and floured 9x5x3-inch loaf pans. Bake in 350° oven for 55 to 60 minutes. Good to eat one now and freeze one for later.

Mayonnaise Cake

1 cup mayonnaise
1 cup cold water
1 tsp. vanilla
2 cups flour

1 cup sugar
2 tsp. soda
4 Tbsp. cocoa

    Combine mayonnaise, water and vanilla. Sift together flour, sugar, soda and cocoa. Add to mayonnaise mixture; mix thoroughly. Pour into 2 greased 8" cake pans; bake at 350° for 30 to 35 minutes.

Fruit Cocktail Cake

1 No. 303 can fruit cocktail
2 cups sugar
2 cups self-rising flour

2 tsp. baking soda
pinch of salt
1 egg

    Mix dry ingredients. Add fruit cocktail, then add egg. Beat well. Pour into a greased 9x13" pan. Bake for 35 minutes at 350°. Cool in pan.

Topping:

1 stick margarine
1 cup sugar, granulated
1/2 cup canned milk

1 tsp. vanilla
1/2 cup coconut
1/2 cup chopped pecans

Cook margarine, sugar and milk 10 minutes until thick. Remove from heat. Add coconut and pecans and vanilla. Mix well. Spread over warm cake.

Hurricane Oatmeal Cake

1 cup oatmeal
1 1/4 cups boiling water
2 eggs
1 cup granulated sugar
1 cup brown sugar

1/2 cup vegetable oil
1/2 cup flour
1 tsp. soda
1 tsp. salt
1 tsp. cinnamon

    Combine oatmeal, boiling water, set aside. Beat together eggs, two sugars, and oil until blended. Add sifted flour, soda, salt and cinnamon; add oatmeal. Pour into greased 13x9" baking pan. Bake at 350° for 30 to 36 minutes.

Topping:
1 cup coconut 1/2 cup chopped pecans
1 cup brown sugar 1/4 cup evaporated milk
6 Tbsp. melted shortening

    Mix all topping ingredients together until moist. Spread over cake; broil until topping is light brown and crunchy, about 2 minutes.

Bride's Orange Butter Cake

1 cup butter 2 cups sifted sugar
1 cup milk 1/2 tsp. salt
3 1/2 cups cake flour 4 level tsp. baking powder
1 tsp. vanilla 1 tsp. orange flavoring
6 eggs whites

    Cream butter, add sugar gradually. Cream until smooth. Sift flour, measure, and sift with baking powder and salt. Add, alternately with milk (flour first) to first mixture. Add flavorings. Fold in stiffly-beaten egg whites. Pour into 2 well-oiled 9" cake pans. Bake in moderate (350°) about 35 minutes.

    Cover with white butter icing. Decorate with colored rosebuds, or use seven-minute icing and sprinkle with a can of angel-flake coconut.

Chocolate Cake

    Years ago, chocolate cake was yellow layers with chocolate frosting. A cake that was chocolate was devil's-food cake.

1/4 cup margarine or butter 3 1/2 cups all-purpose flour
2 cups sugar 2 1/2 tsp. baking powder
1 tsp. vanilla or 1/2 tsp. lemon extract
3 eggs 1/2 tsp. baking soda
1 3/4 cups buttermilk

Beat margarine or butter in a large mixer bowl on medium speed of electric mixer for 30 seconds or until softened. Add sugar and vanilla or lemon extract. Beat until well combined.

Add eggs, one at a time, beating well after each. Stir together flour, baking powder and baking soda. Add to creamed mixture alternately with buttermilk, beating just 'til combined. Spread batter in greased 13x9x2" baking pan. Bake in a 350° oven for 40 to 45 minutes. Cool and frost with fudge frosting.

Fudge Frosting:

4 3/4 cups sifted powdered sugar 1/3 cup boiling water
1/2 cup unsweetened cocoa powder 1 tsp. vanilla
1/2 cup margarine or butter, softened

Mix powdered sugar and cocoa. Add margarine, boiling water and vanilla. Beat with an electric mixer on low speed until combined. Beat 1 minute on medium speed. Cool and frost cake.

Buttermilk Pound Cake

1 cup margarine   2 cups sugar
4 unbeaten eggs   1 tsp. lemon extract
1/4 tsp. mace   3 cups flour
1/2 tsp. soda   3/4 tsp. salt
1/2 tsp. baking powder   1 cup buttermilk
1 tsp. vanilla

Cream margarine (or butter if used) and sugar. Add eggs, one at a time. Add milk and sifted dry ingredients alternately beating well but not long. (You get more volume by working quickly and not overbeating.) Bake 1 hour in well-greased, floured tube pan in 325° over.

Santa Claus Fruit Cake

This is a recipe that I got from a magazine over fifty years ago. I made several for all the family before Christmas. My brother-in-law, Kerby Walker, used to hide his and dole out. He said that it was so good that you could sit in front of the fire, eat cake and pat your foot.

1 cup buttermilk   1/2 lb. raisins
2 cups sugar   1/2 lb. blanched almonds
1 cup butter   1/2 lb. English walnuts
2 1/2 cups flour   1/2 lb. pecans
6 eggs   2 cups candied pineapple
1 tsp. soda   2 cups candied red cherries
1/2 cup candied citron   1/4 cup lemon peel
1/4 cup orange peel   1 can angel-flake coconut

Cream the butter and sugar. Add egg yolks. Mix soda

with half of the flour, add alternately with the buttermilk. Toss flour over cut up fruits and nuts and add last. Fold in the well-beaten egg whites.

Bake in tube cake pan at 350° for about 1 hour. Test for doneness and do not let get too brown.

Take out of oven and place on wire rack. Pour the juice of 2 oranges and 1 lemon and 1 cup of sugar (which has been boiled to a light syrup) over and let cool. Store in tight container in refrigerator. This is more like a confection than a cake.

When I first made these cakes, I blanched my own almonds and grated a fresh coconut. I do think it was better. One could add hot water to already blanched almonds so they would not be dry.

In the magazine this recipe was given in cents worth of citron, candied pineapple etc. I had to work on it and arrive at the proper amounts.

Orange Nut Cake

1 cup sugar	1 cup sour cream (or 1 cup canned milk with 1 1/2 tsp. vinegar)
1/2 cup Crisco	
2 eggs (separated)	1 level tsp. soda in sour cream or milk
1 tsp. baking powder	1 cup nuts (chopped) 1 tsp. grated orange rind

Cream Crisco and sugar; add egg yolks and beat well; add flour and baking powder alternately with milk or cream and soda. Stir in orange rind and nuts. Last, fold in stiffly-beaten egg whites. Bake in stem (tube pan) for 45 minutes at 350°. (Preheat oven.)

When done, remove from oven and pour following mixture over cake and let cool in pan.

1/2 cup orange juice   3/4 cup sugar

Bring this to a boil before pouring over cake.

This cake is delicious and quite moist. For a party, it can be served with whipped cream.

Banana Cake

3/4 cup shortening
1 1/2 cups sugar
3 eggs, beaten
1 cup sour cream
1 tsp. vanilla
1 tsp. baking soda

2 cups flour
1/2 tsp. salt
2 bananas, mashed
1 cup chopped nuts
1/2 cup chocolate chips

Preheat oven to 375°. Cream together shortening and sugar, mixing well. Add beaten eggs, sour cream and vanilla.

Sift together baking soda, flour and salt; add to creamed mixture. Beat until creamy. Add bananas, nuts and chocolate chips and mix. Bake in a 15x10" pan for 45 minutes.

Hint: To keep nuts and chocolate chips from drifting to the bottom of the pan, sift a little flour over them before adding them to the mixture.

Tex-Mex Sheet Cake

1 cup butter or margarine
1/4 cup cocoa
1 Tbsp. instant coffee
1 cup water
1 1/2 cups firmly-packed light brown sugar
2 cups unsifted flour
1 tsp. baking soda

1 tsp. ground cinnamon
1/2 tsp. salt
1/3 cup sweetened condensed milk

2 eggs
1 tsp. vanilla extract

Preheat oven to 350°. In small saucepan, melt butter; stir in cocoa and coffee, then water. Bring to a boil; remove from heat. In larger mixer bowl, combine sugar, flour, baking soda, cinnamon and salt; add cocoa mixture. Beat well. Mix in condensed milk, eggs and vanilla. Pour into lightly greased 15 by 10-inch jelly roll pan. Bake 15 minutes or until cake springs back when lightly touched. Spread with Tex-Mex Frosting. Cool before serving.

Tex-Mex Frosting:
1/4 cup butter or margarine
1/4 cup cocoa
1 Tbsp. instant coffee
1/2 cup toasted slivered almonds

1 cup sweetened condensed milk
1 cup confectioners sugar

In small saucepan, melt butter, stir in cocoa and coffee. Remove from heat. Add condensed milk. Stir in sugar, then nuts. Spread on warm cake.

Gloria's Christmas Orange-Coconut Layered Cake

2 and 1/3 cups sifted cake flour   1 tsp. salt
1 1/2 cups sugar   1/2 cup Crisco
2 tsp. double acting baking powder   1/4 tsp. baking soda
Grated rind of orange (about 1 tsp.)

Sift dry ingredients into mixer bowl, add shortening and orange rind. Beat at slow speed until shortening is cut into mixture.

Measure into measuring cup 1/4 cup unstrained orange juice and 3/4 cup water or milk.

Add this to dry ingredients slowly with mixer on slow to medium speed for 2 minutes.

Add 2 medium eggs and beat 2 more minutes. Batter should be light and fluffy.

Pour batter into prepared pans, 2 round layer 8" pans. (I grease pans with Crisco, line with waxed paper (bottoms only) then flour the pans).

Bake about 30 minutes with oven temperature at 350°.

Remove from oven, place on wire racks to cool 5 minutes, then run knife around edges, turn out on wire rack and peal the wax paper off.

Put layers together with cream filling and frost with boiled frosting, or 7 minute double boiler type, if that is what you do best. Scatter a can of angel flake or southern-style shredded coconut over top and sides.

Decorate with red and green colored coconut-tree design, Santa, or your favorite Christmas design.

This cake, displayed on a pedestal-type cake server will take care of your table centerpiece decoration.

Since my husband did not like a lot of sweet icing on a cake, I built this one to his specifications and it has been a hit with our family for years not only for Christmas, but all birthdays, Easter and other special occasions.

Boiled Icing:

1 1/2 cups sugar	1/8 tsp. cream of tartar
3/4 cup boiling water	2 eggs whites, stiffly-beaten (reserve the yolks for the filling).

Combine sugar, water, and cream of tartar. Stir until dissolved. Boil to softball stage, or until a little mixture dropped in beating constantly over egg whites. Beat until thick and creamy. Should stand in peaks.

Cream Filling:

3/4 cup sugar	1/3 cup flour
1/8 tsp. salt	2 egg yolks, beaten
2 cups milk	grated rind of orange
2 Tbsp. butter	

Combine sugar, salt, flour and egg yolks. Add milk slowly, stirring constantly. Cook over low heat until thick and smooth. Stir in butter. Put between layers of cake and stick toothpicks through layers so that they will not slide off. Finish off with the icing and shredded coconut.

Orange Syrup Cake

Beat well 4 eggs, add 2 cups sugar and 2 cups flour. (Sift flour and measure, then sift again). Over low heat, melt 1/4 lb. of butter, add 1 cup of milk. Let cool to lukewarm. Add 1/2 tsp. vanilla, sprinkle over batter 2 tsp. baking powder. Fold into mixture. Do not beat. Grease and flour baking tins. Fill tins about two-thirds full. Bake at 450° for about 11 minutes, until golden brown.

Syrup:

1 1/2 cups sugar, juice of 2 oranges. Grate lightly the orange peel, then juice it. Do one lemon the same way.

Dip hot cakes quickly into juice and drain. After draining, sprinkle with confectioners sugar.

These tiny cakes can be arranged on lace doiles, stacked in pyramids, or use your imagination.

A cousin came to my house and helped me make these for a special party. I have a very large round aluminum tray which we covered with lace doilies and arranged on each 7" doily. It was lacy and very beautiful. It would be good to serve at a wedding. These are to be baked in tiny "gem" pans-12 to a pan. The batter is very thin.

Hot Water Pastry

1 cup shortening
1/2 cup boiling water
1 tsp. salt
2 tsp. baking powder
3 cups flour

Pour boiling water over shortening. Stir until melted and creamy. (Who says oil and water won't mix?) Cool-not in refrigerator. Sift dry ingredients together and add to shortening mixture. Mix well. Refrigerate to stiffen. Roll and use as other pastry. May be kept in refrigerator for several days. (If soft, do not add flour; let stand in refrigerator.)

This was my mother's recipe and the only recipe she or I used for pie crust–always good.–Olive Marrical–Charleston, Beckley, now California.

Molasses Pecan Pie

3 eggs, slightly beaten
1/4 cup molasses
3/4 cup light corn syrup
2 Tbsp. butter, melted
1/8 tsp. salt
1 tsp. vanilla
1 Tbsp. flour
1 cup pecans
1 unbaked 8" pastry shell

Combine eggs, molasses, corn syrup, melted butter, salt and vanilla in mixing bowl. Make a paste of a small amount of mixture and flour, stir into remaining mixture. Add pecans. Turn into unbaked pastry shell. Bake in 325° over about 1 hour or until firm.

Creamy Pumpkin Pie

1/2 cup sugar
1 tsp. cinnamon
1/2 tsp. nutmeg
1/4 tsp. cloves
2 eggs
1-9" unbaked pastry shell
1/2 cup molasses
2 cups strained pumpkin
1 can (14 1/2 ounces) evaporated milk
1/2 tsp. ginger
1/2 tsp. salt

Mix sugar and remaining dry ingredients. Stir in molasses, then pumpkin and evaporated milk. Separate one egg. Beat yolk with remaining whole egg and stir into pumpkin mixture. Beat white until stiff but not dry with rotary beater and fold into pumpkin mixture. Pour into unbaked pie shell. Bake at 400°, 40 to 50 minutes or until knife inserted into center comes out clean.

Molasses-Pumpkin Pie

This is a quick recipe. Since pumpkin and molasses were in good supply "in the old days" cooks made good use of them. In a mixing bowl combine 2 cups masked, cooked pumpkin, or 1-16 ounce can pumpkin, 2 cups milk, 3 eggs, 1/2 cup packed brown sugar, 1/2 cup molasses, 2 teaspoon ground cinnamon, 1/2 teaspoon ground ginger and 1/2 teaspoon salt. Beat mixture until well blended. Pour into unbaked 10" pastry shell with edges crimped high. Bake in 400° till knife inserted off-center comes out clean, about 40 to 50 minutes. Serve plain or with whipped cream.

Jason Jarrett's Favorite Apple Pie

From the desk of Jason Jarrett, I bring you his favorite apple pie. My niece, Linda Jarrett, is a good cook and baker. Several years ago she gave me the recipe for the following apple pie which is her son Jason's favorite. I have eaten the pie at her house and can attest to his good taste.
Here goes:
3 pounds (about 10 medium) tart apples
1 1/4 cups sugar
1/8 tsp. salt
1 small lemon, sliced
1/4 cup water
1 Tbsp. flour and 1/2 tsp. cinnamon blended with small amount of water
1 Tbsp. butter, or margarine
Pastry for 2 crust 9" pie, chilled
1 egg yolk beaten with 1 Tbsp. milk
Peel apples, cut in eighths and core. Combine sugar, salt, lemon and water in large skillet. Cover and cook over low heat until sugar starts to dissolve. Add apples a few at a time in single layers and simmer covered until tender (do not overcook), 5 to 7 minutes. Remove with slotted spoon to plate or waxed paper to

cool. When all apples are done, discard lemon. Stir flour cinnamon mixture into syrup and cook until thickened and smooth and reduced to about 1/2 cup. Stir in butter and cool. Place apples in pastry-lined pie plate and add syrup. Cover with top crust, slit, trim edges and flute firmly. Brush with egg yolk mixture. Bake in lowest rack in preheated oven at 400° about 40 minutes or until golden brown. Serve slightly warm or preheated.

This pie is made different from the standard apple pie and is a little more trouble, but it is worth it. Use your favorite pie crust recipe or Crisco crust for "Real Apple Pie".

Real Apple Pie

Crisco Crust: (use 9" pie plate)
2 cups all-purpose flour
1 Tbsp. sugar
1 tsp. sugar
11 Tbsp. butter-flavored Crisco shortening
5-6 Tbsp. water (ice)
1/2 tsp. salt
1 egg
3-4 Tbsp. milk

Combine flour, salt, and sugar in mixing bowl. Cut in shortening with pastry blender or 2 knives until mixture is uniform. Sprinkle with water, 1 Tbsp. at a time; toss lightly with fork. When all the water has been added, work dough into a firm ball. Divide dough into 2 parts and refrigerate for 3 hours.

Preheat oven to 400°. For apple filling, combine all of the ingredients in a large mixing bowl and toss lightly until apple slices are completely coated.

On a lightly-floured board roll bottom crust into a circle 1/8-inch thick and about 1 1/2 inches larger than inverted pie plate. Gently ease dough into pie plate, being careful not to stretch the dough. Trim edge evenly with pie plate. Spoon filling into unbaked pastry shell.

Moisten pastry edges with water. Roll top crust and cut small round hole in the middle to allow steam to escape.

Apple Filling:
5-6 large Rambo autumn apples, peeled and sliced
2 Tbsp. tapioca
1/8 tsp. nutmeg
1/4 tsp. cinnamon
1 tsp. vanilla extract
1/2 to 1 cup brown sugar (depending on apples' tartness)

2 Tbsp. butter, melted   1 Tbsp. real lemon juice
This is a prize winner!

Chocolate Cream Pie

This is really a good chocolate pie. Those who make chocolate pie from a "mix" will never do so again once they try this recipe and see how a real chocolate pie should taste! (And it is easy to make, too).

3 Tbsp. cocoa   3 Tbsp. flour
3/4 cup sugar   2 cups milk, 1 cup of which
Yolks of 3 eggs   should be canned evaporated
Dash of salt   milk-undiluted
1 tsp. vanilla   1 baked 8" pie shell
1 cup heavy cream, whipped   2 Tbsp. butter

Mix the dry ingredients with a little of the milk until smooth; add rest of the milk and cook over boiling water until thick and about the consistency of mayonnaise. Beat the egg yolks slightly, add to them about 3 tablespoons of the chocolate mixture, stir and return to pan; stir well and cook a few minutes more.

Remove from heat, stir in butter and vanilla and cool a bit. Pour into pie shell. When completely cool, top with the whipped cream-unsweetened and refrigerate until serving time. If you plan to take this to the reunion picnic, use the three egg whites to make a meringue and brown slightly in a moderate oven.

Mom's specialty was butterscotch pie. She made the best ever. She browned white sugar in a black cast iron skillet, added water to make a syrup, then added milk, eggs, a little flour and a big chunk of butter. Stirred it and cooked it rapidly. She really didn't measure, so I cannot give you her exact recipe. I did find a recipe that matches hers in taste.

"Real Butterscotch Pie"
BROWN THAT BUTTER!

6 Tbsp. butter	1/2 tsp. salt
1 cup dark brown sugar	1 2/3 cup milk
1 cup boiling water	3 egg yolks
3 Tbsp. corn starch	1 tsp. vanilla
2 Tbsp. flour	9 inch baked pie shell

Melt butter in heavy skillet over low heat. When butter is golden brown, add brown sugar. Boil until foamy, 2-3 minutes, stirring constantly. Stir in boiling water; remove from heat.

In sauce pan, mix cornstarch, flour and salt. Stir in milk gradually until smooth. Stir in brown sugar mixture. Cook over low heat, stirring constantly. Boil 1 minute. Remove from heat. Stir a little of hot mixture into slightly-beaten egg yolks. Then blend it all back into hot mixture in saucepan. Boil 1 minute longer. Remove from heat. Blend in vanilla. Cool, stirring occasionally. Pour into pie shell. Chill.

Top with meringue made of the 3 egg whites beaten until stiff with 3 tablespoons of white sugar added. Brown lightly in oven.

Sweet Milk Doughnut Dough For Fried Apple Pies

1 cup sugar	1 tsp. salt
2 Tbsp. melted shortening	3 tsp. baking powder
2 eggs, slightly beaten	1/2 tsp. cinnamon
1 cup milk	1/2 tsp. nutmeg
1/2 tsp. vanilla flavoring	1/8 tsp. ginger
4 3/4 cups flour	1/2 tsp. lemon flavoring

Combine eggs and sugar, blend carefully. Sift flour, measure and sift with salt, baking-powder, and spices. Add alternately with combined milk, shortening, and flavorings to first mixture. Chill dough. Turn onto lightly-floured board and roll in sheet 1/2-inch thick. Cut with biscuit cutter. Roll each into a circle, put tablespoon (or more if circle is large) in center and fold over, pinch edges to seal and fry until golden brown in hot oil or Crisco, turning once.

Remove to platter, covered with paper towel–dot tops with paper towel to soak up extra oil–sift confection or regular sugar over tops, if desired.

Molasses Drop Cookies

1/2 cup shortening
1 cup sugar
2 eggs, well beaten
1/2 cup milk
1/2 cup molasses
3 cups sifted flour
3 tsp. baking powder
1/2 tsp. salt
1 tsp. ground cinnamon
1/2 tsp. ground cloves
3/4 cups seeded raisins, cut fine

1. Cream shortening, add the sugar gradually, creaming until light and fluffy.
2. Add eggs, then the milk, molasses and raisins.
3. Sift flour, baking powder, salt and spices and add to creamed mixture, beating until smooth.
4. Drop by teaspoonfuls on greased baking sheet 1 inch apart and bake in moderate oven (350°) 10 to 12 minutes. Makes 4 dozen cookies.

Secret Treat Molasses Cookies

1/2 cup butter or margarine, softened
1/2 cup packed brown sugar
1 egg
1/2 tsp. ground cinnamon
1/2 tsp. ground ginger
1/2 cup strawberry pre serves
1/2 tsp. salt
3/4 tsp. baking soda
1/2 cup molasses
2 1/2 cups all-purpose flour

Glaze:
1-2/3 cups confectioner's sugar
1/4 tsp. vanilla extract
2 Tbsp. water

In a large mixing bowl, cream butter and sugar. Add egg; mix well. Beat in molasses. Combine flour, baking soda, salt, cinnamon and ginger; add to creamed mixture and mix well. (The dough will be very stiff.) Cover and chill several hours or overnight. On a lightly-floured surface, roll dough to 1/8" thickness. Cut into 2 1/4" to 2 1/2" circles. Place 1/2 tsp. preserves on the circles; top with remaining circles. Pinch edges together to seal. Place on greased baking sheets. Bake at 350° for 10 minutes or until lightly browned. Cool on a wire rack. Combine glaze ingredients and frost cooled cookies. Yield: 4 dozen. If cooking for two: freeze unfrosted cookies in airtight containers or freeze bags.

They will keep for several months.

These cookies are good for special occasions. They're fun to decorate and delicious to eat, with a "surprise" flavor inside.

Soft Molasses Cookies

1 cup molasses	1 tsp. soda
1 cup shortening	1/2 tsp. salt
1/2 cup sugar	1 1/2 tsp. cinnamon
1/2 cup mashed potatoes	1 1/2 tsp. ginger
1/2 cup buttermilk	4 cups flour

Heat molasses and add shortening. Cool slightly and add sugar, mashed potatoes and milk. Mix and sift 2 cups flour with other ingredients. Add enough more of the flour to make a dough as soft as can be handled. Chill. Roll to a quarter of an inch in thickness. Use a biscuit cutter so you will have large round cookies. Bake at 350° for about 15 minutes, or until brown.

Three Spice Oatmeal Cookies

1 cup shortening	3/4 tsp. baking powder
2 cups brown sugar	1 tsp. cinnamon
2 eggs	1 tsp. ground ginger
2 Tbsp. milk	1/2 tsp. ground cloves
2 cups sifted flour	1/2 cup quick cooking oatmeal

Blend shortening and brown sugar. In separate bowl combine flour, salt, baking powder, cinnamon, ginger, cloves and oatmeal; set aside. Add eggs to sugar-shortening mix, then add flour mixture alternately with milk. Add raisins and nuts if desired. Bake at 375° for 10 to 12 minutes. (These are drop cookies).

Baker's Dozen Cookies

3 cups sifted flour	1/2 tsp. nutmeg
1 1/4 cups sugar, divided	1 cup margarine
1 1/2 tsp. baking powder	2 eggs
1 1/4 tsp. salt	6 Tbsp. milk
1/2 tsp. baking soda	1 tsp. grated lemon rind

Preheat oven to 350°.

Sift together flour, 1 cup sugar, baking powder, salt, baking soda and nutmeg into large bowl. Cut in margarine with pastry blender or two knives until crumbly.

Beat eggs slightly with milk in small bowl and stir into flour mixture. Mix well. (Batter will be thick).

Drop by rounded tablespoons 4 inches apart on lightly-greased cookie sheet. Flatten into 3" rounds using a spatula dipped in water. Sprinkle lightly with mixture 1/4 cup sugar and lemon rind. Bake for about 15 minutes or until browned at edges. Cool completely on wire racks. Makes 13 dozen cookies.

Sweet Revenge Cookies
The $250.00 Cookie Recipe

2 cups butter	2 cups sugar
2 cups brown sugar	4 eggs
2 tsp. vanilla	5 cups blended oatmeal*
4 cups flour	1 tsp. salt
2 tsp. baking powder	2 tsp. baking soda
24 oz. chocolate chips	1 Hershey bar, grated
3 cups chopped nuts	

Cream butter and sugars. Add eggs and vanilla. Mix together with flour, oatmeal, salt, baking powder and baking soda. Add chips, candy and nuts. Roll into balls and place 2 inches apart on cookie sheet. Bake for 6-10 minutes at 375°. Makes 112 cookies, but the recipe can be divided.

*Blended oatmeal: Measure and blend in a blender to a fine powder.

A friend of a friend had lunch at a posh department store restaurant in November, and for dessert she had a cookie. She thought that it was the most wonderful cookie that she had ever tasted, and asked if the recipe were available. She was told it was, but there was a charge of two fifty. She said that was fine. She took the recipe and told them to charge her account.

In December, when she received her bill, there was a charge of $250.00. She called and told them there was a mistake–the charge should be $2.50. She was told the charge was indeed correct–there was no mistake.

She has vowed to get the pricey place back. She would like to give everyone she knows this very expensive recipe, and for those people to pass it on.

This recipe was printed on the back page of the October 1994 issue of "The Torch of Beta Sigma Phi." I tested these for my Christmas party in 1994. Just made half of the recipe. They are very good.

Gloria

Healthy Apple Walnut Muffins

Made with no added fat or sugar, these tasty muffins use fruit and buttermilk to keep them moist.

2 cups all-purpose flour
1 tsp. baking soda
1/4 tsp. ground cinnamon
1/4 tsp. ground ginger
1/4 tsp. ground allspice
1/4 tsp. ground nutmeg
1/4 tsp. salt
1/3 cup chopped walnuts

2 large eggs
1 cup plus 2 Tbsp. frozen, thawed apple juice concentrate
2/3 cup buttermilk
2 Tbsp. oat bran
2 small Granny Smith apples, peeled, cored, and chopped

Garnish:
1 small Granny Smith apple, peeled, cored and cut into 12 thin slices.

1. Preheat oven to 375°. Grease 12 standard muffin pans cups or line with paper liners.
2. Mix together flour, baking soda, cinnamon, ginger, allspice, nutmeg, and salt.
3. Mix together eggs, apple juice, and buttermilk.
4. Stir flour mixture and oat bran into egg mixture until dry ingredients are just moistened. Do not overmix. Gently stir in chopped apples and nuts.
5. Spoon batter into prepared pan, filling cups 2/3 full. Garnish each muffin with apple slices.
6. Bake muffins until lightly golden and tops spring back when pressed, 25 minutes. Transfer pan to a wire rack to cool slightly. Turn muffins out onto rack to cool completely.

Baked Apples

3/4 cup sugar
1 tsp. cinnamon
1 Tbsp. margarine
1 Tbsp. lemon juice
6 cups sliced and cored apples (leave peel on)
1 Tbsp. cornstarch

Mix together and put in casserole dish. Bake 425° for 50 minutes.

Molasses Short 'nin' Bread

2 cups all-purpose flour
1/4 tsp. ground nutmeg
1/2 cup buttermilk
1 cup molasses
1 egg, slightly beaten
1/2 tsp. ground cinnamon
1 1/2 tsp. baking soda
1/4 cup plus 3 Tbsp. butter or margarine

Combine flour, cinnamon and nutmeg in a large bowl; mix well and set aside. Dissolve baking soda in buttermilk; stir well and set aside. Combine butter or margarine and molasses in a heavy saucepan; bring to a boil, stirring constantly. Add to the flour mixture. Stir in buttermilk mixture and egg. Pour batter into a greased and floured 10" cast iron skillet. Bake at 350° for 25 to 30 minutes. Cool in skillet 10 minutes. Invert bread onto plate. Cut into wedges to serve. Makes 8 servings.

Boiled Apple Dumplings

2 cups milk
1 Tbsp. vinegar
1/2 tsp. baking soda
1 tsp. salt
1/2 cup butter, melted
flour
6 to 8 apples
brown sugar
cinnamon

    Combine milk, vinegar, baking soda and salt. Mix in melted butter. Add enough flour to make dough a little stiffer than a biscuit dough.

    Divide the dough into 6 to 8 portions. Peel and core apples, leaving them whole.

    Roll out each portion of dough. Set an apple in the center of each portion of dough and fill apple with brown sugar and a sprinkle of cinnamon.

    Wrap dough around apple and pinch edges together

tightly. Take a white cotton cloth the size of a man's handkerchief and set the dumpling in the center of it. Bring up the four corners of the cloth and tie them together, (easier to use a piece of string). Have water boiling in a big kettle. Add 1/2 tsp. salt to the water. Put dumplings into boiling water and keep them covered with water throughout cooking. Boil 40 minutes. Remove cloth and serve warm with rich milk poured over or with ice cream.

Recently, while reading some of my cookbooks, I came across the above recipe for boiled apple dumplings which were tied in a cloth. I had completely forgotten watching Mom make the dumplings early in the Spring. She made them with the first yellow transparent apples and served them with country milk. The evening meal might consist of just these dumplings. What more could we want? When I can "get around to it", I plan to try to re-create this confection and hope that it tastes as heavenly as it did when I was a child. Sometimes, these dumplings would puff right out of the sides of the cloth.

Baked Apples

Baked apples signal the arrival of autumn

8 apples (suitable for baking)   candy red-hots
sugar   butter
whipped cream or vanilla ice cream   cinnamon

Core apples, cutting out center to form well. Pare a strip from top of each. Pour 1 cup water into large baking pan to keep apples from burning. Place apples well-side up in pan.

Fill apple wells with 1/2 tsp. butter, sugar and cinnamon and candy red hots to taste. Sprinkle some sugar cinnamon mixture on pared areas. Bake uncovered at 350°. Frequently baste apples with juice that bubbles out into the pan.

Bake until tender, about 20 to 25 minutes. When tender and golden brown remove from oven and serve warm with rich milk, whipped cream or vanilla ice cream.

You can store baked apples in the refrigerator; they are also delicious cold.

Joe Froggers

These big, soft, fat molasses cookies, known as Joe Froggers in New England and Bolivars in New York, are a happy inheritance from the Gay Nineties.

Lightly grease cookie sheets; sift together and set aside.

4 1/2 cups sifted flour	1 1/2 tsp. salt
1 tsp. baking powder	1 tsp. baking soda
1 1/2 tsp. ginger	1/4 tsp. ground cloves

Cream until softened.

2/3 cups shortening

Add gradually, creaming until fluffy after each addition.

1 cup firmly-packed brown sugar

Mix together:

1 1/4 cups molasses   1/4 cup water

    Alternately blend dry ingredients in fourths, molasses mixture in thirds into creamed mixture, blending well after each addition. Finally blend until well mixed. Divide dough into halves and roll 1/4 inch thick on lightly-floured surface. Cut with lightly-floured 3-inch cookie cutter. Using a pancake turner, gently lift cookies and place about 2 inches apart on cookie sheets.

Bake at 375° 10 to 12 minutes. With pancake turner, carefully remove cookies to cooling rack. Yields about 2 1/2 dozen 3-inch cookies.

Angel Biscuits

5 cups flour (approximately)	1 pkg. Fleischman's active dry yeast
1/4 cup sugar	
1 tsp. salt	2 cups buttermilk
3 tsp. baking powder	1/4 cup water
1 tsp. soda	3/4 cup shortening

    Mix 1 1/2 cups flour, sugar, salt, baking powder, soda and dry yeast. Combing buttermilk, water and shortening in pan, heat until very warm. Shortening does not need to melt. Gradually add to dry ingredients and beat for 2 minutes at medium speed of electric mixer, scraping bowl occasionally. Add 3/4 cup flour, or enough to make a thick batter. Beat at high speed for 2 minutes, scraping bowl occasionally. Stir in enough flour to make a soft dough. Turn out on lightly-floured board and knead about 20 to 25 times to form a round ball. On a well-floured board, roll dough out to 1/2 inch thickness. Using a 2-inch biscuit cutter, cut dough into circles and place on ungreased baking sheet. Cover and let rise in warm place, free from draft, about 1 hour. Bake at 400° about 20 minutes, or until done. Preheat oven. Best when served warm. Makes about 2 1/2 dozen.

Buttermilk Biscuits

Makes 12 biscuits
2 cups all-purpose flour   1/2 tsp. baking soda
2 tsp. baking powder   5 tsp. chill vegetable shortening
3/4 tsp. salt   1 cup buttermilk

1. Preheat oven to 425°. In a large bowl, sift together flour, baking powder, salt, and baking soda. Using a pastry blender or 2 knives, cut the shortening into the flour mixture until coarse crumbs form.
2. Add the buttermilk, tossing with a fork until a dough is formed.
3. Turn dough out onto a lightly-floured surface. Gather into a ball. Knead lightly a few times just until smooth. (The dough can be made up to 2 hours ahead, wrapped in plastic wrap, and refrigerated until ready to use.)
4. Pat the dough to 3/4-inch thick. Using a biscuit cutter dipped in flour, cut out biscuits. Place the biscuits, 2 inches apart, on an ungreased baking sheet. Gather dough trimmings, pat to 3/4-inch thick, and cut out more biscuits.
5. Bake the biscuits until golden, 12 to 15 minutes. Serve hot.
Baking tips: to produce flaky biscuits, take care not to overhandle the dough. For less waste and a speedier preparation, pat the dough into a square, then cut into square-shaped biscuits with a floured knife. Bake as directed above.

Sour Dough-Old Time Starter

This starter gathers yeast from the air to provide leavening.
2 cups unsifted flour   1 1/2 cups water
2 Tbsp. sugar   1 Tbsp. vinegar
pinch of salt

        Combine flour, sugar and salt in a stone crock, jar or

bowl. Mix well. Add water and beat to a smooth batter then add vinegar. Put lid on or cover with cloth; set in a warm place until bubbly and sour. This you can tell by the yeasty odor. Takes about 12 hours.

Sourdough Biscuits

1 1/2 cups flour   1/4 cup melted shortening
2 tsp. baking powder   1 cup starter
1/3 tsp. baking soda

    Mix dry ingredients in bowl, add shortening and starter and mix.

    Turn dough out on lightly-floured board. Knead and pinch off a small amount of dough, placing in a greased Dutch oven. Crowd biscuits and set in a warm place and let rise for about an hour. Set Dutch oven in a hot bed of coals and cooks in about 20 minutes. (If you don't have a bed of hot coals, use your oven.)

Sourdough Pancakes
(for three)

1 cup starter   Milk–just enough to make a batter
2 cups flour   Salt–a dash, too much ruins action of starter

    Let above stand overnight (6-8) hours in a warm room in crock bowl large enough to allow for an increase in the bulk. When it's ready to use, the batter will look like a sponge and have a pleasant odor.

    Next morning take out one cup of the batter and put aside, in a cool place. This is your starter for the next time. To the remainder in the crock bowl, about 2 cups of spongy batter, add:

2 eggs   1 tsp. soda (moistened with water)
2 Tbsp. melted fat   1/2 cup sugar

    Mix well with fork to a smooth batter. If too thin add a little sponge starter, but **never** flour. Cook on hot griddle.

Recipes with oatmeal can be exciting!

Oatmeal Bread

1 1/2 cups boiling water	2 eggs
1 cup quick-cooking oats	1 3/4 cups flour
1/2 cup margarine, softened	1 tsp. baking soda
1 cup sugar	1/2 tsp. salt
1 cup packed brown sugar	1 tsp. cinnamon

Pour boiling water over oats in bowl; set aside. Cream margarine, sugar and brown sugar in mixer bowl until light and fluffy. Beat in eggs, one at a time. Add mixture of flour, baking soda, salt and cinnamon; mix well. Stir in oats. Spoon into greased and floured 5x9" loaf pan. Bake at 350° for 1 hour or until loaf tests done. Cool in pan 10 minutes. Remove to wire rack to cool completely.

Zucchini Bread

3 eggs	1 tsp. soda
2 cups sugar	1/4 tsp. baking powder
1 cup oil	*2 cups grated zucchini
1 tsp. vanilla	2 1/2 cups sifted flour
1 tsp. cinnamon	1/2 cup wheat germ
1 tsp. salt	1 cup chopped nuts (sliced almonds)

*Beat until foamy in bowl. Add sugar, oil, etc. zucchini last. Makes 1 lg. loaf 3 sm. or 1 bundt cake. (I use 2 loaf pairs-1 hr. Bake 1 hr. 20 min. 350° (I spray pans with *Pam*, no flour) remove from pan and cool on rack .

NOTE: I go a little light on the sugar so it won't be quite so sweet. I'm generous with the cinnamon, cause I love cinna-yum-yum-yum! And I use 1/2 whole wheat flour to make the calories nutritious!

1 cup of brown sugar is enough-*Gloria*. I have never made it with the nuts. Might be nice if you wanted to slice thin and spread with soft cream cheese, but I like it better plain.

I had a hard time last summer finding a recipe as this one was in Florida. This is not in cookbooks or at least the earlier ones. Also had trouble finding banana bread until I finally found Mom's old one on a piece of paper.

Onion Upside-Down Bread

Onion Upside-Down Bread is a little something special.

2 to 3 medium sweet Spanish onions
3 Tbsp. butter or margarine
2 Tbsp. brown sugar
2 cups flour
4 tsp. baking powder
1 tsp. salt
1 tsp. sugar
1 egg beaten
1 cup milk
1/4 cup oil

Peel and thickly slice onions. Saute in 2 tablespoons butter until golden and fairly soft. Spread remaining 1 tablespoon butter in 9-inch round baking dish. Sprinkle with brown sugar. Arrange onion slices in baking dish. For topping, combine dry ingredients. Add egg, milk and oil. Batter should be a little thinner then biscuit dough. Spread over top of onions. Bake 35 to 40 minutes in a 350° oven. Let stand 5 minutes. Loosen edges and turn out on serving plate. Cut in wedges to serve and eat with a fork. If you are in a hurry, 2 cups of a packaged baking mix may be used for the dry ingredients.

Dilly Bread Casserole

(No kneading. Just mix the savory batter. Let it rise. Turn into casserole dish. Makes one round loaf.)

1 packet active dry yeast
1/2 cup warm water
1 cup creamed cottage cheese, heated to lukewarm
2 tsp. sugar
2 Tbsp. minced onions
1 Tbsp. butter
2 Tbsp. dill seed
1 tsp. salt
1/4 tsp. soda
1 egg, unbeaten
2 to 2 1/2 cups all-purpose flour

Soften yeast in warm oven. In mixing bowl, combine cottage cheese, sugar, onion, butter, dill seed, salt, soda, egg, and softened yeast. Add flour gradually to make a stiff dough, beating well after each addition. (For first addition use mixer on low speed.) Cover, let rise in warm place until light and doubled in size, about 50 to 60 minutes. Stir dough down. Turn into well-greased eight-inch round casserole. (1 1/2 to 20 quarts.) Let rise in warm place 30 to 40 minutes. Bake at 350° 40 to 50 minutes, until golden brown. Brush with butter.

I have no excuse for giving you the following recipe, except for a chuckle. I don't think any of our family ever made this recipe (unless one was a navy cook) and I don't remember anyone ever bringing it to one of our family reunions.
Here goes:

Resape for Bred (Navy Style)

The following is an exact copy of a famous bread recipe by a navy cook.

Furst you take 5 handfulls of sugar. Enuff lard to make havy paist when you mix it with the sugar. 4 or 5 good pinches' of salt. If you use seawater, forget the salt. 5 helmits of flour. Handfull of spud yeast (which you gotta make yerself). Sumtimes this is too much and then agin it ain't. If its rainin, you gotta use more. 1 helmit of water size 7 1/4. If using swamp water, boil furst. Directions for puttin all this together. It don't make much difference how you mix this but do it for quite awhile. It will get reel thick. When it gits to where you can't hardly gitcha hands out, then its done. The mixin, that is.

Now it will start puffin up. (If it don't that won't hurt none). Us bakers calls this fermentin. There's a mess of little bugs inside making alcohol. I think---inway. From this point on you gotta start bein more careful cause this doe is reel delicut. After it puggs up reel big, nock it down. Sometimes it will fall all by itself and save you the trouble. Cut it off in chenks with your bayonett and wad it up in balls about the size of yer hed. You shood git about 3 balls. It shood rise again, then its reddy to eat after you bake it sum.

If you can't find iny bred pans you can mash up sum tin cans and use them. Yu'll find that the bottoms will burn furst so about 1/2 way thru you gotta turn them over. The furst time you make this bred it mite not be so hot but its easy after a while.

This is enuff stuff for about 30 min but if the furst few min in chow line duz a lot of bitchin you'll have enuff for the hole iland........

O yes, if yer bakin this for the C.O. its gotta be nicer and richer so thro in an extra handfull of sugar.

Zucchini Cobbler

8 cups chopped seeded zucchini (about 3 lbs)
2/3 cup lemon juice   1 tsp. ground cinnamon
1 cup sugar   1/2 ground nutmeg
Crust:
4 cups all-purpose flour   1 tsp. ground cinnamon
2 cups sugar   1 1/2 cups cold butter or margarine

In a large saucepan over medium-low heat, cook and stir zucchini and lemon juice for 15-20 minutes or until zucchini is tender. Add sugar, cinnamon and nutmeg, simmer 1 minute longer. Remove from the heat; set aside.

For crust, combine the flour and sugar in a bowl; cut in butter until the mixture resembles coarse crumbs. Stir 1/2 into zucchini mixture. Press half of remaining crust mixture into greased 15x10x1" baking pan. Spread zucchini over top; crumble remaining crust mixture over zucchini. Sprinkle with cinnamon. Bake at 350° for 35-40 minutes or until golden and bubbly.

This tastes like apples and will fool people.

Grandma Mills' Rhubarb (or Pieplant) Breakfast Dumplings

In the crisp Spring mornings, Grandma would go out to the garden and cut half a dozen tall rhubarb stalks, bring them in, wash them and cut into pieces which she dropped into a boiling pot of water. She added sugar and proceeded to make buttermilk biscuits, which she dropped into the boiling pot and cooked 5 to 10 minutes, then served in big bowls with more sugar and country rich milk. Sure made a delicious breakfast.

These can be duplicated in these modern times by using a package of frozen rhubarb and the *Bisquick* recipe for dumplings listed on the box and then serving with *Half and Half* cream.

Molasses Taffy

1 cup molasses	3/4 cup sugar
2 tsp. vinegar	1 Tbsp. butter
1/8 tsp. salt	1/8 tsp. baking soda

Boil molasses, sugar and vinegar to hard boil stage. Remove from fire. Add butter, baking soda and salt. Stir only enough to blend. Pour into well-buttered pan. When cool, pull until light and porous. Cut in 1-inch pieces.

When Aunt Hessie came to our house, she almost always made her special "Vinegar" candy for us. I believe that the recipe below is what she made.

Old Fashioned Vinegar Candy

1 cup sugar	1 Tbsp. white vinegar
1 cup dark corn syrup	1 Tbsp. baking soda

Combine sugar, syrup and vinegar in a large pan. Cook, stirring constantly until sugar dissolves. Cover and cook 1 minute. Uncover and insert candy thermometer. Cook without stirring until temperature reaches 300°. Remove from heat. Stir in soda. Pour into 9-inch square pan. Mixture will bubble and spread. Cool in pan. Break into pieces. Store in tight container.

I do not believe that Aunt Hessie used corn syrup. To the best of my memory, she just used white sugar and when she was making the candy, we kids always watched and waited. Of course, she never heard of a candy thermometer at that time, but she knew how to time it.

Aunt Dessie's Molasses Butter

1/2 cup molasses   2 Tbsp. milk
1 egg yolk

Mix well the egg yolk and milk, and stir into the molasses. Cook over very low heat, stirring constantly until thick. Good on hot buttered biscuits.

Molasses Cake

1/2 cup brown sugar	3 tsp. baking powder
1/2 cup butter	1/2 tsp. salt
1/2 cup molasses	1/4 tsp. soda
1/2 cup milk	1 tsp. mixed spices
2 cups flour	1 egg

Cream butter, and gradually cream in the sugar; add molasses and beaten egg, and mix; sift and measure flour, add baking powder, salt, soda and spices. Re-sift together; add flour and milk alternately and mix well. Bake in well-greased shallow pan in a moderate oven–baking time about 40 to 45 minutes. Serve while yet warm. Ice if desired.

Cooks made good use of molasses since almost everyone grew cane and made their own.

Dandelion Wine #1

First, you go out and pick a lot of dandelion yellow blossoms. You pick all on your own lawn, all the neighbors lawns and then go out into the fields and pick some more. Try to pick where they have not been sprayed. You will need 3 quarts of flowers, 4 pounds of sugar and 1 gallon of water. Place the clean flowers in a large clean crock. Use flowers only, no stems. Dissolve the sugar in boiling water and add to flowers with 2 whole lemons. Let stand 3 days and nights in a cool place. Slice the lemons and boil mixture about 15 minutes. Cool. Strain out the lemons and add 2 tablespoons of yeast. Put in cool place to ferment. Strain the wine slowly through several layers of clean cloth. Bottle and keep for special occasions.

Dandeline Wine #2

Pour 1 gallon of boiling water over 2 quarts clean flowers. Let stand 24 hours. Strain, then add 3 pounds of white sugar and 1 cup yeast. Let stand 18 hours. Add the juice of 2 lemons and 2 oranges, then strain and bottle uncorked until fermented.

After being served some of my nephew Randy Walker's wine, I made a batch several years ago. I still have a pint jar in my refrigerator. It was good the last time I tried it. Think I had better go in the kitchen and check it out! (1994)

Homemade Furniture Polish

2 Tbsp. olive oil 1 qt. warm water
1/4 cup vinegar

Combine all ingredients. Dip clean cloth in solution and wash furniture. Dry completely with another clean cloth. This will not only remove all dirt, but will leave a satiny luster that will remain until the next week's time rolls around.

Cough Syrup

juice of 1 lemon 1/2 tsp. glycerin
2 Tbsp. honey 2 cups boiling water
4 tsp. Bourbon (for preservative)

Combine lemon juice, honey, liquor and glycerin and add to boiling water. Store in refrigerator. Can flavor with a piece of horehound candy.

My Sister Lorena's Soft Gingerbread

1 cup molasses 1 cup water
1 cup sugar 4 cups flour
1/2 cup shortening, melted 1/2 tsp. salt
1 level tsp. ground ginger 1 level tsp. baking soda
1/2 tsp. ground cinnamon

(I notice that she did not list eggs. Don't know if this was an oversight when she was writing it for me, or if she really did not use eggs. Most recipes of this size would call for 2 eggs).

Stir the molasses, sugar and shortening together; add the water then the flour, salt, soda and spices sifted together, and beat hard. Bake in 2 well-greased pans in a moderate oven about half an hour.

Now, this is gingerbread, but I use the same recipe for a stacked cake. I just add a little more flour to make it thick enough to roll it out. I divide it into 4 or 5 balls of dough and roll it very thin, cut it out with scalloped pie pans. If you have a wide pan that would hold layers at once, it won't take too long.

The dried apples, I was them good and put water to come to about the top of them and let them soak overnight and add some sugar and cook in the water that they soaked in. Can flavor with allspice if desired.

I have this on a piece of lined note paper in Lorena's own handwriting and I treasure it. It sure tasted good when it came out of her oven and we ate some before it cooled off.

Mom, Grandma and my aunts made pickled beans the old fashioned way. In a large crock or barrel with salt brine, but I am going to give you a quick easy way to make in smaller quantities.

Pickled Beans

1 cup vinegar   1 gallon water
1 cup salt

String and break beans. Wash and drain. Add water to cover and cook about 15 minutes. Drain and pack into sterilized jars. Bring the water, vinegar and salt to a boil and pour over beans. Seal and set aside in cool place.

Remember the ground cherry preserves? I didn't mind picking those sweet, yellow little cherries up. They lay flat on the ground and you had to do a lot of stooping over, but it was worth it. The big, blue or purple ones were not very good–more plentiful and you could fill a bucket quicker, but they did not make good preserves. Here's a recipe, should you be lucky enough to harvest any of these little goodies.

Ground Cherry Preserves

6 cups ground cherries
6 cups sugar
1/4 cup lemon juice
1 cup water
(We did not use that, since lemons were not plentiful in the country and also we had never heard of adding lemon juice.) I suppose it would make the preserves a little more tart.

Husk and wash ground cherries. Make syrup by bringing remaining ingredients to a boil. Simmer 5 minutes. Take from heat and let stand overnight to plump ground cherries. Continue boiling next day until mixture thickens. When desired thickness is obtained, seal preserves in sterile jars.
It was easy to tell which ground cherries to pick up, the ones where the husk had turned a light brown and looked like lace. Then, you knew the ground cherry was nice and yellow and ripe.

Hot Peppers in Sauce

1/2 peck hot peppers
1/2 cup vegetable oil
1 cup vinegar
1/4 Tbsp. salt
1/4 Tbsp. garlic
24 ounce bottle catsup

Clean the seeds from the peppers and then cut the peppers into rings. Mix the oil, vinegar, salt, garlic and catsup in a kettle. Add the peppers and boil for 4 minutes. Ladle into hot jars; seal. Process in hot water bath for 15 minutes.

Loma Comb's Hot Peppers and Weiners

1 peck hot banana peppers
1 pint vinegar
32 ounce bottle ketsup
8 or 10 sweet peppers
1 pint Crisco oil

Put all in large pot and cook until peppers change colors. Add 10 pounds weiners, cut into 2-inch pieces. Bring to a good boil. Pack in pint jars and seal. You now have several jars of delicious peppers and weiners to take to reunions all summer. Loma cans these and lots of other vegetables from her garden. She always has plenty of homegrown and canned "goodies" on hand.

Wild Meats
Squirrel Stew

3 squirrels
2 onions, chopped
1 green pepper, chopped
2 medium potatoes, chopped
1/4 cup diced celery
4 Tbsp. chili powder
salt and pepper to taste
Dash hot sauce
1 cup cooked rice

Cover squirrels with water and cook until tender. Remove meat from bones and put back into broth. Bring to a boil and add all other ingredients, except rice. Cook for about 45 minutes or until vegetables are tender. Add cooked rice. Serve hot.

Venison Stew

3 pounds venison (boned)
1 cup water
1 cup vinegar
2 cups chopped carrots
2 cups chopped onions
1/4 cup butter
1/2 cup red wine
1/2 pint sour cream
rosemary
salt and pepper

Marinate venison for 8 hours in mixture of water, vinegar, salt, and pepper. Drain and put into baking dish with carrots, onions, dash of rosemary and 1 cup water. Cover and bake in oven at 350° for 2 hours. Braise occasionally. When cooked, remove venison; add flour and butter and stir until thick. When thickened, add sour cream and wine, and stir again. Slice venison and pour mixture over meat.

Barbecued Bear

3 pounds bear steak, cut in 2" cubes
1 slice salt pork, cut up
1 cup catsup
1/3 cup steak sauce
2 Tbsp. tarragan vinegar
1 onion diced
1 tsp. salt
1 Tbsp. chili powder
1 Tbsp lemon juice
(fresh or frozen)

Trim all fat from bear steak and cut in 2" cubes. Sear meat on all sides with salt pork in a heavy frying pan. Then place meat in a casserole. Add rest of ingredients to fry pan and bring to a boil, stirring constantly. Pour sauce over meat in casserole. Cover and bake for at least 2 hours in a 325° oven, stirring occasionally until meat is tender.

In his book, *The History of the Walker Family*, Glennis Walker tells of Great-grandmother Martha Adeline Sizemore Walker killing a bear with a knife. With the help of her children, she dressed out the bear and had some cooked and ready to serve Great-grandfather Numa when he returned at a late hour that night.

I don't believe that she went to all the trouble of the preceding recipe. I imagine the bear meat was put into a large black cast iron kettle hanging over the fire in the fireplace and boiled until it was tender.

Roasted Opossum and Sweet Potatoes

1 opossum (2-2 1/2 lbs)
salt, pepper and sage
apple and raisin stuffing
1/2 to 1/3 cup flour
3-4 sweet potatoes
2 Tbsp. brown sugar
2 cups stock (or water)

Rub inside of dressed opossum with seasonings; fill with stuffing; truss season and place on greased rack in shallow pan. If lean, brush with fat and cover with cloth dipped in melted fat. Roast uncovered in slow oven at 300-325° for 1 1/2 to 2 hours, allowing 30-35 minutes per pound. Remove cloth the last half hour and place parboiled sweet potatoes (peeled and halved) around opossum; baste several times with drippings in pan. Dust meat with flour and potatoes with brown sugar after each basting. Place potatoes around opossum on heated platter, garnish and serve with butter peas and turnip cubes, french fried green pepper rings, brown bread and cranberry sauce.

We always had FAT ones, so we roasted them, seasoned with salt and pepper. We kept draining the fat out of the pan, so that when completely roasted, the skin was brown and crusty.

Fried Venison

2 lbs. venison steak cut 1-inch thick
1/4 cup flour
1 tsp. salt
Fresh ground pepper to taste
3 Tbsp. bacon fat
1 piece of celery, cut up
3 medium onions, sliced
1 Tbsp. Worcestershire sauce
2 cups tomatoes

8 oz. of noodles

Cut venison steak into serving-size pieces. Mix flour with salt and pepper. Coat venison with flour mixture.

Heat bacon fat in skillet and brown venison on both sides.

Add celery and onions and brown. Add remaining ingredients and cook, covered 1 to 2 hours, or until tender. Serve over noodles.

Baked Squirrel Pot Pie

3 squirrels, cooked and boned
Pot pie dough
1 medium carrot, chopped
1 medium onion, chopped
3-4 medium potatoes chopped
salt and pepper to taste
parsley
pie crust

In baking dish, place layers of pot pie dough, boned squirrel meat and a layer of vegetables. Continue in such layers to top of dish. Add salt, pepper, basil or parsley to broth: heat, then add to baking dish. Cover top with regular pie crust. Bake at 350° for 1 1/2 to 2 hours.

Now, the first problem about this recipe is getting 3 squirrels! I could probably find a dozen in my backyard, jumping from tree limb to tree limb, but I couldn't kill them.

When we lived at Egeria, people would come from Besoco, Odd and all over to hunt. When the squirrel season came around, they closed the mines because the miners did not show up. Lots of times just at daylight men would come to the house with a lot of squirrels for Mom to cook. We cooked them until tender, then added milk and butter and some "thickening" (flour dissolved in a little water or milk). This would go good over hot biscuits and could feed a number of people. Cousin Arbrie Mills and his friend, Corbit Wood would usually show up.

Daddy was a good hunter and I think he gave Corbit a rifle and taught him at the age of ten or under, so we usually had our share of wild game.

Some hunters could skin the squirrel pretty clean, but no matter how good you were, there were always tiny hairs sticking to the skin like glue. It was a major job to wash them and I am sure that a few hairs got cooked with the stew. It didn't hurt the flavor.

Dandelion Salad

Large bowl of fresh dandelion greens
4 slices thick bacon, diced
1/4 cup country butter
1/2 cup thick cream
2 hen's eggs, beaten (or 1 wild turkey egg)
Dash of black pepper
Small handful salt (heaping tsp.)
1/4 tsp. paprika
1 tsp. brown sugar
1/4 cup apple cider vinegar

Carefully wash dandelion greens; use only the tender, new growth. Shake dry and place in bowl. Pan-fry bacon, crumble into small pieces and place over greens. Warm butter and cream in same skillet (after pouring off the grease) using low heat. Add remaining ingredients to cream mixture. Increase heat and cook until mixture thickens, stirring constantly. Pour hot dressing over greens. Toss and serve real "back to nature" salad.

When the dandelions were plentiful in the spring, we picked and made a salad, but we only used vinegar and bacon fat, getting it to the boiling state and pouring over greens. We usually added some green onions also; the same way that we made wilted lettuce salad.

Gloria's 4-Bean Salad

This is a good one to serve a large crowd.

1/2 cup salad oil
1/2 cup cider vinegar
1/3 cup sugar
1 large sweet onion, chopped
1 large green pepper, chopped
1 number 2 can green beans
1 number 2 can kidney beans
1 number 2 can yellow wax beans
1 number 2 can Garbanzo beans (chick peas)

Drain liquid from beans (let water run through strainer and wash the kidney beans) and marinate all ingredients over night. If you want the salad to be more tart, add more vinegar. Also, a red and yellow pepper add color.

Yum Yum Salad

1 can pineapple #2 (large)
1 cup sugar
juice of 1 lemon

Combine and heat until sugar is dissolved; dissolve 2 envelopes

(2 tablespoons) Knox gelatin in 1/2 cup water. Add to above mixture. Put in refrigerator and let thicken slightly. (Thick enough to hold the pineapples suspended). Add 1 cup grated American cheese.

Gently fold in one pint whipping cream, whipped until very stiff. Pour into large *Pyrex* oblong or square pan. Let set in refrigerator 8 to 10 hours. Place Maraschino cherry halves on top so one will be in the center of each square when cut to serve. This has a beautiful white top and with the red cherry in the center of each square looks real Christmacy, so I usually make it for my family Christmas party.

Frozen Strawberry Salad

1 8-ounce package cream cheese
3/4 cup nuts (pecans)
2 small pkgs. strawberry *Jello*
2 cups boiling water
2 tsp. lemon juice
1 large can crushed pineapple
2 10-oz pkgs. frozen strawberries (sliced)

Put cream cheese out to soften in advance. Roll into bite-sized balls (less than 1/4 teaspoon). Roll the balls in the nuts which have been crushed with a rolling pin. Put cream cheese balls on wax paper to use later.

Drain crushed pineapple. Mix strawberry *Jello* and boiling water. Add lemon juice. Add frozen strawberries direct from freezer. Mix strawberries well in *Jello* and lemon juice mixture, until you are sure that the strawberries have thawed. Add drained pineapple and cream cheese balls. Stir gently until all mixed. Pour into long *Pyrex* dish. Chill until firm.

This was made by one of my B.P.W. Club member's husband and brought to our pot-luck dinners. Sure furnished a fancy ending, more of a dessert than a salad.

Buckwheat Pancakes

Basic Yeast Batter:

1 pkg. dry yeast, or 1 cake fresh yeast
2 cups warm water
1 cup buckwheat flour
1 cup unbleached flour
1 tsp. salt
1 Tbs. butter, melted
1/4 tsp. baking soda

For Sweet Cakes:
2 Tbsp. molasses

About 12 hours before cooking time, dissolve yeast in warm water in a large bowl, then stir in both flours and salt. Cover and set in warm place. Just before using, add melted butter and baking soda (and, if you are making sweet pancakes, the molasses). You may need to thin the batter with up to 1/3 cup more warm water.

To bake, brush a large heavy skillet with softened butter. Heat until almost smoking, then pour in about 1/2 cup of batter, depending on how big you want to make the cakes. Turn when bubbles appear all over and bake until lightly browned on the other side.

These would probably taste like Grandma made. She just left enough batter to use as a "starter" the next time.

Buttermilk Pancakes

3 cups sifted flour
3/4 tsp. baking powder
1 tsp. salt
2 eggs, separated
2 1/2 cups buttermilk
2 Tbsp. melted butter

Sift together flour and baking soda and stir in salt. Beat egg yolks then add to flour mixture with buttermilk and melted butter and beat until smooth. Beat egg whites stiff enough to form peaks and fold into batter. Drop spoonfuls of batter onto hot griddle, making 12 pancakes; turn and brown on other side.

Cornmeal Griddle Cakes

3 cups milk
2 eggs
1 cup yellow cornmeal
1/2 cup all-purpose flour
1 tsp. baking powder
1/2 tsp. salt
1/2 cup melted lard, bacon fat or butter
1 1/2 tsp. sugar

Mix well and pour on griddle in sizes you want.

Mexican Burgers

1 lb. lean ground beef
1/4 teaspoon garlic powder
1/4 cup chopped onion
1 1/2 tsp. chili powder

4 slices Monterey Jack cheese   1/4 tsp. salt
with jalapeno peppers

Heat coals on outdoor grill or preheat broiler. In a medium mix just enough to combine beef, onion, chili powder, salt and garlic powder (over-mixing can cause toughness); shape into 4 patties.

Place on a rack either over hot coals or in a broiler pan about 4 inches from heat; cook to desired doneness, about 4 minutes per side for medium.

Top each burger with a cheese slice; heat until cheese melts, 30 seconds to 1 minute.

Serve in toasted hamburger buns with lettuce and sliced tomato if desired.

Greek Burgers

1 pound ground lean beef   1/2 tsp. salt
1/2 cup finely-chopped onion   1/4 tsp. ground black pepper
2 Tbsp. lemon juice   1 cup chopped tomato
1 tsp. oregano leaves, crushed   1/2 cup crumbled feta cheese
1/2 tsp. garlic powder

Heat coals in an outdoor grill or preheat broiler. In a medium bowl mix just until beef, onion, lemon juice, oregano, garlic powder, salt and black pepper are combined, (over-mixing can cause toughness); into 4 patties.

Place on a rack either over hot coals or in a broiler pan about 4 inches from heat; cook to desired doneness, about 4 minutes per side for medium. Meanwhile in a small bowl combine tomato and feta cheese; set aside.

Serve burgers in warm pita pockets or in toasted hamburger buns, if desired. Top each burger with cheese mixture.

German Burgers

1 pound ground lean beef   1 Tbsp. prepared brown mustard
1/4 cup chopped onion   1/4 cup ground black pepper
1/4 cup pickle relish   4 slices Muenster cheese with
1/4 tsp. salt   caraway

Heat coals in an outdoor grill or preheat broiler.
In a medium bowl mix just until beef, onion, relish, mustard,

salt and black pepper are combined, (over-mixing can cause toughness). Shape into 4 patties. Place on a rack either over hot coals or in a broiler pan about 4 inches from heat; cook to desired doneness, about 4 minutes per side for medium.

Top each burger with a cheese slice; heat until cheese melts, 30 seconds to one minute.

Serve in toasted hamburger buns with sauerkraut, if desired.

Swedish Meat Balls

1 medium onion chopped 1 green pepper, chopped
1 tablespoon butter 1 can cream of chicken soup
1 can mushroom soup 2-3 pounds ground beef
spices to taste, salt, pepper, garlic and oregano
4 ounces sour cream

Mix ground beef with seasonings, shape into small balls and brown, drain off fat. Saute onions and pepper in butter. Add meatballs to pepper and onions. Add soup with a little milk to mix soup. Mix ingredients good. Let simmer 'til all is hot. Remove from heat and add sour cream. Serve over rice, potatoes, or noodles.

Pork and Cabbage Supper for Two

2 pork lion chops (1/2 inch thick) 1/4 tsp. salt
1 Tbsp. cooking oil 1/4 tsp. pepper
1 can (10-3/4 ounces) 1/2 tsp. garlic powder
condensed cream of mushroom soup, undiluted
3 cups shredded cabbage

In an oven-proof skillet, brown chops in oil on both sides; remove and set aside. To drippings, add soup and seasonings; bring to a boil. Return chops to skillet; add cabbage. Cover and bake at 350° for 50 to 60 minutes or until meat is tender.

Bread Pudding for Two

1 1/2 cups day-old buttered bread cubes (2 slices)
2 eggs 1/4 tsp. ground cinnamon
1 cup milk 1/8 tsp. ground nutmeg
1/4 cup sugar dash salt

Divide bread between two greased 8-oz. baking dishes; set aside. In a bowl, beat eggs, milk, sugar, cinnamon, nutmeg and salt. Pour over bread. Bake uncovered at 350° for 40 to 45 minutes or until a knife inserted near the center comes out clean. Serve warm.

Copper Carrots for Two

3 medium carrots, julienned
2 tsp. sugar
1/2 tsp. cornstarch
1/4 tsp. salt
Chopped fresh parsley, optional
1/8 tsp. ground ginger
2 Tbsp. orange juice
1 Tbsp. butter or margarine

In a small saucepan, cook carrots in water until tender; drain. Remove carrots; set aside and keep warm. In the same saucepan, combine sugar, cornstarch, salt and ginger. Gradually stir in orange juice; bring to a boil. Cook and stir for two minutes. Add butter. Return carrots to pan; heat through. Sprinkle with parsley if desired.

Calico Bean Dish

1 pound hamburger
1/4-1/2 pound bacon, cut in pieces
1/2-1 cup onion
1/2 cup catsup
1/3-1/2 cup packed brown sugar
1-3 tsp. mustard
salt to taste
2-6 tsp. vinegar
one 16-ounce can pork and beans
one 16-ounce kidney beans
one 16-ounce lima beans

Saute hamburger, bacon and onion. Drain a small amount of liquid from the beans and mix thoroughly with all other ingredients. Bake uncovered for 1 hour and 35 minutes in 300° oven. Note: Amount of onions, bacon and spices may vary according to personal taste.

Crowd Pleasing Potato Salad

1 gallon potatoes (about 16 large), cooked, peeled and slices
10 hard cooked eggs   1/3 cup vinegar

1 cup chopped onion	1/3 cup sugar
2 cups salad dressing	3 Tbsp. prepared mustard
1 cup light cream	1/2 tsp. salt

Place potatoes in a large salad bowl. Separate eggs. Chop whites and add to potatoes with onion. Toss gently. In another bowl, mash yolks with salad dressing, cream, vinegar, sugar, mustard and salt. Pour over potatoes and stir to coat. Cover and chill; 16-20 servings.

Low Fat Sour Cream

Mix 1/4 cup nonfat dry milk powder with 1 cup cold water. Add this to 8 oz. uncreamed cottage cheese. Add 2 teaspoons lemon juice.
Blend in blender and refrigerate until ready to use.

From pounds to cups:
If you should find an old cake recipe that you would like to try, but the amount of sugar, butter, and flour are given in pounds. Here's how to convert:
1 pound of flour equals 4 cups
1 pound of sugar equals 2 cups
1 pound of brown sugar equals 2 1/4 cups
1 pound of butter equals 2 cups

Brandied Fruit
(No alcohol)

1 package dry yeast	1 cup diced peaches
1 cup crushed pineapple	1/4 cup Maraschino cherries
1 cup sugar	

Mix together dry yeast and diced peaches, crushed pineapple and Maraschino cherries. Stir with sugar. Let this set a week. As for the container, I use a wide-mouth loose-fitting gallon jug as the fruit accumulates rapidly. Next week add 1 cup sugar, 1 cup of any desired fruit, pears, peaches, apricots, or pineapple or even a cup of drained fruit cocktail and 1/4 cup of the cherries. Now, the third week, add 1 cup of sugar, a cup of fruit you didn't use the previous week plus your 1/4 cup cherries. Stir well.

By the time you have acquired a goodly amount of the fruit and the next week you can begin to take out some to give others as a starter, or use on ice cream or pound cake.

Brandied Fruit Cake

1 cup sugar
1/2 cup butter or margarine
4 large eggs
3 cups sifted all-purpose flour
1 cup raisins, coconut and chopped nuts
1 tsp. each cloves and allspice
1 1/2 cups applesauce
2 cups brandied fruit
2 tsp. soda

Cream butter and sugar. Beat in eggs. Add dry, sifted ingredients, then the applesauce and brandied fruit, mixing well. Gradually add the raisins, coconut and nuts. Bake in a tube pan at 350° about 75 minutes. Cool and store in an airtight container, or freeze.

Recipe for Coal Plant also called Depression Plant

4 Tbsp. blueing
4 Tbsp. salt
4 drops Mercurochrome
4 Tbsp. soda
4 Tbsp. water
piece of soft coal

Place the piece of soft coal in a dish. Mix the blueing, salt and soda together and pour over the coal. Drop Mercurochrome over the top. Every three days add about a tablespoon of water.

It seems the plant is called by different names in different localities. A few of them are: Chemical Garden, Coral Plant, Coal Flowers, Grow Coal, Clinker Depression Flower, and Magic Flower.

In place of the Mercurochrome, some people use dampened raspberry gelatin or lipstick for coloring.

This plant will not stand rough handling. It is best to place the plant where the sun will not shine directly upon it. Porous brick or tile may be used.

Real Scrapple

1 1/2 lbs. lean pork pieces   1 1/2 tsp. salt
1 1/2 cups yellow cornmeal   1 cup cold water

Cook the pork in 2 quarts water until meat is tender. Cool the meat and remove the bones and fat. Chop the meat fine and refrigerate. Chill the broth.

Remove the hardened fat from the cold broth. Place 4 cups broth in a large saucepan and bring to a boil; add the chopped meat. Mix the cornmeal, salt and 1 cup cold water and gradually add it to the boiling broth, stirring constantly until it thickens.

Reduce the heat to low and cover. Cook for 30 minutes. Stir occasionally as it will stick easily to the pan.

Pour into an oiled 9x3" loaf pan, cover and refrigerate several hours or overnight. When very firm cut into 1/2-inch slices. Flour the slices and brown on both sides in hot vegetable oil. Serve with warm maple syrup or pancake syrup.

The following is for people who think that they do not like grits.

Cheese Grits

1 cup quick grits, cooked by package directions
4 1/2 cups grated sharp cheddar cheese (add cheese to grits and mix well)
1 1/2 cups milk   2 tsp. onion flakes
3 eggs yolks   1 tsp. parsley flakes
1 Tbsp. hot mustard   1 tsp. worcestershire
dash of tabasco   salt to taste

Combine all in greased 9x13" casserole. Bake at 325° for 1 1/4 hours. Serves 10. Bake two----its so gooooood.

Oh Suzanna's Grits

4 1/2 cups water   1 tsp. cinnamon (to taste)
2 small Granny Smith apples, peeled
1 1/2 small peaches   1/4 tsp. ginger
1 banana   1/4 tsp. cloves

1 cup raisins   1 cup quick grits
5 Tbsp. butter

Dice apples, peaches and 1/2 banana into bite-size pieces. Add to water and raisins in medium sauce pan. Add cinnamon, ginger and cloves. Boil at medium heat until fruit is tender but not mushy. Add remaining banana, cover pan and simmer for ten minutes. Bring to boil, add grits and butter. Boil until grits are mushy, but small chunks of fruit remain. Stir constantly. Great as a naturally-sweetened breakfast cereal or a snack on a chilly evening.

Grits and Sausage Italian-Style

4 cups water	1 tsp. salt
1 cup grits	1 tsp. oregano
1-16 oz. can peeled tomatoes	1/4 lb. hot Italian sauage
1 small can tomato paste	1/4 lb. sweet Italian sausage
1 onion	3 tsp. grated cheese (parmesan)
1 clove garlic	

Heat oven to 350°. Place sausage in skillet and cover with water. Cook on medium heat. Prick sausage to allow fat to escape. After the water boils down, brown the sausage. Remove sausage and set aside. Place about 1 Tbsp. fat in sauce pan. Saute onions and garlic. Add salt, pepper and oregano. Place tomatoes and paste through food processor. Cook in saucepan with onion and garlic on medium heat. Cook grits according to package directions for about 30 minutes, stirring constantly until it reaches the consistency of porridge. Pour into two-quart casserole. Let stand a few minutes. Spread sauce on top. Sprinkle cheese and add sausage. Place in oven for 15 minutes. Serve with extra sauce.

3-Bean Soup

Saute large sweet onion, finely-sliced, in 2 Tbsp. butter.
Add 1-16 oz. can pork and beans, 1 can garbanzo (or chick peas), 1 can large red kidney beans.
Add 2 cans water.
Season with 1/2 teaspoon pepper and 2 tablespoons dried parsley.

Simmer for 1 hour.
Mash beans lightly with potato masher.
Serve in soup bowls.
This soup can be made with 1 can pork and beans and 1 can red kidney beans. Makes a good main course by adding 1/2 lb. ground beef to the onions and browning.

My father-in-law made a hearty bean soup by soaking beans overnight and cooking up a big pot of beans, then adding onions and ground beef, can of tomatoes (or fresh tomatoes when in season and elbow or shell macaroni). He called this "Pasta Fizoli". Sure was good served with thick slices of my mother-in-law's homemade bread.

Guacamole

2 medium ripe avocados, peeled and seeded
2 Tbsp. reconstituted lime juice   1 tsp. seasoned salt
1 Tbsp. finely-chopped onion   1/4 tsp. garlic powder
1/4 to 1/2 tsp. hot pepper sauce

In medium bowl, mash avocados. Stir in remaining ingredients. Chill thoroughly to blend flavors. Serve as a dip with fresh vegetables or tortilla chips. Makes about 1 1/2 cups.

Quick and Easy Cobbler

1 cup flour   2 tsp. baking powder
1 cup sugar   1/4 tsp. salt
1 cup milk   about 2 cups canned blueberries with juice
2 Tbsp. butter melted in pan

Mix ingredients together, pour in pan, add blueberries and bake at 350° for about an hour. (The crust comes to the top).

A Recipe for Lye Soap

Use two quarts of melted grease from baking drippings or scraps of fat meat. Stir in 1 cup of lye dissolved in 1 quart water. This will get hot during the mixing process. Allow to cool until lukewarm.

At once add 1 cup ammonia and 2 tablespoons *Borax* dissolved in 1/3 cup water. Stir 5 minutes or until too stiff to handle.

Put away to harden it. It is best to let it set for 4 weeks. Nearly all soaps are better when they get older.

One advantage over commercial soaps is that the natural glycerine remains in the mixture. Also, it's cheaper.

Mom used to make soap regularly. She ran the little restaurant that we had in operation while they were building the Veterans Hospital and with all the frying of hamburgers there was always a supply of grease. She was proud of her soap when it hardened and got very white. I can remember when it was soft and brown in color. I believe that it was made then without Borax. It was very good to wash your hair with.